WINE WARS II

WINE WARS II

THE GLOBAL BATTLE FOR THE SOUL OF WINE

MIKE VESETH

ROWMAN & LITTLEFIELD
Lanham • Boulder • New York • London

Published by Rowman & Littlefield
An imprint of The Rowman & Littlefield Publishing Group, Inc.
4501 Forbes Boulevard, Suite 200, Lanham, Maryland 20706
www.rowman.com

86-90 Paul Street, London EC2A 4NE

Distributed by NATIONAL BOOK NETWORK

British Library Cataloguing in Publication Information Available

Library of Congress Cataloging-in-Publication Data

Names: Veseth, Michael, author.
Title: Wine wars II : the global battle for the soul of wine / Mike Veseth.
Description: Lanham, Maryland : Rowman & Littlefield Publishers, [2022] |
   Includes bibliographical references and index.
Identifiers: LCCN 2021048542 (print) | LCCN 2021048543 (ebook) | ISBN
   9781538163832 (paperback) | ISBN 9781538163849 (epub)
Subjects: LCSH: Wine industry. | Globalization—Economic aspects.
Classification: LCC HD9370.5 .V475 2022 (print) | LCC HD9370.5 (ebook) |
   DDC 338.4/76632—dc23/eng/20220208
LC record available at https://lccn.loc.gov/2021048542
LC ebook record available at https://lccn.loc.gov/2021048543

♾™ The paper used in this publication meets the minimum requirements of
American National Standard for Information Sciences—Permanence of Paper
for Printed Library Materials, ANSI/NISO Z39.48-1992.

CONTENTS

CONTENTS

PRELUDE
GRAPE EXPECTATIONS?

1

A TALE OF TWO GLASSES

It was the best of wines, it was the worst of wines (apologies to fans of Charles Dickens). The global wineglass, it seems, is both quite empty and full to the brim. We live today in the best of times for wine if we evaluate the situation objectively, as economists like me are trained to do. Never before has so much good wine been made and so many wine choices offered up to consumers. For someone who loves wine, the glass is very full, indeed; it is hard to imagine better days than these. The global markets deliver a world of wine to your door. Drink up!

And yet many enthusiasts are anxious about the future of wine. The good news we find in our wineglasses and on the supermarket shelves is often accompanied by disturbing rumors, feelings, and forecasts. It is the worst of times, too, you see—especially if you are a maker of cheap wine in France, Italy, or Spain, the largest wine-producing countries. Everything about wine is wrong for you. Consumption at home has been falling for decades and squeezing your market share, and import competition has increased. The rise in global wine drinking that you counted on to power your export business has unexpectedly stalled at exactly the wrong moment. You find yourself making the wrong wine in the wrong style from the wrong grapes at the wrong price and trying to sell it in the wrong places. You are betrayed at every turn by the markets that once treated you so well. You hold an empty glass, or so it must seem.

Times are troubling in Australia, too, where a wine boom was followed by a wine bust, when consumers around the world have seemingly turned away from the muscular Aussie wines they enjoyed so much just a few years ago. So the Aussies turned to China and, through lots of hard work, turned it into their number 1 export market, bigger that either the United States or the United Kingdom. Then the lucky country's luck turned again. Driven by political disagreements that have nothing to do with wine, China imposed tariffs of more than 200 percent on Aussie wine, choking off this promising market.

Wine producers are optimists by nature, but they face serious challenges. Recession, pandemic, falling consumption, rising antidrinking lobbies, water shortages, global warming, and even raging brush fires all threaten the livelihoods of winegrowers and producers in many parts of the globe.

It is the worst of times for consumers, too, if they seek that special taste of a place that wine geeks like me call *terroir*. The wine in your half-empty glass is free of any technical flaw, but so what? Does it have a soul? Does it express any particular place or any producer's distinct vision of what wine should be? This is the age of McWine, I have heard people say: wine that is all the same. When everything is the same, then it is all nothing! And what's worse than that?

These are good times and bad ones, too, for the world of wine—what a contradiction! What about the future? Will wine's tale of two glasses have a happy ending? Or will our (excuse the Dickensian pun) "grape expectations" be crushed? I'm an optimist about the future of wine, but as an economist, I am trained to pay close attention to the dismal side of any situation. I wrote this book to try to find out just how empty or full the global glass really is and how the world of wine is likely to change.

The first thing to understand about wine is that it is many things, not just one, in terms of both wine itself and the economic forces that drive the wine industry, so the story of the future of wine will necessarily be a complicated one. Although hundreds of factors will come into play as the wine world evolves, three big forces will almost certainly shape the overall pattern: globalization; brand-driven commodification; and resistance to these powerful winds, which I call the revenge of the terroirists. Globalization and commodification are economic push forces that are transforming the world of wine. The revenge of the terroirists is all about pushing back.

GLOBALIZATION: REDRAWING THE WORLD WINE MAP

Globalization comes first. It isn't something new, as you will see, but it is a powerful force that is becoming even stronger. It is quite literally redrawing the world wine map, pushing it out from the Old World, where most of the earth's wine is still produced, to many New Worlds, where both production and consumption are on the rise.

Wine has become a global or nearly global phenomenon, produced and widely consumed in a growing number of countries (except where religious edicts forbid it). The International Organisation of Vine and Wine (OIV), a sort of United Nations of the wine world, reports that 45 percent of the world's wine crosses at least one international border on its way from grape to glass. Interestingly, wine is both global *and* local. Wine drinkers have a strong home country or region bias. Most of the wine consumed in France comes from France, for example, and Californians drink mostly California wine.

Ironically, the most global wines live at the top and bottom of the "wine wall," my name for the various real and virtual spaces where wine enthusiasts confront the vast and often confusing supply of available wine. The top shelf holds Champagne, of course, and iconic wines that can sell for hundreds or even thousands of dollars. These wines travel the world, reaching collectors, investors, connoisseurs, and upwardly mobile wine snob wannabes wherever they live.

The bottom shelf of the wine wall holds inexpensive generic wines that can sell for as little as two dollars in the United States. In the European Union, you can get a liter of this wine for a single euro coin (VAT included). Some of these wines are packaged in traditional 750-milliliter bottles, but most of them come in other sorts of packages: 1.5-liter bottles; foil-lined cardboard tubes that look like exaggerated juice packs; and 3- and 5-liter "casks" of wine, cardboard boxes containing special plastic bags. You get to the wine through a spigot, not by pulling a cork, with these box or bag-in-a-box wines.

Whereas status and prestige pull iconic wines to the four corners of the globe, cost concerns drive the generic wine trade. Cost is key on the bottom of the wine wall, and there is always cheaper wine somewhere in the world. With the advent of efficient bulk-wine shipping (huge FlexiTank bags of wine in big ocean-shipping containers), even relatively small differences in price can unleash tidal waves of wine. Thus, cheap wine in China often makes a long journey from Chile, while the Pinot Noir sold by a California-based brand might come from the South of France, northern Italy, Chile, or somewhere else. It's a small world after all down there on the bottom shelf.

The vast majority of wines made today are neither top-shelf trophies nor bottom-bin bulk. These midwall wines are numerous enough to create a kaleidoscopic if slightly misleading image of wine globalization, especially if you live in Great Britain or the United States, the two most important markets for global wine today. Some specialist retailers in the United States, for example, offer shoppers more than five thousand wine choices from around the world. Incredible.

If globalization simply meant that more of the world's people are drinking wine and more of the earth's surface is covered with vine, then it wouldn't be very controversial. But it doesn't; money and power are at stake. Money, of course, because vanity vineyards aside, people make wine to make a living. They may seek personal fulfillment or artistic achievement, of course, but they also need to pay the bills. It's hard to completely avoid the bottom line. So globalization is not an abstract concept to winemakers; it is a steely sharp, double-edged sword: The prospect of new demand comes with the threat of new competition.

Money is an understandable issue, but power? Yes. The battle for the future of wine is all about power—whose idea of wine will dominate and whose tastes and interests will prevail. You don't have to take my word for it; you can see power politics at work for yourself the next time you purchase wine.

The wine wall has many political divisions, each with its own internal power structure. The French wine part of the wall, for example, is organized according to French geography, with Rhône here, Bordeaux there, and Burgundy somewhere else. Power resides (or is meant to reside) with producers in this part of the wine world, and the wine wall makes it clear. But if you move over to any of the New World shelves (California, for example, or Chile or Australia), you'll find a different political organization, dominated by branded varietal wines like Yellow Tail Shiraz or Mondavi Woodbridge Chardonnay.

Globalization has brought these political systems into direct conflict. It's like the Cold War all over, only it isn't just capitalism versus communism; it's more important than that. It's the soul of wine at stake. Who will call the shots in the wine market of the future? Who will set the price? Whose palate will prevail? To paraphrase the Chairman on *Iron Chef*, whose idea of wine will reign supreme?

BRAND POWER: TWO-BUCK CHUCK

Many fear that power and taste will shift from the Old World to the New and *vin de terroir* (wine from the earth) will be replaced with *vin du marché* (market wine)—wine designed by marketing executives and engineered to appeal to least-common-denominator palates shaped by long exposure to vast quantities of fizzy, sweet, ice-cold Diet Coke. This is the world, wine snobs say, of products like Two-Buck Chuck (TBC), the simple, inexpensive wine sold in the United States at Trader Joe's supermarkets. Every country has its Two-Buck Chuck (sometimes at prices significantly below two dollars!), although they are not always as drinkable or successful as the wine found at Trader Joe's, and every wine snob worries that the global market has unleashed a race to the bottom, where taste and terroir are endangered species and Chuck and his even cheaper cousins will someday rule.

TBC is a phenomenon; Trader Joe's sells hundreds of thousands of cases of this low-cost wine each year. TBC is a classic element of the tale of two wines. It has drawn thousands of consumers to the wine wall, introducing them to wine as an affordable, quotidian pleasure, but by focusing their attention on the bottom shelf, has it encouraged an epidemic of arrested development? TBC has raised the floor on bulk wine in terms of quality, but has it simultaneously lowered the sensory or aesthetic ceiling?

The story of Two-Buck Chuck, as it is usually told, is all about price, quantity, and quality—the economist's familiar playground—but there is more to it than that. The miracle of TBC is not that millions of bottles can be produced at low cost—that's surprisingly easy to do; it is that consumers are willing to buy it! You see, wine is a mystery to most consumers. They have little confidence in their ability to tell what's in the bottle as they stare at the wine wall or puzzle over a restaurant wine list. Some of them are adventurous and treat it as a treasure hunt, but far too many buy the same thing over and over (that arrested development problem again) or, worse, walk away in frustration, buying nothing at all.

Just cut the price if you want to sell wine—that's what Econ 101 teaches us. Ah, but there is a problem. Insecure wine buyers often read price as a proxy for quality. They are afraid to pay too little for a bottle of wine because they are worried that it will be horrible. Paying more, they believe (falsely, as a general rule), guarantees a better product—but they are also afraid of paying too much. No wonder so many people don't purchase any wine at all! So selling cheap wine is trickier than you might think.

The Two-Buck Chuck syndrome is the problem created both by wine's confusing complexity and the logical response: to simplify and rationalize by creating such branded products as TBC, Barefoot, Yellow Tail, 19 Crimes, and the many other labels that try their best to stand out on the crowded wine wall. The miracle of Two-Buck Chuck is that it has given millions of Americans the confidence they once lacked as they try to stare down the wine wall and make a purchase. The wine business is really a confidence game, if you get my drift, and the future of wine—and the money and power that it brings—will be influenced by how the game is played and who plays it.

THE REVENGE OF THE TERROIRISTS

For many people, globalization and the Two-Buck Chuck syndrome are wholly positive forces: more wine; better wine (or at least fewer bottles that are really, really bad); wine that is easier to understand, purchase, and drink. What could be better? But not everyone shares these happy thoughts. The terroirists sure don't.

Terroirists are people who see the new global wine map and shudder. Terroirists seek to preserve and protect an idea of wine that is more natural, more connected to the earth, more deeply embedded in culture. It would be easy to say that this is an Old World vision of wine, but nothing in wine is ever as simple as Old versus New. Many of the forces that terroirists oppose most vehemently were invented in France, the queen of Old World wine.

Do you oppose simple, maybe even stupid wines that exist only because marketing campaigns can sell them? Then you may oppose Yellow Tail or Two-Buck Chuck, but you must first confront Beaujolais Nouveau, France's most successful *vin du marché*. Are you against wine that is highly processed and manipulated, wine that is almost manufactured? Then it is understandable that you may dislike many New World wines because there are often fewer restrictions on winemaking techniques, but you should hold your greatest contempt for Champagne, a wine that is made underground (not in the vineyard), processed, blended, and sold for huge sums by French luxury-goods conglomerates.

The Old World is home to both terroirists and the wines, winemakers, corporations, and critics they oppose. And the New World is, too. It's hard to find Old World winemakers who are more committed to the idea of terroir than, say, Randall Grahm, founder of Bonny Doon, or John Williams of Frog's Leap. In truth, you won't learn much about terroirism by looking at a physical map; mental maps or moral ones have more to say. But the physical map will tell you something if you stare at it long enough. *Terroir*—the idea that wine is deeply rooted in a particular place—is now a moving target.

The problem is global climate change. Now, I know there are climate change doubters who think that Al Gore's contribution to world peace (he shared the Nobel Prize in 2007) is overrated. But I've never met anyone in the wine business who has the slightest doubt that climate is changing. The world is getting hotter overall, and the weather, more variable and extreme (which means, ironically, that some places are getting cooler, too). Global climate change makes set notions of wine terroir pretty problematic. Interestingly, it both undermines the terroirists' case and makes it stronger.

WINE'S TRIPLE CRISIS

The global wine industry is in the midst of a triple crisis, and I am not sure how it will end. The climate change crisis comes first. It affects everything if we consider both direct and indirect effects, so it may seem odd to think of it as a *wine* crisis. Wine grapes generally can be made to grow under quite extreme conditions; in some colder regions, they actually *bury* the vines in the winter to protect them and unearth them each spring so that they can come back to life (you might call this Lazarus viticulture). But specific wine grape varieties thrive in only very narrow bands of average temperature, and wine regions defined by particular grapes or wine styles are threatened by relatively small changes in environmental conditions. Wine is, therefore, the canary in the coal mine when it comes to climate change. It will feel the impacts before many other industries, and so it is not a surprise, as I explain later, that wine businesses are among the strongest advocates for progressive environmental action.

The climate change crisis dwarfs everything else in the long run, but because the long run can seem far away and we often misjudge how fast it is approaching, climate concerns do not get the attention they deserve. Indeed, as the global reaction to the coronavirus pandemic crisis has demonstrated, climate change generally isn't treated with the "drop everything" or "operation moonshot" urgency that real crises warrant. But even if the climate change threat were to disappear tomorrow, wine would still be in trouble.

The second crisis is economic. Wine is a magical beverage, but it is a crazy business. Wine's economic environment is characterized by cyclical, structural, and "wild card" forces that make it difficult to prepare for or successfully execute a business plan.

Global wine consumption grew steadily for the twenty years that ended in about 2008, the date we associate with the global financial crisis. Rising wine sales were important because they slowly soaked up a surplus of wine. Too much wine? Well, for many years the European Union in effect subsidized wine production to stabilize agricultural economies, especially in France, Italy, and Spain. Wine farmers were paid to grow grapes and to make wine that could not be sold, so some of it was distilled into industrial alcohol. Yuck! Those policies are history, and European winegrowers turned from government subsidy wine to wine aimed at global markets. This is a good thing, but it happened just as wine production increased in other parts of the world, too. The result: a lot of grapes, a lot of wine, and a lot of jobs and incomes at risk.

Rising global wine sales were most welcome in this context, and when sales dropped a bit in 2008, no one was very concerned. "It's just the economy, dummy," they said. "Wine will spring back when the economy improves." But it didn't, and the next ten years were what I have called "wine's lost decade." Why did wine lose its mojo? There are many possible reasons (I explain them later), but the sudden loss in momentum changes the nature of the game from a positive-sum tide that raises all ships, to a zero-sum fight for market share. And the battle isn't just between Old World and New World or among the growers and producers in these regions; the opponents are now more diverse and unexpected than ever before.

The reason? Wine's identity crisis. Wine has never been just one thing. It is, after all, both that fancy French Champagne at the top of the wine wall and that big box of Franzia at the bottom. Wine is healthful (think Mediterranean diet) and dangerous (read the government required warnings on wine labels in the United States). It is culture to some and just another commodity to others.

The cartoon character Pogo famously said, "We have met the enemy, and he is us," and this is true in a way for wine. The biggest threat to wine's identity is something inherent to wine's existence: alcohol. You might think that wine is just grape juice with alcohol, but wine doesn't taste much like the grapes it is made from except for in a few specific cases. Fermentation doesn't just add an alcoholic kick; it transforms the product in complex ways. It's the same with the way that fermenting yeast makes bread different from flour and water. So wine as we know it is impossible without alcohol, but it may also be impossible with it if antialcohol forces have their way.

Wine's identity crisis is significant because it seems like those who see wine as a social or health problem, not an essential element in our culture, have seized the momentum. If wine doesn't know who it is and what it is and cannot tell its story to the world, then how can it survive?

HOW I STUMBLED INTO THE WINE WARS

People often ask me how I became a wine economist, an economist who studies the global wine markets. The answer is rooted in a particular time and place. Sue and I were still newlyweds, taking a low-budget vacation in the Napa Valley back in the day when that was still possible. We were headed north on the Silverado Trail late on our last day, pointed toward our economy motel in Santa Rosa, when we decided to stop for one last tasting.

The winery name was very familiar, and I had high hopes for our tasting. If I had known more about wine back then, I would have recognized this as one of the wineries that kicked French butt in the 1976 Judgment of Paris wine tasting. We pulled off the road and went in to find just the winemaker and a cellar rat at work. No fancy tasting room back then, just boards and barrels to form a makeshift bar. They stopped what they were doing and brought out a couple of glasses. Had I known more about wine back then, I would have been in awe of the guy pouring the wine, but I was pretty much in the dark. So we tasted and talked.

I started asking my amateur questions about the wine, but pretty soon the conversation turned around. The winemaker found out that I was an economics professor. Suddenly he was very interested in talking with me. What's going to happen to interest rates? Inflation? Tax reform? He had a lot of concerns about the economy because his prestigious winery was also a business and what was happening out there in the financial markets (especially interest rates and bank credit, as I remember) had a big impact on what he could or would do in the cellar. Wineries, especially those that specialize in fine red wines, have a lot of financial issues.

In addition to the initial investment in vineyards, winery facilities, equipment, and so forth, each year's production ages for two or three years, quietly soaking up implicit or explicit interest cost as it waits to be released from barrel to bottle to marketplace. The wine changes as it ages, but the economy changes, too. It's impossible to know at crush what market conditions will be like when the first bottle is sold. Wine economics is a serious concern. Few winemakers are completely insulated from the business side, and sometimes the economy can have a huge effect on what winemakers get to make (if they have the resources to stick with their vision) or have to make (if they don't). And so a famous winemaker taught me to think about wine in economic terms and to consider that supply and demand sometimes matter as much as climate and soil when it comes to what's in my wineglass. I should have known.

Although my interest in wine and economics merged on that Napa day, it sat on its lees for a long time, as I waited for an opportunity to link my personal passion with my professional research agenda. The two naturally converged a few years ago when I began writing what turned out to be a four-volume series on the global economy. My 2005 book *Globaloney: Unraveling the Myths of Globalization* includes a chapter called "Globalization versus *Terroir*," my first attempt to write about wine economics for a general audience. *Globaloney* argues that complex global processes shouldn't be reduced to a few simple images. Globalization and food are more than just McDonald's, for example, and globalization of wine isn't just McWine.

The wine chapter in *Globaloney* gave me confidence that I had more to say about money, wine, and globalization, so I launched a website called *The Wine Economist* (WineEconomist.com), where I could work out my ideas in public, make connections, and develop a wine voice. After several years and nearly 200,000 words of blog posts, *The Wine Economist* evolved into the first edition of this book.

THE ROAD TO *WINE WARS II*

I wasn't sure if anyone would want to read about the business of wine, but I was wrong. *Wine Wars* was warmly received by both critics and readers. It turns out that while wine is good, wine and a story is even better, and stories about the business side of wine can be very interesting. A number of wine industry readers have said that *Wine Wars* helped them connect the dots and see things more clearly. Consumers, who have no particular business connection, say they just like knowing the backstory of their favorite drink.

I've spent the last decade on the wine road speaking at wine industry conferences around the world and learning more about wine and the people who make it. It is a tough job, but someone has to do it, and apparently I am that lucky someone! I have recorded my impressions and experiences in hundreds of columns on *The Wine Economist*. *Wine Wars* has been joined by three other books that continue my analysis of global wine: *Extreme Wine* (2013); *Money, Taste, and Wine* (2015); and *Around the World in Eighty Wines* (2017).

Wine Wars celebrated its tenth birthday in 2021, and that occasion made me stop and think (as round-number birthdays sometimes do). The powerful forces that I identify in *Wine Wars* are still important, but they've changed in ways both big and small. Environmental and demographic shifts, for example, are now much more clearly understood as wine industry challenges. There is a lot to think about and to write about. And so I have written this new book, *Wine Wars II*, which updates the first edition and extends its argument to address wine's global crisis.

In a way, this journey has brought me back to that dark cellar on the Silverado Trail in Napa Valley, the great wines we sampled that day, and my "aha!" moment when I realized that wine and economics are a perfect pairing. I've learned much more about wine and wine economics, and I appreciate now more than ever the many challenges that the world of wine faces. But I remain an optimist, as I show in this book. I still have grape expectations!

2

GOT WINE?

No one can be certain what the future of wine holds, but we can be sure of one thing: When it comes around, we will be surprised. The future of wine will bear only a superficial resemblance to its present state. You may still be able to find wines in bottles with corks and fancy labels, of that I am sure. But almost everything else about wine is an open question. How do I know this? Not because I can see the future. It's because I have seen the past.

Imagine what the wine wall—the wine department of your local supermarket or wine store—must have looked like fifty years ago. If you lived in the United States, then chances are the wine wall was pretty small—maybe a single, narrow supermarket shelf—and kind of grim. Not a place where a wine enthusiast could work up much passion. If you lived in Great Britain, the supermarket wine wall basically didn't exist at the start of the 1960s. Wine, if you wanted to buy any, was something you found in specialist drinks shops. Government regulations strictly separated wine and food sales in Britain in those days, as they still do in several US states today. The convenient global market for good-quality wine that we take for granted today did not yet exist fifty years ago.

THE PRESENT AS AN UNLIKELY FUTURE

What do you suppose was offered in the 1960s on a representative American wine wall? There was probably some sweet, strong, fortified wines—ersatz Port and Sherry from California and proprietary blends like Thunderbird—and then perhaps a few rather pretentious French labels from obscure domains and châteaux. Italian wines? Maybe—Soave, Chianti in a raffia-wrapped flask. Australian wine? No. New Zealand? No. Spain? Probably not, unless there was a bottle of authentic Sherry alongside the California-made fortified wines. Chile? Argentina? No. No. Germany? Regrettably, yes. Blue Nun.

Down toward the bottom of the shelf, if you were in the United States, you'd find the jug wines, like Gallo or Italian Swiss Colony. The wines were identified by style, not grape variety. No Pinot Noir, Chardonnay, or Riesling. It was Burgundy, Chablis, and Rhine wine—Old World names that had nothing in common, not even the grape varieties used, with the New World brands that paid tribute to them and took a free ride on their reputations.

You could tell the good wines from the cheap ones easily—cork (good) versus crude, old-fashioned screw cap (bad)—but there weren't many good choices except in big-city specialty shops. It was hard to get good wine in the heartland because its movement and sale were so tightly regulated by state and local authorities. (A wine lover in Washington State, I am told, was jailed for having a cellar full of wine he had illegally smuggled in from California.) The sorry state of the wine wall in 1960 reflected very well the condition of the world of wine. A thin layer of spectacularly good wines floated like cream on a cloudy sea of red and white plonk.

Standing in the wine aisle fifty or sixty years ago, staring down that bottle of Thunderbird or jug of Gallo Hearty Burgundy, what would you have thought about the future of wine? Certainly, the present, as we know it today, represents an unlikely future when viewed from the past. Here are a few examples to make my point clear.

OLD IS NEW: THE NATURAL WINE PHENOMENON

One important trend sixty years ago was the rise of science and technology in winemaking. The French wine scientist Émile Peynaud is often said to be the godfather of modern winemaking, with its focus on strict hygiene, temperature-controlled fermentation, and careful control of the winemaking process from start to finish. Peynaud revolutionized winemaking, with the result that even inexpensive wine today is for the most part free of the defects that plagued all wines to one degree or another before him. Bravo!

Given the obvious benefits of wine's scientific revolution, a counterrevolution and return to some of the practices of the past is probably the last thing that an observer in the 1960s and 1970s would expect. And so the recent growth of the natural wine movement would come as a complete surprise. Natural wine is a global movement that seeks to return wine to its roots as a cultural product, and for that reason, many in the movement eventually make a pilgrimage to Georgia. I'm talking Georgia, the country, the cradle of wine—not Georgia, the US state, the cradle of Coca-Cola. Wine is a powerful cultural force in Georgia. Everyone drinks wine. Most families make wine. Wine and grape symbols are everywhere.

What kind of wine do Georgians make? Well, lots of kinds. Sweet red wines are made for export to Russia and former Soviet markets, where they are very popular. Georgia was the vineyard of the old Soviet Union—Stalin was Georgian and favored wines from his home. Dry wines in the international style, often made from such international grape varieties as Sauvignon Blanc, are also produced for export to European markets. But natural wine pilgrims come to Georgia for its *qvevri* wines.

Qvevri are large, egg-shaped earthenware pots that are buried in the ground with only the circular mouth showing. In the fall, grapes are loaded into the *qvevri* and then sealed without any chemical additives—not even yeast. The wild yeasts that cling to the grape skins in the vineyard do the fermentation job. When the seal is broken in the spring, what you have is a very natural wine indeed. And sometimes there's a party to celebrate breaking the *qvevri* seal because wine without antibacterial additions can spoil quickly in some circumstances. Best to drink it up while it is fresh! It is a method that is literally thousands of years old and simultaneously at the cutting edge of wine today.

You don't have to have a *qvevri* to make natural wine, and you don't need to visit Georgia for inspiration. Natural wine is still a niche but a growing one, with many winemakers experimenting with natural techniques. Poke around the next winery you visit, and there's a good chance you'll find a clay pot or amphora over in the corner alongside a tank of wine being made with low or no-added sulfur and native yeasts. There are natural wine bars all around the world where like-minded wine lovers gather to share a vision of wine that would be hard to imagine just fifty years ago.

KIWI JUICE, SHANGRI-LA, ENGLISH FIZZ

If you zoomed back in time fifty or sixty years ago and asked a wine expert to name the most important wine-producing countries, you would have received a fairly short list. Most of the world's wine was produced in Europe, and most of that, in France, Italy, and Spain. These were the global wine powerhouses. Algeria was important, too. You may be surprised to learn that Algeria was the world's largest exporter of wine until its colonial ties with France were broken in the 1960s and its wine industry faded away. Dark, strong Algerian wine fortified lighter, weaker French products. Wine was made elsewhere in Europe and in a few other regions, too, including South Africa, Australia, Chile, Argentina, and even the United States. But France, Italy, and Spain dominated the scene.

And they still do in terms of wine production statistics, but momentum has shifted in several ways, and three countries that you would absolutely have to include somewhere on your wine power list today would have been unimaginable fifty or sixty years ago. I'm talking about New Zealand, China, and merry old England.

New Zealand is a small island country far away in the South Pacific Ocean. A wine powerhouse? Yes and no. No in terms of quantity. New Zealand is only the fourteenth-largest wine-producing country by volume, sandwiched between Romania and Hungary on the global league table. But it is perhaps the world's most successful wine producer, with rising export sales year after year after year. New Zealand's signature wine—Marlborough Sauvignon Blanc—is known the world over. For many years, New Zealand has topped the table for highest export price for still wines.

And consumers just can't seem to get enough of the stuff. This was literally true in 2021, when a poor wine grape harvest combined with rising demand produced a shortage; there just wasn't enough Kiwi Sauvignon Blanc to go around. Producers resorted to allocation lists to ration the precious liquid. How did New Zealand go from unknown to superstar so quickly? It's an interesting story I tell you all about in chapter 4.

Many people today are surprised to learn that China makes wine and Chinese consumers drink wine, so you can imagine how radical this thought would have been back in the days of Mao jackets, Little Red Books, and the Cultural Revolution. I'm just fascinated with China's unexpected rise in the world of wine. The first edition of *Wine Wars* features an entire chapter on China, and *Wine Wars II* does, too. China was the world's tenth-largest wine-producing nation in 2020, just above Old World stalwart Portugal and below Germany. China was the sixth-largest wine consumer, with total sales greater than Russia but less than the United Kingdom.

China is the wild card of global wine. With its huge population and rapid economic growth, China has long been the object of global wine dreams. And nightmares, too. French producers dreamed, for example, of the big sales they could make in China as upwardly mobile urban consumers discovered the glories of wine. French producers have been so enthusiastic about China that they've invested small fortunes to make wine there as well as to sell it.

We've tasted delightful Chandon sparkling wines from the Ningxia region, for example, and a remarkable red wine called Ao Yun made high up in the Himalaya Mountains near a place called Shangri-la (really!) by the French wine and luxury-goods conglomerate LVMH.

The dream came true. Chinese wine sales have grown and grown. But so did a nightmare of fake bottles and counterfeit wine. As China gained steam as both producer and consumer in the twenty-first century, many thought that China was the solution to wine's growing economic crisis. But China is a wild card, remember? It changes its colors constantly. Pandemic lockdowns knocked the stuffing out of Chinese wine consumption, for example, as the social occasions where wine was a featured element disappeared. Wine drinking—especially of imported products—declined enough for the OIV to suggest in its 2020 global market report that a growing Chinese wine market was unlikely to be the rising tide that lifted the wine world's boats after all.

England would definitely not show up on that 1960s list of top wine countries, and you might be surprised to see it included here today. The United Kingdom is one of the most important wine markets in the world, as I explain later in this book. But isn't England too cold and rainy for wine grapes? Well, yes—for many types of wine. But, powered by climate change and patches of the same chalky terroir as Champagne, England has become known as a producer of sparkling wines. In this case, climate change is a double-edged sword. It makes England's vineyards viable for sparkling wines while at the same time pushing temperatures up in France, where the extra heat is detrimental to Champagne production.

Will England be the Champagne of the future? No, because wine regulations specify that Champagne can only come from the Champagne region of France. But, yes, if climate change continues, English sparkling wines may rival and then—who knows?—surpass those of France.

AMERICA'S HANGOVER

Perhaps the most unlikely feature of the present-day world of wine when viewed from the past is this: The United States, the land of Mountain Dew and Diet Coke, has become the world's largest wine market measured by dollars spent. Even more amazing, America achieves its number 1 rating despite the fact that about 35 percent of the adult population doesn't consume alcohol at all and another 20 percent drink alcohol but not wine. Only about 15 percent of the adult population drinks wine with any frequency. And yet the United States is number 1 in global wine sales. This is such an unlikely situation that we should examine it in some detail.

Why does America's awkward embrace of wine come as a surprise? The answer is that American wine was (and to a certain extent still is) suffering from a hangover. But it isn't a hangover created by some barrel-draining, bottle-gulping Bacchanalian binge. America is still recovering from the Prohibition era (1920–1933), when production and sale of wine and other alcoholic beverages was all but banned. Prohibition's impact on wine in America and the peculiar pattern the market took once wine was legal again continue to shape the world of wine today.

Wine, the "temperance beverage," according to its advocates, was banned along with all other alcoholic beverages during the "Great Experiment" of Prohibition. Or at least that's what most people think. Banning wine—letting the vineyards go to ruin, allowing America's wine culture to shrivel—would have been bad. But what actually happened to wine in America during Prohibition was even worse.[1]

Wine consumption increased during Prohibition. How is this possible because wine was illegal? Well, the truth is that the Volstead Act provided three loopholes that wine producers and consumers exploited for all they were worth. It was legal for commercial wineries to make and sell wine for religious and medical purposes. Sacramental wine and prescription wine kept a few American wineries in business, albeit at low production levels. (I suppose it is possible that some of this legal wine might have made its way onto the black market.)

The biggest loophole, however, was the provision that allowed for limited home production of wine. It was against the law for an Italian American family in Brooklyn to buy wine, but they could legally make two hundred gallons of it at home for nonintoxicating family use. Two hundred gallons! That's about a thousand bottles a year, a lot more wine than most Americans were drinking before Prohibition.[2] Plenty of wine for the family and maybe a bit left over for friends and even under-the-table sales. Okay, a lot left over for other purposes. The wine loopholes, combined with attempts for tighter regulations of other forms of alcohol, encouraged wine production and consumption during the long Prohibition years but in a way that corrupted the idea of wine and crippled the development of a sustainable wine culture.

Wine is many things to many people, which is why it is so interesting, but during Prohibition, it was really just one thing: a widely available, semilegal buzz. Wine was reduced to its alcoholic content in the minds of many producers, consumers, and (especially) regulators. The idea that it was a valuable cultural component or temperate, healthful food product—well, those notions basically disappeared. We still suffer from the hangover effect of this transformation, with wine that is heavily taxed and regulated and subject to tight distribution controls.

America's taste for wine changed, too. Wine that is consumed with meals is different from wine that you drink to get numb. Sweet, high-proof wines were the beverage of choice, and it took decades after 1933 for drier table wines to reestablish themselves in American life in an important way.

Most important, however, is the fact that the wine itself changed. Because of the two-hundred-gallon loophole, much of the wine that Americans drank during Prohibition was utterly revolting. It was made by fumbling amateurs, not trained professionals. It was made at home, with rudimentary equipment, not in clean and well-supplied cellars. And it was made with grapes that traveled hundreds and sometimes thousands of miles by truck and rail to get to the cities and towns where home winemakers lived.

I can only imagine what the grapes must have looked like when the amateur winemakers got them home. My friends who make wine pick their grapes in the early-morning hours and then rush them to the cellar to process them at the peak of freshness and before bacteria have a chance to do their smelly work. I'll bet the grapes that were loaded onto railcars in California were in sorry shape when they reached their final destinations in Chicago and Philadelphia!

So wine consumption rose during Prohibition, but the culture of wine went into a steep spiral of decline. Wine drinkers changed (into alcohol drinkers), the wines changed (they got much worse), and even the grapes themselves changed. Given the realities of the Prohibition wine market, winegrowers focused on thick-skinned grapes that would survive shipping in place of more delicate varieties that would make better wine. It made sense in the short run, of course, but it added one more barrier to the revival of wine once the Prohibition era came to a close.

A lot of my wine snob friends turn up their noses at Gallo wines and others like them, but I think you have to appreciate the role they played in the rebirth of wine in America. Ernest and Julio Gallo founded their eponymous California winery in 1933 at just the moment when production and sale of wine became legal again. The American wine industry, as you can probably appreciate, was in a sorry state indeed.

In addition to all the problems I've just listed, add one more. The death of Prohibition did not mean the end of wine market controls. The federal government turned over wine distribution regulation to state governments while retaining certain controls in the Treasury Department's Alcohol and Tobacco Tax and Trade Bureau. This act did even more to fragment the wine market by subjecting it to both several layers of regulation (federal, state, local) and multiple systems of distribution controls. Interstate wine trade was subject to a maze of rules and regulations, and each state's internal wine market was different. In theory, the end of Prohibition created a huge potential market for wine in America, but in practice, the new regime replaced one huge barrier to wine with hundreds of smaller ones.

Gallo and the other wine pioneers of the era evolved around the bottlenecks they confronted. The most obvious key to their success was that their professionally made wine was of much higher quality than the rotgut homemade stuff that buyers had grown accustomed to. But you shouldn't imagine that their aim was to make fine wines to rival the best of Burgundy and Bordeaux. The fragmentation of the American market and the corruption of the American palate meant that American wine needed to be targeted at the mass-market middle, where a broad enough consumer base could be found to make the big investment in multistate distribution worthwhile, not the fine wine heights.

The early strategy for Gallo and other post-Prohibition pioneers was to make large quantities of wine and ship them in bulk (in railroad tanker cars for the most part) to clients across the country who would bottle the wine and sell it under their own label. It was an economical system because the extra weight of the bottle was added close to the final buyer's market, and that put most of the burden of meeting local liquor regulations on the local bottlers and distributors who were best situated to deal with them.

Wineries like Gallo grew quite large, with storage capacity denominated in the millions of gallons, but they were not household names and didn't promote national brands. They supplied commodity wines to local firms that bottled and sold wine but rarely made it. Growing grapes (under contract to a winery) and making wine and selling it were surprisingly discrete links in the mass-market-wine commodity chain.

World War II changed all that. More than half of the fleet of wine tanker railcars that were key to the prewar wine system were conscripted—used to transport industrial alcohol to make armaments. The best way to get wine to market during World War II was to bottle (and brand) it at the winery and use readily available boxcars to ship cases of wine across the country. In a matter of months, the tank car shortage turned companies like Gallo from anonymous bulk wine producers into nationally distributed bottled-wine brands.

This pattern persisted in the early postwar years and is responsible for the way the wine wall looked in the 1960s. A pretty thin selection, except in big-city specialty stores, because the fragmented market structure made national distribution cost-prohibitive for most winemakers. Top-shelf wines came from the Old World. American wines were aimed at the mass-market middle and below, wine drinkers whose palates were still recovering from the Prohibition hangover.

AMERICAN WINE'S UNLIKELY REBIRTH

Zoom ahead a few years to 1970. Hugh Johnson, the eminent British wine writer, visited California and said he was impressed. He tried to persuade skeptical Americans (especially, I suspect, Eastern elites) that their homegrown wines were good enough to drink: "It seems curious that I, a visitor from Europe, should be telling Americans about the unrecognized glories of some of their country's produce."[3] His eyes were opened, he said, by the very first glass . . . of Gallo Chablis (poured from a half-gallon jug). He praised the Gallo Vin Rosé and Hearty Burgundy, too, as "clean, fresh and in perfect condition," in contrast to French wines, which were so highly variable—filled with peaks and depressing troughs compared to the consistent American goods. Johnson visited other winemakers, Mondavi, Mirassou, and Louis Martini among them, but it was that clean, inexpensive Gallo Chablis that lingered in his memory. There certainly was fine wine being made in California in the 1970s. The question was, Would anyone buy it? And then came Robert Mondavi.[4]

I like to say that Robert Mondavi tried to do for American wine what Julia Child (public television's *The French Chef*) tried to do for American cuisine: revolutionize it by convincing Americans that they could not just imitate the French but also maybe better them at their own game. Julia Child succeeded, although not by herself, of course. American cuisine was transformed by her books and *The French Chef*, which aired from 1963 to 1973. She changed the idea of food in America. American ingredients, French techniques. Bring them together, and cooks could be chefs.

Robert Mondavi did the same thing for wine. He was convinced that American grapes and Old World techniques could produce world-class wines. And he was right. When the Robert Mondavi Winery opened in Oakville in 1966, it was the first major new investment in Napa Valley in decades, and it changed everything (not by itself, of course) and paved the way for a distinctly American vision of fine wine that coexists today along with a Gallo-tinted image of mass-market wines. The Mondavi winery wasn't just a vineyard and production facility; it was a destination. Mondavi knew that wine and a story sold better than wine by itself, so he set out to create a facility that would glow with a particularly California aura. It stood alone in the 1960s as an outpost of fine wine, and it stands alone today, even though it's surrounded by other wineries it inspired.

It took one more event to shake up perceptions of American wine and accelerate the country's hangover cure. We call it the Judgment of Paris, although it has nothing much to do with Greek mythology. Here's what happened. To celebrate the bicentennial of American independence, a Paris-based British wine merchant organized a comparative tasting of leading French and American wines. George Taber, then a *Time* magazine correspondent in Paris, recorded the event for posterity.[5] A popular 2008 film, *Bottle Shock*, may be more fiction than fact in the details, but it amusingly passes on the shocking result to today's audience.

The judges were French experts, and the French wines were first rate. Fortunately, the American labels were not Gallo, Almaden, and Paul Masson, although that would have been interesting, too. Instead, Steven Spurrier rounded up California Chardonnays from Chateau Montelena, Chalone, and Freemark Abbey and Cabernets from Stag's Leap Wine Cellars, Ridge Vineyards, Clos Du Val, and Heitz Cellars, among others.

Given the low expectations, it would have been surprising if the California wines simply held their own in this exalted company. In fact, however, the French judges were stunned to find, when the bottles were revealed, that they had awarded top marks to two California wines. Suddenly, and to everyone's surprise, California was on the map. Nothing was proven at the 1976 Paris tasting, but much was revealed about both the wines on the table and the winds of change that were sweeping around the world. And so began the slow, then quick, emergence of American wine and the vast unexpected wine wall of today.

WINE BY THE NUMBERS

One way to understand how much wine in America has changed is to look at the number of wine choices consumers enjoy, which is vastly greater than just a few decades ago. The US wine industry has absolutely exploded. There were a little more than one thousand bonded wineries in the United States in 1940. The number fell to about nine hundred by 1950 and just five hundred by 1960. That's the Prohibition hangover effect. The number of wineries then fell again and did not return to five hundred (half the 1940 figure) until about 1975. I think you could have put a bottle of every single different wine produced in the

United States in 1970 onto the shelves of a modern wine megastore like Total Wine & More and still have had room to spare.

The winery count recovered to about 1,000 by 1980–1981 and finally grew to more than 1,600 by 1990. Then came the growth years, with the number of wineries nearly doubling to three thousand by 2000–2001. That's fast growth, but the wine surge was only beginning. The Wine Institute reports that between 2000 and 2005, more than two thousand new wineries were added to the US total, about eight hundred in California and the rest in other parts of the country.

Wine Business Monthly calculates that at the start of 2021, there were wineries in every one of the United States, adding up to 9,352 total American bonded wineries. Add to this the 1,657 "virtual" wineries that sell wine that others produce, and you have a grand total of 11,009 wine producers. What a change in a relatively short time. But that's just part of the story because these are only the domestic wine producers, and 30 to 40 percent of the wine on American store shelves comes from other countries. No wonder upscale supermarkets can stock hundreds or even thousands of different imported and domestic wines, and some restaurant wine lists are as thick as a book. Five hundred wineries to 11,000 and growing. Did anyone back in the 1960s see this explosion coming? I doubt it.

GOT WINE?

I think the future of wine holds many twists, turns, and surprises. If we look back in twenty or thirty years, we'll be amazed at how much has changed and probably surprised, too, at what hasn't. Why do I think this? Partly, as we've just seen, because wine has changed so much in the last few decades. The who, what, when, where, how, and why questions all have different answers today than they did just a few decades ago. That's reason enough to believe that wine, with its many quaint traditions, is still changing fast.

But there's another reason I see change ahead. I've seen what's happened to milk. Do you remember those "Got Milk?" advertisements that were everywhere a few years ago? That "Got Milk?" promotion campaign ran for twenty-five years and attracted lots of attention. All sorts of celebrities posed with milk mustaches (aka moo-staches) to draw attention to milk and its broad appeal. Everyone enjoys milk—that was the message. The Whoopi Goldberg ad was my favorite. But memorable as these advertisements are, they were fighting a losing battle. Increasingly, American consumers don't follow the "Got Milk?" path.

I first realized this a few years ago when I heard wine economist guru Karl Storchmann talk about trends in various consumer beverages. He examined Google data about searches for wine, tea, coffee, milk, and water and concluded that, while water was rocking it, milk was fading fast. "Milk is all over," Karl proclaimed.[6] Karl wasn't wrong. Dean Foods, America's largest milk producer, filed for bankruptcy in November 2019. Milk sales fell for four years in a row as Americans shifted to plant-based cow milk alternatives, including oat milk and almond milk. Got milk? Yes. Always. But increasingly it doesn't come from a cow. Maybe milk really is all over, at least compared to its old status. And if it can happen to milk, maybe it can happen to anything.

When you think about it, what happened to milk is a little bit like what seems to be happening to wine. There are lots of new products available that compete with wine, including craft beer, craft spirits, and fruit-flavored alcoholic sparkling water. Some of these products are popular in part because they have less alcohol than wine, addressing a health concern in the same way that almond milk avoids a health problem for some dairy-intolerant consumers. Is wine all over? I don't think so. But could big changes be in the cards as consumer preferences for all kinds of products shift with the times?

The comfortable traditions of wine haven't changed very much since the 1960s, but just about everything else has. Wine is different now. There are more choices from more places at more price points. Everyday wine is better now and cheaper for the quality you get, although iconic wines from legendary producers are often priced beyond the means of ordinary people. Wine's social role has changed, too, especially in the New World, where it has become as much a lifestyle expression as a beverage. At the same time, however, concern that wine is being commercialized and homogenized—McDonaldized, in short—continues to be voiced.

The wine wall today could not look more different from the dismal product patch of the 1960s, don't you agree? It is, as I explain in the coming chapters, the semiglorious creation of globalization, which has broadened the world of wine; brand-driven commodification, which has deepened its commercial core and shifted power within it; and the revenge of the terroirist resistance, who seek to preserve and protect a particular idea of wine and its meaning. These are three forces that have created today's wine world, and I think they will continue to shape its future.

The future of wine? Who knows? But it won't hurt to do some research to try to figure out where wine is going. In fact, I think it will be fun! You've got to pull lots of corks to get any answers in the world of wine. To try to get a feel for the future, let's look more closely at the present. This will require a short trip to one of your favorite places, the familiar wine aisle of your supermarket.

But first we should taste wine. Turn the page to find your first wine-tasting assignment, a sampling of special wines that illustrate this book's main themes. Grab your wineglass and follow me. We have work to do!

A TOAST TO
WINE WARS II

Each of the main sections of *Wine Wars II* (I call them "flights," after the term for a selection of wines to be tasted together) concludes with a suggested wine tasting intended to allow you to consider these ideas in a different way, one that draws on all your senses. Wine is the perfect choice, don't you think?

Our first tasting is centered around Champagne, that magical sparkling wine that comes from the Champagne region in France. Why Champagne? Well, because it is a celebratory wine, and what better occasion to celebrate than the start of a new book. Besides, for many of us, Champagne was the first wine we ever tasted when we joined a toast to celebrate a holiday like New Year's or a special event like a birthday, wedding, anniversary, or graduation. The taste of Champagne, the special effect of the bubbles, and the sound of a popping cork and clinking glasses all come together in happy memories.

But there is another reason for this Champagne toast. Champagne embodies all the important themes of *Wine Wars II*. It is, first of all, a global wine. Although Champagne is not an especially large winegrowing region, you will find its products almost everywhere around the world. Some of the most important Champagne producers have global reach. Möet & Chandon is famous for its luxury Champagne wines, for example. But its parent company, the global luxury-goods conglomerate Möet Hennessy Louis Vuitton, also makes sparkling wine under the Chandon label in California, Argentina, Brazil, Australia, China, and India.[1] All are high-quality sparkling wines, but each differs from the others. And only one is Champagne.

That's because (this is the second theme of this book) Champagne is more than just a region; it is also a brand that is protected with fierce determination because of its enormous market value. Having that word *Champagne* on the label makes the wine inside worth more than other sparkling wines. You can see this effect at the wine shop if you look closely. Some say that the special technique for creating the bubbles in Champagne was actually developed in another region of France, Limoux. Crémant de Limoux is a delicious wine. Different—made in the same way as Champagne but from different grapes in different conditions. And it is usually much cheaper than Champagne because it lacks that brand's cachet.

Champagne is more expensive than many other wines because consumers are willing to pay the higher price. But cost is also a factor. Not just the cost of producing the wine, however, but also the cost of promoting the brand. Some say that the largest single contributor to the cost of a bottle of Champagne is marketing.

The rise of luxury Champagne brands has generated a number of interesting reactions, including one that is a sort of "terroirist" resistance movement. Grape growers do very well in Champagne. They get high prices for the Pinot Noir, Chardonnay, and Pinot Meunier grapes they sell to the big Champagne houses. But some of them would like to capture more value from their labors and express their winemaking abilities, too. So they make what are called "grower Champagnes." These wines are made by the same methods using the same grape varieties as the luxury brands but without the big marketing budgets. Look for "RM" on the label. That stands for Récoltant Manipulant, the French term for a grower-producer.

Champagne thus symbolizes the globalization, brand-driven commodification, and "terroirist" resistance themes of *Wine Wars II*. Champagne is also a victim of wine's "triple crisis," which we examine in the final flight of chapters. Champagne experienced an economic crisis, for example, during the COVID-19 pandemic, when the celebratory occasions it is most closely associated with suddenly disappeared. It was already dealing with an environmental crisis as climate change raised growing-season temperatures, making it more and more difficult to consistently produce the grapes to make the wines that we know and love as Champagne.

And Champagne has to deal with an identity crisis, too. The French want us to know that Champagne can only come from Champagne, but in fact, delightful sparkling wines are made all around the world (sometimes, as we've just seen, by the French themselves). When people toast to health and happiness, they increasingly choose other sparkling wines from other regions. Cava from Spain, for example, is made from indigenous Spanish grapes using the classic method in Champagne. Prosecco is made in northeast Italy from the Glera grape using a different technique. Prosecco has become incredibly popular in the last dozen years, undermining Champagne's fizzy hegemony.

The question of Champagne's special status was brought to the fore on July 2, 2021, when Russian president Vladimir Putin signed into law new wine regulations. Sparkling wines made in Russia can describe themselves with the common Russian term *Shampanskoye*, which sounds a lot like *Champagne* and is sort of the brand name for this type of wine in Russia. It is what you would ask for at a bar or restaurant, for example. Imported Champagne is free to use its French name but is forbidden to call itself *Shampanskoye*. Worse yet, Champagne is required to identify itself as mere "sparkling wine" on the back label, putting itself on the same level as Cava, Prosecco, and other fizzy wines from around the world. With one stroke, Champagne is demoted and Russian sparklers elevated, at least in this context. It is kind of a big deal because the Russian market buys a lot of sparkling wine, including Champagne. French producers and officials are outraged.

Can Champagne keep its special place in the shifting world of wine? Or has its identity been undermined by its own success, combined with the complex political, economic, and natural forces at work in global wine today?

To celebrate our beginning, I propose that you get a few friends together and pull three corks. Let me suggest two strategies for your tasting. The first is to try wines from three different countries made using the same grapes as Champagne and the same method: the second bubble-producing fermentation in the bottle that the wine is sold in. Look for indication of "classic method" or "fermented in this bottle." Only Champagne producers are allowed to call it "méthode champenoise." Whichever wines you choose, I think you will discover that although Champagne only comes from Champagne, some pretty fine non-Champagnes are made elsewhere.

A second strategy, and I think you will find this even more interesting, is to taste a Champagne from France, a Cava from Spain, and a Prosecco from Italy. I guarantee that you will taste the difference and find one wine that you like above the rest. And, I hope, each taste will make you think of the themes of this book.

Cheers, to the start of a new book adventure. Cheers to *Wine Wars II*.

FLIGHT 1
GLOBALIZATION—
BLESSING OR CURSE?

3

THE DA VINO CODE

The Metropolitan Market on Proctor Street in Tacoma, Washington, is a typical upscale American supermarket. It has all the upscale basics: a delicatessen, a fishmonger, fresh seasonal local produce, a coffee bar, and a gelato stand. You can buy cat food, cornflakes, and laundry soap at competitive prices. There is sushi, too, along with various panini and espresso drinks that pair nicely with a proprietary chocolate chip snack called "The Cookie." Or, for $6.99, you can take home a quarter of a 1.9-kilogram loaf of Poilâne whole-grain sourdough bread, flown in fresh from Paris every Wednesday. Eat it plain—it is delicious—or topped with European butter and a swish of raw monofloral Manuka honey from New Zealand. You can find them all on the Met's generous shelves.

The Metropolitan Market is the kind of store that is increasingly common in American cities, patronized by people like me, who take their culinary cues from celebrity chefs on the Food Network. It is to foodies what Home Depot is to the DIY set: an adult toy store where imaginations can run wild.

You probably have a store like the Met in your town, and because you are reading this book, you probably go there frequently so that you can check out the wine wall. I'd like you to go there now (or, if that's not convenient, to imagine that you are there) because this chapter requires your participation. I don't want to *tell* you what the wine world looks like, although that's easy enough to do. I want you to see for yourself—and to be surprised.

I'm sending you to the supermarket because that's where the battle for the future of wine is being waged. It isn't the only battlefield; the idea of wine is contested wherever and whenever wine is bought and sold. Restaurants and bars. Wine shops and auction floors. Tasting rooms and cellar doors. Shoot, I've even bought wine in the middle of the night, directly from the maker, from the back of a pickup truck on a dark city street. (Don't ask.)

But the supermarket is the central stage of this story, and that's where we need to begin. And to understand what's going on there, we will need to inspect it closely, looking for the key to its secret code.

THE GRAPE WALL OF WINE

So let's walk the wine wall together. I want you to get a personal sense of the world of wine that global markets bring to your door every day. So first, please just stand back and try to get a sense of the scale of the place. There are probably more than forty linear feet of wine bins, boxes, shelves, and racks stocked from toe to tip with bottles, jugs, cans, and boxes of wine. There are more than 1,500 different wines on display at the Met—1,500 different answers to the question, What should I drink tonight? It's like searching for a needle in a haystack if you don't have a strategy.

The wine wall is really the Grape Wall (pardon the pun) of the upscale supermarket empire. But wait, there's more: more wine, and more wine choices, scattered around the store—in the cooler; by the bakery; and around the meat, fish, and produce displays. How does the wine wall compare with other product venues in the store? There are clearly more choices for wine than for any other type of product, don't you think? Look around. Beer? Lots of choices but nothing like wine. Milk? Not even close. Breakfast cereals take up a lot of room and there are sure a lot of them to choose from, but the variety can't compare to wine. What seemed to be an overwhelming variety of gourmet cheeses is nothing compared to the wine selection. Your upscale supermarket brings the world to your doorstep, it's true, and showers you with choice. The wine wall is its crowning achievement. No wonder people spend so much time staring at it, trying to make sense of the choices.

Fifteen hundred wines is a lot, but it is not an exceptionally large collection for a retail store. The Tacoma Boys farm store a few miles away has a lot of space to fill in its big barn-size facility, so it can afford to give more room to wine. It stocks more than three thousand different wines. The nearest Total Wine & More big-box alcoholic beverage superstore always carries at least five thousand wines. Your store may have fewer wines or more, but in any case, it sure has a lot of them.

You've stared at this wine wall dozens of times; did you really appreciate the embarrassment of riches here, at least compared with the rest of the store? Now that you have a quantitative sense of this abundance, I would like you to walk through the wine aisle a couple of times to get a more qualitative feeling for what's going on.

First, try to get a sense of the types of wines offered. Yes, I know—red and white. But there are really many more types of wines here than you think. Red and white table wine, for sure, and also sparkling wines, dessert wines, and several types of sherries and ports. You will find wine in bottles; half-bottles; double-bottle "magnums"; 1-liter Tetra Pak containers; and 1.5-, 3-, and 5-liter boxes. You can find wine and wine spritzers in cans, too. Wine in small "single-serving" containers like cans is one of the fastest-growing categories in the United States, but there's a problem. Because wine typically has more than twice the alcohol of beer or hard seltzer, the recommended serving size is proportionately smaller. Chugging down a whole can of wine, which might seem natural if you are used to cans of beer or soda, can produce an unexpected and unwanted buzz very quickly.

The alcohol content of these wines ranges from 0 to nearly 20 percent, and prices are as low as a couple of bucks per bottle to, well, the sky's the limit, depending on your store's clientele. I once saw a $100 bottle of Champagne on the shelf of a grocery store in a blue-collar neighborhood. Anything can happen here.

THE WORLD WINE WALL

Because this section of the book is about globalization, where does the wine come from? Assuming that your supermarket is in the United States, you will certainly find California wine. A lot of these wines are Gallo products (Gallo is the world's largest winemaker), although they won't all say Gallo on the label. One of the dark secrets of the wine wall is that many products are not actually made by the winery on the front label. They are made by others under contract, for example, or blended up from bulk wines from many different sources. Private-label wines bottled specifically for particular retailers or restaurants are a fast-growing phenomenon.

You should also be able to find products from Washington State, the number 2 US producer. Many of these wines are Ste. Michelle Wine Estates products, although they won't necessarily say this on the label, either, because Ste. Michelle also has many brands (such as Columbia Crest and 14 Hands) in its stable.

Keep looking for US wines. Wine is made and sold commercially in all fifty states, so you may well find wine from other parts of the United States on the shelf. Oregon has zoomed to prominence, for example, powered by its iconic Pinot Noir wines. New York, Virginia, and Michigan have important wine industries, and Ohio and Missouri are historically important wine regions.

Time to travel to the wine wall's Old World region. You should see wines from France, Italy, Germany, Portugal, and Spain and maybe Hungary, Greece, and Austria. Madeira, a wine from the Portuguese island off the Moroccan coast, is frequently seen on the fortified patch of the wine wall along with Port and Sherry.

Now find the New World section of the wall. These are wines from Australia, South Africa, New Zealand, Chile, Argentina, and maybe Canada, especially if there is a dessert wine section. Canada is famous for its sweet and expensive ice wines, although it makes good table wines, as well. These countries are not new to wine (wine has been produced in South Africa, for example, for more than 350 years); they are simply new in grabbing our attention after having been left off the wall for many years because of its focus on France, Italy, and California. Now they are back with a vengeance.

The only continent (apart from Antarctica) not well represented on your wine wall is Asia, unless you count Sake, which is made from rice. Japan has a small but thriving grape wine industry, and its wines can sometimes be found at larger Asian grocery stores, along with products from Thailand, India, and China, which sometimes are featured in restaurants that specialize in these countries' cuisines.

I predict that your upscale supermarket or wine shop will have wines from at least ten different countries and possibly as many as fifteen, which is amazing when you think of it. What is the next most "global" part of your grocery store? Fruits and vegetables? Maybe. Cheese? Possibly. The deli? Could be. Modern superstores are wonders of globalization, but there is no single product that routinely features more different international choices than wine.

All markets are local, even when they are global like wine, so your wine wall may feature some unusual labels based on local demand. Many immigrant families have settled in my part of town, for example, so some local stores carry specialty products, including wine, to bring them a sense of home. That's why I can sometimes find wines from Romania, Bulgaria, Georgia, and Moldova in certain stores. These are all major wine-producing countries (Georgia is the "cradle of wine," they say) that are trying to break into the world wine market. Occasionally, I find wines from Lebanon, Israel, and Croatia.

VINO EXCEPTIONALISM

This much choice demands organization, so look closely at how the wine wall is arranged, and compare it to other parts of the store. Is wine arranged like the beer, cereal, and snack aisles—by producer? Lots of aisles in the store rent shelf space to manufacturers, who array their products together in competition with other suppliers. Thus, Kellogg's Corn Flakes are in the Kellogg's section, not in some grouping of everyone's cornflakes. Ditto for Post cereals. It would make it easier to compare price if all the cornflakes were on the same shelf instead of scattered in different brand sections, but that's not the system. Kellogg's paid for this shelf, and it doesn't want any Post or General Mills products there.

Now, I have seen some wine walls organized this way—with all the Mondavi wines here (part of the Constellation Brands territory) and all the Turning Leaf wines there (in Gallo-ville)—but that's not how it works at my supermarket. State law stands in the way. Supermarkets make money renting shelf space to manufacturers, who then put all their products together on their "property," like hotels on a Monopoly board, but wine suppliers aren't allowed to pay for space in my state because their product contains alcohol. Alcoholic beverage sales are highly regulated in my state (as in most others). Distributors can't pay their way onto the shelves here, so they can't lease shelf acreage and must fight for position bottle by bottle.

Chances are that your wine wall is organized more like the General Assembly of the United Nations than the pasta or breakfast cereal section of the store. The American wines will be seated here, in one section, and arrayed according to the vocabulary of American wine, which is based on branded grape varietal wines. This is the language used by New World wine: brand/grape/region as in Mondavi/Cabernet Sauvignon/Napa Valley or Dancing Bull/Zinfandel/California.

The New World wine section is seated separately from the American wines, but the label identifiers use the same brand/variety/region system. You'll find Yellow Tail/Shiraz/southeastern Australia; Monkey Bay/Sauvignon Blanc/Marlborough, New Zealand; and Santa Rita/Cabernet Sauvignon/Maipo Valley, Chile. Apart from relatively trivial translation issues (Syrah = Shiraz), it is pretty easy to move back and forth among the various New World wine producers, which is without doubt a fact that has helped all of them increase global sales. Brand/variety/region is the lingua franca of the wine world today, just as English is the common tongue of the World Wide Web.

LOST IN TRANSLATION

It would simplify your wine wall choice if every wine were to identify itself according to a common classification system like brand/variety/region. This would be the vinous equivalent of a universal language—Esperanto for wine lovers. It would make choosing wine and understanding it much simpler than it is today.

And so, of course, nothing of the kind exists. Old World and New World speak different languages, both literally (how good is your German?) and figuratively in terms of product identification systems. The standard vocabulary of Old World wine is based on geography, and there are hundreds and hundreds of wine-producing regions and locales: Chablis, Bordeaux, Burgundy, and Beaujolais, for example. The wines of the regions are each based on a dominant grape variety or designated blend (Chardonnay, Cabernet Sauvignon and Merlot, Pinot Noir, and Gamay, respectively), but the wines are identified by their place of origin rather than grape type because the geographical designation is a sort of brand.

Brands come in many forms. In the New World, we are accustomed to private or corporate brands (Robert Mondavi, Yellow Tail, Cloudy Bay). The businesses that own these brands have an interest in maintaining consistent quality, and the brand is a way to communicate this to customers. In the Old World, appellations (official geographic designations) serve the same purpose, although they are collective brands ("owned" by the winemakers in the region) rather than private brands. Geographic designations define, more or less, as the case may be, what is in the bottle.

Old World geographical "brands" like Chianti and Beaujolais, therefore, advertise the quality of wines made by many different producers in a given region using the same basic grape inputs in the same way that New World brands like Mondavi and Penfolds identify the quality of wines by a single producer, sometimes but not always from a particular region and often using many different grape varieties.

A look at the Italian zone of your wine wall will illustrate the point. Many of the wines you find here are Chianti, which is both a style of wine and a geographic designation. Chianti wines must come from a particular geographic area in Tuscany and be made according to a particular recipe. In Chianti's case, the traditional recipe was set almost two hundred years ago by Baron Ricasoli and required the use of Sangiovese, Canaiolo, Trebbiano, and Malvasia grape varieties (Trebbiano and Malvasia are white grapes, unusual for a red wine). Until this recipe was revised a few years ago, winemakers could not legally use other grape varieties (or grapes from outside the Chianti zone) and call their wine Chianti. There are several subzones within Chianti (Chianti Classico is the most famous), and the wines come in differing quality levels, such as Superiore and Riserva. Chianti is a brand (and a valuable brand to producers in this region) but a complicated one that requires some study to master.

Old World brands are like foreign languages—powerful communication tools once you have mastered them but lofty barriers to entry for the uninformed. One reason the wine wall often seems much narrower than it really is (weren't you surprised to learn how many wines your supermarket stocks?) is that significant portions of it are terra incognita.

THE DA VINO CODE

Once you have learned the Old World language of wine, it is a tremendously useful tool because the differences between and among geographical areas and their wine traditions allow for subtle but important differences in wine to be expressed and appreciated. The problem is that the price of admission—the time and expense of mastering the hundreds of valley and village labels for each Old World nation—is very high and so discourages consumers. For the uninitiated, the language of European wine labels is an indecipherable code—not the *Da Vinci Code* but the Da Vino Code. One reason New World wines have become so popular, even in the Old World, is that you don't need to break the Da Vino Code to understand them. There is still a lot to know—Who are the best winemakers? What are the best vineyards? Which year is most reliable?—but the New World lingo is a much more transparent entry point to the world of wine.

A lot hides behind those European labels if you don't understand them, including most importantly the real diversity of the world of wine. I frequently hear that wine is being dumbed down and homogenized, and I think this is because New World wine labels make wine seem very simple, while the Old World labels are lost in translation. The best way to see this is to pick up some unfamiliar bottles from the Old World shelf and read the back labels. Many will tell you only the maker and importer names, but some at least will provide more information. What you will see if you persevere is a world of grapes and grape varieties that you possibly never knew existed. Rioja wines, from Spain, for example, are blends of Tempranillo, Garnacha, Mazuelo, and Graciano grapes. Valpolicella, from northern Italy, is a blend of Corvina, Rondinella, and Molinara grapes. The wines of Chinon, in the Loire Valley in France, are Cabernet Franc (or Breton, as it is known in the region).

If you spend enough time reading the back labels of the hundreds of bottles of wines in your supermarket, you will soon accumulate material to fill a book about the tremendous diversity of wine available to us today. You don't have to write the book, however, because it has already been done and by several different authorities. Jancis Robinson, the British wine critic, is author of one of the best: *Vines, Grapes and Wines: The Wine Drinker's Guide to Grape Varieties*, which has been continuously in print with frequent updates since 1986.

And so you can see that the wine wall is a very confusing space if you don't understand its secret code. Some of its territory is ruled by private brands that compete with one another to tell their story in the grape varieties that went into each bottle. The New World vocabulary is simple and clear and heavily marketed by the brand owners. The Old World of wine, however, is a kind of turf war among wine appellations. The appellation is the brand, and the product it defines is embedded in its name. Pinot Noir and Sauvignon Blanc are known by these names on the New World parts of the wall (California, Chile, or New Zealand, for example) but are classified as Burgundy and Sancerre, respectively, in French Old World territory.

TREASURE HUNT

Now it is time for a little treasure-hunting practice to help you appreciate the wine wall's complexity. Suppose that you'd like a smoky, spicy red wine to go with dinner—a Syrah! What choices do you have? Well, first you'll need to understand that Syrah also has an alias, Shiraz, which is used in Australia, South Africa, and occasionally the United States (to suggest an Aussie style of Syrah). So you will need to go to these parts of the wine wall to see what's on offer. Get a cart and start filling it with the Syrah wines you've found.

Syrah is called Syrah on the labels of wine from the United States, New Zealand, and Chile, just to name a few countries that produce wine from this grape, so you will need to visit each of these wine wall territories in turn. When you have finished (and by now you ought to have dozens and dozens of bottles in your basket, with prices ranging from very low to quite high), you will still have missed the most famous Syrah wines of them all—those from France. For these great wines, you must look for names associated with the northern Rhône region—Hermitage, if you can find it, along with Crozes-Hermitage, Cornas, and St. Joseph.

Don't get northern Rhône confused with the wines down the river, however. Wines of the southern Rhône feature the Grenache grape, although they aren't called Grenache, of course. These wines can be great, too, but they are different. Châteauneuf-du-Pape is based on Grenache, which is confusingly also called Garnacha in Spain, where it originated.

Now that you have a proper big pile of Syrah in your shopping cart, you still face the biggest choice: Which one? Obviously, they come from many different places, reflecting different climates and styles, and are made for different markets according to different practices and philosophies. You need to be a geographer (to chart the wine wall's curious map) and a linguist (to translate from Old World to New) if you are going to understand the future of wine. But that won't be enough. You'll also need to be a geologist who can read through the hidden strata that divide the wine wall into key market zones because price is the final part of the Da Vino Code puzzle.

NAVIGATING THE WINE WALL

The takeaway message of this chapter is that globalization has brought us an embarrassment of riches when it comes to wine. We have more choices from more places at more price points than can be imagined. And we want more.

But wine is changing in part because of the Da Vino Code problem. A world of global wine demands a global language of wine, and that language, for good or bad, is the New World vocabulary of brand/variety/region. As new buyers seek out wine labels they can understand, they will be drawn toward wines that identify themselves this way (and, if recent experience is any indicator, have cute animals on the label). The rise of these new brands will be stiff competition for a myriad of old, complicated geographic brands. What will they have to do to compete?

But before we think about that question, we need to consider a more basic one. How did all this wine get here in the first place? It takes two chapters to answer this question, and you'll need to leave the supermarket and come with me. We are going to two unlikely corners of the world of wine: New Zealand and London.

4

MISSIONARIES, MIGRANTS, AND MARKET REFORMS

The wine in my glass tonight is from New Zealand. It's a Sauvignon Blanc from Marlborough, on the South Island. It's a very good wine—fragrant, fruity, with a nice acid bite—but not a particularly rare wine. You can find it and other New Zealand wines in restaurants, wine shops, and supermarkets everywhere. You should probably pour yourself a glass to sip while you read this chapter.

What are the odds that a *New Zealand* wine would end up here? New Zealand is a former British colony, inhabited, according to popular stereotype, by fun-loving, beer-drinking rugby players, not Sauvignon-sipping socialites. Why would Kiwis make wine like this when they are so unlikely to drink it? Its wine production is small, as you would expect from a narrow island nation. New Zealand accounted for less than 1.3 percent of global wine production in 2020, according to OIV statistics, which put it at number 14 on the global wine table. That's not much wine in the global context, but in fact, it represents the result of more than thirty years of rapid growth.

When I wrote *Wine Wars* just a few years ago, New Zealand was a teeny-tiny wine power, with 0.3 percent of world wine output, and ranked number 25 in the world. Back then, New Zealand made less wine than Brazil, Uruguay, and Mexico. Gallo made more than eight times as much wine each year as did all New Zealand producers put together. Still very small compared to the big three of Italy, France, and Spain, New Zealand has zoomed up to the next tier of total production, along with Romania, Hungary, and Austria—small European countries with thousands of years of wine history.

New Zealand punches above its weight on global markets. The OIV reports that New Zealand ranks seventh in the world in the value of its wine exports. Only France, Italy, Spain, Australia, Chile, and the United States have higher export sales. The value of tiny New Zealand's exports is more than twice the exports of much larger Argentina.

New Zealand is just a drop in the global wine bucket. No doubt, the odds against finding a New Zealand wine in your glass or on the supermarket wine wall would seem to be spectacularly long. And yet here it is—and abundantly so. On a visit a few years ago to Richmond, Virginia, to give a talk, I went with my wife's parents, Mike and Gert Trbovich, to try to find New Zealand wine at a typical suburban Kroger store. We counted thirty-six different Kiwi bottlings! Clearly something is going on. So how did it happen?

The short answer is globalization, the process that delivers so many products from unexpected places to your doorstep each day. But it wasn't easy. It took an accident of geography and three waves of globalization to bring New Zealand wine to your table.

AN ACCIDENT OF GEOGRAPHY

The conventional wisdom is that global products like wine are made everywhere, sold everywhere, and consumed everywhere. Globalization covers the earth like a coat of paint, whether we're talking about wine, hamburgers, or reality TV programs. We imagine that globalization works like this, but we know it isn't so. Even McDonald's isn't really global, although it is an oft-used symbol of globalization. It has stores in only 119 of the 200 or so recognized nations of the world today. McDonald's restaurants spring up when a country achieves a moderate standard of living and adopts a legal system that protects private property and encourages markets. About 40 percent of countries have unfriendly economic and political environments; Big Macs just won't grow there.

Wine is even more dependent on the environment because it is an agricultural product. *Vitis vinifera* grapes—the ones that make the wines we love—are even more finicky than Ronald McDonald. They grow best within two relatively narrow bands that circle the earth, between latitudes 30°N and 50°N and 30°S and 50°S. The northern ribbon of wine is the most familiar. Thirty degrees of latitude marks the southern wine boundary in the Old World, for example— Morocco, Algeria, Israel. It's too warm for wine grapes below this line, although high elevation (which brings temperatures down) can sometimes compensate for low latitude. Fifty degrees is about the northern limit—Germany's Mosel vineyards, for example. It is very difficult to ripen wine grapes farther north than this (and cold winters can damage the vines), although exceptions can be made. Wine grapes love to perch on steep hillsides in northern climes; the slanted aspect acts like a solar panel to collect more heat in the summer and helps cold air slide down and away in the winter.

If you follow the 30°–50° wine belt around the Northern Hemisphere, you see that it embraces the main vineyard areas of Europe and North America and wraps around to pick up Chinese and Japanese wine regions, too. Wine is consumed north or south of this band, but little is made. The northern wine belt covers a lot of area and includes about 85 percent of the wine made in the world. Why so much? Because it includes France, Italy, and Spain, which together make about half the world's wine. But the map reveals an even better reason.

The 30°–50° wine belt in the North includes a lot of land, much of it suitable for vines. The southern wine belt, however, is mainly ocean. Only a little territory (Chile, Uruguay, Argentina, and a bit of Brazil in South America; the tip of Africa; New Zealand; and parts of Australia) have environments friendly to wine. Geography blessed the North with vast vineyard resources. The main land areas of the Southern Hemisphere—much of Brazil, most of Africa, the Indian subcontinent, and two-thirds of Australia—are too close to the equator to reliably produce wine grapes without some natural or technical offsetting factor. Even South Africa's vineyards would be too warm for fine wine grapes were it not for a cold current that flows up from Antarctica and keeps a lid on the heat.

The two wine belts are where wine was first born and where wine-drinking people migrated, the Greeks and Phoenicians first (to Italy and Spain), then the Romans (to France and Germany), followed later by conquerors and colonists from Portugal, Spain, and France to the rest of the world—or, rather, to other parts of the wine belt, north and south. European settlers went outside the wine belt when necessary (drawn by oil or gold, for example), but they mainly moved within and between the wine belts, where they found the climate friendly and could taste the food and wine of home.

As an economist, I find the wine belt fascinating. It is where most of the wine in the world comes from. It is, in fact, where most of *everything* in the world comes from! That 30°–50° band holds much of the world's nonoil wealth and produces most of its GDP. It is possible for a nation to be poor in this wine belt (Moldova comes to mind), but it is hard for a country to be *rich* (except for natural resource wealth) outside it. Geography isn't destiny, but it has some effect on the choices that destiny gets to make.

That wine (and a high standard of living) should be made in New Zealand is, therefore, at least in part a happy accident, for if these islands had been placed a few degrees' latitude farther north or south, *Vitis vinifera* grapes would have been an unlikely crop. Wine grapes didn't get to New Zealand by accident, of course, and the wine didn't make itself. So as much as geography and destiny played a part, the miracle of your wineglass is a people story.

FROM MISSIONARIES TO DALLY PLONK

Bibles and wine grapes came together to New Zealand in 1816, both planted by the British missionary Reverend Samuel Marsden at Kerikeri on the Bay of Islands on the North Island. This fact serves as a reminder that many of the roots of today's complex global economy can be traced back to seeds planted by missionaries, who were often the most enthusiastic and determined globalizers of their day. French missionaries, Marist priests from Lyon, brought their own Bibles and grapes in 1830, planting them first at Poverty Bay and later at Hawke's Bay.

Commercial wine production started in the 1830s, when James Busby made wine to sell to British troops before leaving for Australia to operate a similar and more successful business there. It took a while for a real wine industry to develop, however, because British soldiers, settlers, and visiting sailors were all more interested in beer and spirits than wine. The colonial government didn't put much emphasis on wine or wine exports in part because of a strong temperance movement in New Zealand but also because Australia had been chosen to serve as the "vineyard of the British Empire," thereby reducing British dependency on the hated French.

No one seems to have had any doubts that grapes would grow in New Zealand (thanks to that lucky accident of geography). Natural conditions were favorable, but market conditions were not. Many growers experimented with wine with greater or lesser degrees of success, but the industry didn't achieve a critical mass.

The wine industry in New Zealand didn't really take off until the next great wave of globalization in the years on either side of 1900. Immigrants from central and eastern Europe came to New Zealand, trading depression and war at home for jobs as farmworkers and gumdiggers. They brought with them both a thirst for wine and the know-how to make it—supply *and* demand.

Thus, many of the most famous names in New Zealand wine—their Gallos and Mondavis—are not British, as you might expect, or even French, as might be the case given French influence in the South Pacific, but Lebanese and Croatian. Assid Abraham Corban with his sons, Wadier and Khaleel, built

Corban wines into the dominant New Zealand producer through the 1960s. Dalmatian gumdiggers Josip and Stipan Babic created the wine that bears their name today; Zuva and Nikola Nobilo did the same. Ivan Yukich was the most successful of them all, however, building his Montana brand to be the country's largest, absorbing Corban's before being absorbed itself by Seagram's of Canada and then ultimately by the French drinks conglomerate Pernod Ricard, which eventually changed the brand name to Brancott Estate.

The inexpensive workingman's drink of a hundred years ago was called "Dally plonk" in New Zealand because the producers (and possibly also the consumers) were Dalmatian immigrants. The era of globalization that brought Dalmatian gumdiggers to New Zealand planted the roots of the cultural vines that grew the grapes that made the wine in your glass.

This period also produced New Zealand's first "flying winemaker," although "sailing winemaker" is more accurate historically. Flying winemakers are wine consultants who travel back and forth between the Northern and Southern Hemispheres, giving advice and encouraging winemaking enterprises.

New Zealand's great winemaking consultant was Romeo Bragato. Born in what is now Croatia and trained in Italy at the Regia Scuola di Viticoltura ed Enologia at Conegliano, he sailed first to Australia in 1889, where the government employed him to advise winegrowers, before moving to New Zealand in 1902, where he held a similar post until 1909. Excerpts from Bragato's reports indicate that he recognized New Zealand's great wine potential, even singling out Central Otago as an ideal place to grow the Pinot Noir that it is celebrated for today. Interestingly, he promoted vineyard plantings just about everywhere in New Zealand except Marlborough, which didn't impress him. Chances are good that the wine in your glass is from Marlborough, Bragato's undiscovered country.

THE THIRD WAVE

It would be nice to be able to say that New Zealand's comparative advantage in fine wine was quickly developed once Bragato and others identified it, but that wasn't the case. While some good wine was made, the bulk of production lacked distinction apart from sugar and alcohol. When Kiwis drank wine, they went for the same sweet, fortified productions that their Australian neighbors were gulping down.

It took one more wave of globalization to put this particular wine in your glass. Seagram's investment in Montana in the 1970s gave the firm the capital it needed to expand production. On the recommendation of another consultant—this one, I'm told, from California—Montana planted the first Sauvignon Blanc vineyards in Marlborough at the Brancott Estate, virgin wine territory at the time. The wines were immediately recognized for their distinctive quality. It is tempting to say that the rest is history, but in fact, just the opposite was the case.

The birth of Marlborough wine had the bad luck to coincide with an era of spectacularly misguided economic policy in New Zealand. Like many less developed countries, New Zealand adopted the policies that political economists call import-substituting industrialization. In an attempt to emulate Japan's postwar success, New Zealand raised import barriers, subsidized domestic production, picked "winning" sectors, and generally tried to grow a modern economy from the inside out. This is never an easy task and more so given New Zealand's limited population and resources.

The result in the wine industry was a vast increase in plantings of high-quantity, low-quality grapes as everyone aimed for the captive domestic bulk wine market—the market for Dally plonk. This led, predictably, to a glut of bad wine that could not be sold at home or abroad, falling prices, and a general collapse of the industry. Having failed to develop by keeping imports out, New Zealand changed course and liberalized its economic policies, lowering trade barriers, eliminating agricultural subsidies, and embracing competition and global markets. The wine in your glass owes its existence—dare I say it?—to these neoliberal market reforms!

NEW ZEALAND WINE TRANSFORMED

A transformation of the New Zealand wine industry followed. Cheap bulk wines from Australia and then also Chile flooded in, capturing the bottom end of the market. Domestic Dally plonk was replaced with imported Aussie wine. The government paid winegrowers to rip out their old vines (a process called grubbing up) and replant with high-quality classic varieties like Pinot Noir and Sauvignon Blanc. Winegrowers began to focus on quality, both because quantity no longer paid and because, with good imported wines now readily available, quality was the only way to compete. The crisis of the 1980s finally created the foundation for the wine industry that Romeo Bragato envisioned eight decades before. That's how these great New Zealand wines came to be produced, but how did they get from way over there to way over here, in your glass? How did

New Zealand supply connect with you and me, the demand-side market? Globalization is the answer again.

In 1985, a Marlborough winemaker named Ernie Hunter entered his Sauvignon Blanc in the *Sunday Times* of London's annual wine festival competition, where it was unexpectedly voted the top wine. His Chardonnay scored big the next year, showing that Hunter's wines weren't flukes. This public success opened up the world's most important wine market, British supermarkets like Tesco and Sainsbury's, to Hunter's wines and soon to Marlborough wines and New Zealand wines generally.

At the same time, Cloudy Bay, a Marlborough wine produced by the quality western Australian firm Cape Mentelle (now owned by LVMH—Moët Hennessy Louis Vuitton), also hit the British market through the parent company's distribution network and achieved spectacular success. A firm foundation for New Zealand wine exports was established.

Today the New Zealand wine industry is remarkably globalized, with huge (given the scale of the industry) exports of both bottled and bulk wine. The United States, the United Kingdom, and Australia are its biggest export markets. Foreign ownership dominates the wine sector: Pernod Ricard of France (Brancott Estate and Corban's, plus other brands) and the US conglomerate Constellation Brands (market leader Kim Crawford). Other important brands, including Cloudy Bay, Craggy Range, Clos Henri, and Whitehaven, have international owners, too. New Zealand is both a destination and a home base for dozens of "flying winemakers." British missionaries, Dalmatian gumdiggers, Canadian investors, California consultants, British supermarkets, French multinationals—and three waves of globalization: That's the unlikely story of how Marlborough Sauvignon Blanc came to be poured into your wineglass.

IT TAKES THREE WAVES

I would like to say that it always takes three transforming M waves—missionaries, migrants, and market reforms—to bring a country's wine to the global market, but that's not always true. Missionaries did introduce wine to Chile and Argentina, two important New World producers. Jesuit missionaries brought wine to these countries in the sixteenth century, both for their own consumption and for use in religious observances. Missionaries were important in Mexico and California, too.

Merchants more than priests were responsible for the early wine industry in South Africa; the Dutch East India Company established the first vineyards there around 1652. The Cape of Good Hope was an obvious provisioning stop for ships sailing between Europe and Asia. Food, water, and especially wine were much in demand. Wine was especially valuable because its antibacterial qualities made it safer to drink than much of the water available at the time. By the seventeenth century, South African wines had developed a global reputation and were a precious commodity in Europe. Constantia, a sweet South African white wine, was one of the three most famous wines in the world (along with Tokaji from Hungary and Grasă de Cotnari from Moldova). It comforted Napoleon, who specifically requested it, during his exile on St. Helena.

The British developed a taste for wine hundreds of years ago when Bordeaux became English territory in 1152. For three hundred years, Bordeaux was Britain's vineyard, and the wines that the British call Claret were everywhere to be found. When Bordeaux returned to French hands, the British began what turned out to be a long search for a secure source of good wine. Wine grapes were introduced to Australia around 1800 to create an alternative to France. Australia was envisioned as the vineyard of the British Empire, something that it became in the 1930s (and is again to a certain extent today), despite the long shipping distances involved, due in part to imperial preferential trade policies.

Early wine production in Chile was so successful that the Spanish government tried (unsuccessfully) to forbid new plantings (just as the Romans did centuries before in France) in order to limit competition for their own wines.

Missionaries are not always needed to create a vibrant wine industry, but migrants nearly always are. In California, some pioneers were migrants who came with the Gold Rush and then discovered they would make more money selling wine to prospectors than panning for nuggets in the rivers and streams. Spanish and Italian migrants established a major wine industry in Argentina, simultaneously importing supply-side know-how and demand-side wine-drinking habits. Migrants also played an important role in Australia. Swiss immigrants planted vines in the Yarra Valley; Dalmatians, in western Australia; and migrants from Silesia, in the Barossa Valley.

Migrants were even important in China. Changyu, China's oldest winemaker, was founded in 1892 to make wine for the large population of European expatriates in China at that time. Now its wine finds a market among China's growing urban capitalist class who express their worldliness in part through upscale consumer goods.

CRISIS AND CHANGE IN GLOBAL WINE

Missionaries and migrants were key components of the first two waves of globalization that swept wine to the far corners of the earth. They planted the grapes, but they didn't build the global markets. That was the role of the third global wave, which was powered by market reforms. And one thing that I have learned from studying wine economics is that market reforms seldom happen without a crisis to focus the minds of growers and policy makers.

We've already seen how crisis and reform were crucial to the development of New Zealand's wine sector. Protectionist policies encouraged overproduction of low-quality wines. Too much wine to sell at home. Not good enough to sell abroad. Collapse, grubbing up, replanting, reform. New Zealand wine has done much better as a global competitor than it did as a protected industry.

Argentina, one of today's hottest wine regions, also endured a great wine crisis in the 1970s and 1980s. See if this story sounds familiar. Import protection and agricultural subsidies encouraged the production of huge quantities of cheap, strong, sweet wines. There was no incentive for quality production because quantity was all that mattered in the captive domestic market. (There was no export market—who would buy such poor-quality plonk?) The crisis, when it came, was severe. Import restrictions were removed, and a "grubbing up" program removed about a third of the existing vineyard area. The new market environment encouraged investment in quality production, both for the home market and for export. That's how Argentine wines came to live on your supermarket wine shelf.

The story is much the same for Chile, except that the reforms were more extreme. Half of Chile's vineyards were grubbed up in the 1990s, and the focus was even more clearly on exports because of the collapse of the domestic market.

The story is different in South Africa and Australia, but the need for market reforms was much the same. South Africa had its great wine crisis in 1918, when overproduction and falling demand drove the industry to the edge of collapse. The crisis produced a unique solution, the creation of a strong winegrower cooperative, KWV. KWV allocated production quotas, set minimum prices, and made and marketed wine. With government help, it stabilized the protected Cape wine market and kept grower incomes high.

KWV was forced to abandon its cooperative structure in 1997 as part of South Africa's adjustment to post-apartheid realities, which included access to previously closed export markets. Wine production was privatized, and investment increased. KWV regulatory and administrative functions were transferred to the Wine Industry Trust, which aims, among other things, to use the wine industry as a tool to promote Black Economic Empowerment (BEE). The reappearance of South African wine on global markets can thus be seen as part of a response to a set of crises that reaches well beyond the vineyard.

Australia's surge into global wine markets in the 1990s was the result of intentional policy more than reaction to a crisis. The wine industry in Australia is highly concentrated, with most of the production under the control of a handful of very large firms. These businesses saw an opportunity for export growth and domestic market development. Industry-government discussions produced a 1996 report called *Strategy 2025* that set out a vision for Australia's wine future. The ambitious plan called for an organized push for increased wine volume (1996–2002), rising value as Australian brands attained international stature (2002–2015), and then "preeminence" (2015–2025). Australian wines achieved their initial goals quickly, but the road to preeminence will be difficult. The Australian industry is in crisis once again as these words are written. The future of wine in Australia is uncertain, indeed.

TWO CHEERS FOR GLOBAL WINE

As you can see, the global market we take for granted today is really the result of a long, slow, complicated process punctuated by moments of terrifying crisis and fundamental reform. What should we think as we stand before the wine wall and survey the world of choice before us?

I'd like to give three cheers for global wine, but alas, I fear it only deserves two. Globalization has certainly provided many benefits. As consumers, we benefit from more choices and greater competition, both of which work in our favor. Wine producers gain, too, in a number of ways. The global market for wine has helped create a global market for wine services ranging from technical production matters to financial services to those flying winemakers who help spread winemaking know-how.

Big wine companies also gain from the ability to source globally and sell globally. Increasingly, it pays to read the fine print on wine labels. That Australian-based wine brand's label may be affixed to a bottle containing South African wine when natural or market conditions make that the economic choice. This happened in 2021, when Penfolds sourced wine from South Africa for its Rawsons Retreat export sales to China. The South African product avoided the high tariffs that the normal Australian bottling would have faced. I have seen

"California" wine brands that contain Pinot Noir from Chile, northern Italy, and France. No fraud here—the country of origin is clearly stated. It's just not what you would expect given the brand. The wine world is an increasingly small world, and efficient global sourcing (via 24,000-liter disposable plastic bladders that fit neatly into ocean shipping containers) is doubtlessly here to stay. So what's not to like about globalization? Good for wine drinkers. Good for producers, too. Well, economics is called the dismal science for a reason; economists get suspicious whenever they see a silver lining. They want to know where the dark cloud that goes with it is. So, it should be no surprise that global gains must be weighed against costs.

Terroirists—a group I discuss later in the book—see globalization as a threat to the particular sense of place we associate with wine. Most globally produced goods could be made anywhere; they are defined by their *nowhere-ness*. Terroir is all about *somewhere-ness*.

Wine grapes are particularly sensitive to their growing conditions; they are able to express terroir better than most crops, a fact that Adam Smith notes in *The Wealth of Nations*. Wine drinkers seem to think that somewhere-ness is significant. Wine labels frequently give us much more information about the who, what, when, where, and how of the contents of a bottle of wine than is available for almost any other consumer product. (Ironically, the labels do *not* give the sort of nutritional data routinely found on generic cereal boxes!)

Terroirists recognize that sometimes global markets can save endangered local grape varieties and wine styles from extinction by creating a broader market for them, but they worry that pressure to grow "international" grape varieties like Merlot and Chardonnay and to produce wines that match an international market standard is too strong to resist. Soon, they fear, nowhere will replace somewhere, everywhere! This possibility makes it difficult to award the global market that third hearty cheer.

The creation of the global wine wall was a slow process but not a steady one, punctuated by crises within countries as they adjusted to changing conditions. Global markets may make these crises less frequent but more serious. That's something to consider when you think about the future of wine.

Three waves of globalization—missionaries, migrants, and market reforms—helped create a world of wine, but they don't completely explain how that world came to rest on your upscale supermarket's wine wall. To get the full story, we need to journey to an unlikely place. Grab your hat. Next stop: England!

5

THE CENTER
OF THE UNIVERSE

Take a map (or better yet a globe), and mark an *X* at the center of the wine universe. This is not the simplest task in the world, but you should try anyhow.

The world of wine is usually defined geographically, as you know, by two climate bands that circle the globe, defining the temperate zone between latitudes 30°N and 50°N and 30°S and 50°S, where wine grapes grow best. France, Italy, China, and California are all in the north band. Australia, South Africa, Chile, and Argentina lie in the south. This is where most of the world's wine is made today, although the zone now extends closer to the equator (India, Thailand, Peru, Brazil), as winegrowers adapt varietals and techniques to hotter environments, and nearer the polar regions, too, as global warming pushes vineyard limits. Researchers are seriously developing wine grape clones for the Estonian vineyards of the future.

THE CENTER OF THE UNIVERSE OF WINE

Where is the center of this expanding universe of wine? The answer to this question depends on how you think about the world of wine. If you think about wine in historical terms, for example, then the center is near the Black Sea in what are now parts of Georgia and Armenia. That's where scientists have found evidence of extensive ancient *Vitis vinifera* plantings and even what we would recognize today as a rudimentary wine-production facility.

The answer is different if we frame the question in quantitative terms. Going by number of bottles produced, the center of the wine world lies in Languedoc, the huge Mediterranean arc of vines in the South of France. Languedoc and Roussillon, the adjacent region, make up the world's largest vineyard, where a half-million acres of vines are tended by more than 30,000 *vignerons*.

Languedoc has the numbers when it comes to wine but not the reputation (although many excellent wines are made there). To find the center of the wine world in terms of status, you have to travel from Languedoc 240 kilometers up the Canal du Midi to Bordeaux, the most famous wine region in France and in the world. Although Burgundy and Champagne may cry foul and not without cause, Bordeaux reigns supreme in the minds of many wine enthusiasts, led by the famous *Premiers crus* (first-rated growths) established by the classification of 1855: Châteaux Lafite-Rothschild, Margaux, Latour, Haut-Brion, and Mouton-Rothschild (added to the list in 1973). Not all Bordeaux wines reach these heights (indeed, most fall far short), but the region's reputation is established by these exceptional champions just as Languedoc's low status is due to its noteworthy failures.

Bordeaux, with its classic châteaux and international reputation, is what people imagine when they think about fine wines, but it is not the center of the market when those thoughts become action in the marketplace. No, the center of the world of wine *markets* is the least likely place of all—a place better known for drinking ale and spirits, at about the same latitude as Calgary, Canada, in a climate long thought to be unfriendly to the vine.

My nominee for the center of the wine world in economic terms is in the United Kingdom, on Delamare Road in Cheshunt, Hertfordshire—north of London a few miles past the M25 ring road. What an unlikely place! Why is this the center of the world, and how did it get that way? Read on.

THE WORLD'S BEST WINE MARKET

Britain's consumers have relatively plentiful disposable incomes and are, as I explain, well informed by the wine press and well served by specialists and supermarkets; the wine culture is robust. The British drink about twenty-two liters of wine per capita each year, much less than Italy or France (about forty-six liters per head) or Portugal (almost fifty-two liters) but a good deal more than the United States (about twelve).[1]

There *is* an English winemaking industry, as you have already read, that is growing in quantity and reputation (helped along by global climate change), but it remains small relative to domestic demand. Thus, almost all wine in Britain is imported. This is one reason for the British market's central importance. Almost all the other countries with large wine demand also have large local supplies.

Great Britain is the country with the largest wine imports in the world measured by volume (number of bottles), ahead of Germany and the United States. And it is number 2, after the United States, when wine imports are measured by dollar value, ahead of Germany, Canada, and China. No other country comes close in terms of imported wine opportunities, although the United States and Germany have their own claims to wine market preeminence.

Britain is also a center of the global auction market for fine wines, meaning that it is a key trading center that attracts buyers, sellers, investors, critics, and the wine press. It is no accident that so many of the world's most influential wine writers carry British passports or write for British publications.

THE RISE AND FALL AND RISE OF THE BRITISH WINE MARKET

Britain was not always the pint-and-pie culture popularized by Andy Capp cartoons. Britain had its own vast vineyards for three hundred years, starting in 1152, when the future king Henry II married Eleanor of Aquitaine, which brought Gascony, including Bordeaux, under British control. Low import duties on Gascon wines helped cement cross-Channel relations for a period and encouraged wine drinking, especially among British elites. The eventual loss of those vineyards and then war with France caused Britain to turn away from French wines to those from Spain and Portugal and then, finally, from wine generally.

Faced with the need to generate war revenue in the nineteenth century, Britain imposed high tariffs on wine imports. Significantly, these were not excise tariffs (10 percent or 20 percent of value) but specific tariffs (x number of pence per bottle or gallon). Excise tariffs would have had an equal proportionate impact on wines of all prices, but specific tariffs introduced a bias against cheap wine.

To see this, suppose that the tariff is ten dollars per bottle, for example. The effect on a one-hundred-dollar bottle of imported wine is relatively small—the price rises by 10 percent, and demand declines somewhat. Some people will like fine wine well enough to pay $110 for a $100 bottle, so demand slips but probably doesn't slide away. The impact on a five-dollar bottle of wine is enormous, however. Its relative price rises prohibitively to 300 percent of the pretariff amount. Who will pay fifteen dollars for a five-dollar bottle of wine? Its market evaporates.

The cost of shipping wine abroad, which is more or less the same regardless of the price of the wine, has something of this same effect. If it costs fifty dollars to ship a case of wine from France, for example, then the impact is proportionately greater for wine that sells for five dollars per bottle than the five-hundred-dollar luxury product. This helps explain why that cheap but lovely bottle of local wine you enjoyed on holiday in Provence never shows up on your grocer's shelves here in the United States. By the time the transportation costs are paid—plus whatever import duties apply—it would no longer be cheap, and you might not find it quite so lovely.

The British drinks market was thus split in two. Elites continued to drink and collect fine red Bordeaux wines that they called Claret. The masses switched from wine to now relatively less expensive beer. And Britain acquired its reputation as a beer-drinking nation.

BRITISH WINE RESURGENCE

Wine became cheaper in Britain as import duties were reduced on a wide range of products, including wine, as part of post–World War II trade liberalization. British tariffs on table wine fell in three steps, first in 1949 as part of postwar tariff reform; then again in 1973, upon Britain's entry into the European Community (EC); and once more in 1984, when the EC ruled that British wine tariffs must be "harmonized" or brought into line with those in other member countries. These duty and price reductions stimulated consumption in the price-sensitive British market.

Britain's restrictive retail licensing laws were revised in 1962, giving supermarkets the ability to sell wine and liquor. This was a big change, as previously wine was available mainly through specialized shops with limited hours and distribution. Sainsbury's, the big grocery chain, was the first to take up a wine license, followed quickly by such competitors as Tesco, Waitrose, and Co-Op. This put wine within reach of the everyday buyer, who no longer needed to schlep to such specialists as Berry Bros. & Rudd or high-street merchants like Threshers, Odd Bins, and Victoria Wines to make a purchase.

Wine was more available after 1962, but resale price maintenance agreements prevented true competition in the market for alcoholic beverages. Wine prices were set free in 1966, paving the way for the fiercely competitive market we see today. As the grocery chains expanded, their stores grew bigger, and the wine walls became both larger and more diverse. The economic incentive to sell wine was very strong. The markup for many supermarket items is surprisingly low—just 5 to 10 percent for beer and spirits, for example—but wine prices can be 30 percent over cost and sometimes more.

Selling wine, however, isn't just selling wine (if that makes sense). It also sells complementary items (meat, fish, cheese, gourmet foods) as well as the store's overall image as home to the good life's consumable ingredients. High-end supermarkets scatter wine displays throughout the store as they market lifestyle choices, not just industrial packaged goods.

It worked. British wine consumption increased steadily, from about two liters per person in the early 1960s to more than twenty liters today as consumers shifted from "on-premise" wine consumption (at pubs, restaurants, and wine bars) to "off-premise" drinking at home. Supermarkets account for more than 70 percent of British wine sales today, and their market share continues to grow.

MASTERS OF THE (WINE) UNIVERSE

The conditions were ripe for the rebirth of the British wine market, but one problem remained: sorting out the choices from among the thousands and thousands of wines that came knocking on Britain's door as its supermarket wine sector expanded. Building (or even rebuilding) a wine culture is not a snap in the era of global wine. Education is key, and the British wine industry responded with the Masters of Wine (MW) program.

The MW is not a degree given by Oxford or Cambridge. It is a special designation created by the Institute of Masters of Wine, a London-based, industry-supported nonprofit organization dedicated to wine education for more than sixty-five years. The MW program was originally created for British wine traders, who obviously needed to be very knowledgeable to succeed in their profession, but it eventually expanded in both occupational and geographic terms. Today there are more than four hundred MWs in the world scattered across more than thirty countries (the numbers change each year as new MWs qualify). Not surprisingly, Britain remains the center of MW membership and activities, reflecting its central position in the world wine market generally, with more than two-thirds of the world's wine masters.

The Masters of Wine program created an elite group of wine experts who have played an important role over the years in shaping the growth of British and now global wine markets. Some of the world's most famous wine critics and winemakers hold the MW designation. Jancis Robinson, Michael Broadbent, David Peppercorn, and Serena Sutcliffe are famous British MW wine critics, for example.

It's not easy to become a Master of Wine. There are preliminary evaluations to establish eligibility, independent study, and formal coursework. If you want to be an MW, you'll have to pass exams in five theory areas, stagger successfully through three 12-wine blind tastings, and write a six- to ten-thousand-word research paper on a topic relevant to the wine industry. The research papers cover all sorts of interesting topics, but I've noticed that a lot of them are firmly in the original spirit of the MW program, addressing practical problems facing the wine trade.

Britain thus has just about everything to make it the leading global wine market: rich (by global standards) and educated consumers, expert professionals, a unified wine market, and sophisticated supermarkets to bring all the pieces together. What does the result look like? Well, Google that address I gave you earlier in the chapter (Delamare Road in Cheshunt, Hertfordshire), and you'll find out. That's the address of Tesco House, headquarters of one of the biggest wine retailers in the world, Tesco PLC.

TESCO'S WORLD OF WINE

Tesco employs about 360,000 "colleagues" to staff its stores in Britain, Ireland, Hungary, Czech Republic, and Slovakia and to serve its legions of customers. The Tesco Group includes Tesco Bank; Tesco Mobile; and Dunnhumby, a wholly owned data science subsidiary. Data science? Yes, every time you enter your store loyalty card information when you shop at a market, you are providing data that analysts can mine for valuable insights into buying behavior. I don't know if all the stores in Tesco's global network sell wine, but I'll bet that most of them do. I remember being impressed with the Tesco wine selection on my last visit to Prague.

Tesco was not the first British supermarket to sell wine (Sainsbury's has that distinction), but it has evolved into the largest wine retailer in the United Kingdom because it has aggressively and effectively harnessed the forces of global wine to serve the interests of local consumers. In the course of creating its wine wall, Tesco (and the other British supermarkets) blazed the trail that brings wine to places and people who have never heard of Tesco.

Tesco sources wine from all over the world; the online catalogue lists wines from 203 different brands in a dozen different categories, including red, white, and rosé, of course; sparkling; sweet; organic and fair trade; alcohol-free; and wine in cans. This embarrassment of riches (which you share indirectly, of course, in the form of the wine wall in your local upscale supermarket) is a mixed blessing. More choices aren't always better choices if they are confusing or intimidating. How can you be sure that *this* Chilean Cabernet is any good or what *that* French white wine from an unknown appellation will be like? How can you be confident that your money won't be wasted on an inferior product?

The answer, which Tesco and Britain's other big wine retailers, including Sainsbury's, Waitrose, and the others, have discovered is private-label wines (or "exclusive-label" wines, as a British friend likes to call them). Tesco doesn't grow the grapes or make the wine for its Tesco Finest wine portfolio; it contracts with wineries to make the products sold under its private label. Sometimes the wines are made by wineries that make and sell wine under their own brand, but there are many wine producers who specialize in private-label wines, which are sold by many clients under many brands.

Private-label wines are one of the fastest-growing segments of the wine industry today because they solve a number of economic problems. For the retailer, they are an opportunity to sell a unique product (not available in other stores!) at a lower price but with a higher margin. For the consumer, private-label wines simplify choice. You might never feel confident in buying a mysterious bottle of red wine from South Africa, for example. Who knows what's beneath the cork and if it is drinkable. But you might be willing to purchase Tesco Finest South Africa Pinotage. The Tesco name provides an assurance of quality. Private-label wines are so successful in Great Britain that Tesco has two levels of these wines. You can buy Tesco New Zealand Sauvignon Blanc, for example, for £6.00 per bottle, or you can move up the wall to Tesco Finest Marlborough Sauvignon Blanc for £8.50.

Significantly, buying private-label wines is not necessarily a step to lower quality (although they generally sell at lower prices). Wine critics often surprise their readers (and themselves, I think) by giving high marks to private-label wines from British supermarkets. When that happens, it shows how successful supermarket purchase managers can be in searching out wines and negotiating good prices. Private-label wines are often shipped in bulk to the United Kingdom and bottled (generally in lightweight glass bottles and screwcap closures) close to the final market, which also drives down cost.

Buyers earn ClubCard points, both online and in the stores. The loyalty-card system carefully tracks the purchases of each customer, providing data to guide store strategy and the opportunity to produce individualized suggestions to encourage wine drinkers to buy more or better wines or perhaps to try something different. Tesco was an early pioneer in loyalty cards and is thought to use this data very effectively.

ARRESTED DEVELOPMENT?

The picture I've painted of the British wine scene so far is really quite bright—it must seem much too good to be true. So you should be a little suspicious. Economists hold that if something *is* too good to be true, then it must be false (that's why economics is called the dismal science). The right way to think about Tesco, supermarkets, and the British wine market is that they are part of the incredible transformation of global wine today compared with the sorry state of the wine wall fifty or sixty years ago. The supermarkets have created global supply chains that carry their private-label wines to Britain, along with a great variety of products by winemakers large and small. The cumulative wine wall is perhaps the fullest in the world, and the market for wines has expanded significantly. All silver linings so far; where's the dark cloud? Well, supermarkets are mass merchandisers, of course, and so they need to appeal to a mass market, and although they can shape that market somewhat, they must also reflect it. It's a fact of life.

One of the things I remember best from shopping in British supermarkets when I lived there in the 1990s was the focus on bargains. I was constantly being offered "25 Percent Extra Free" or "Buy One Get One Free." You couldn't walk down a grocery aisle without being offered a bargain of this sort. BOGOF (Buy One Get One Free) was particularly common on the wine wall. This was the way the mass merchandisers tried to get the attention of mass consumers, and I expect that it trained them to expect bargains of this sort and to resist other kinds of incentives.

The problem, therefore, is the possibility of arrested development. Can the British wine market move beyond bargain-priced private-label wines and take advantage of the great potential that those wines have helped create? Some wine critics are pretty pessimistic about this and predict that the future of British wine will be its increasing commodification. Wine will be like soap flakes, a quotidian purchase of unexceptional consequence. Critics are sad when they contemplate the prospect that wine could become so lifeless, so stripped of its finer qualities.

These concerns are especially relevant today because British wine markets and the supermarkets that dominate them are under pressure. Seeking greater tax revenue, the British government has boosted the excise on wine. Finding it hard to pass along the higher tax cost to their price-sensitive British consumers, the supermarkets have put a squeeze on wine producers instead. Some critics worry that the quality of the wine in the bottle has suffered, especially at the bottom of the wine wall.

The British wine industry is also dealing with disruptions caused by Brexit, Britain's decision to leave the European Union. The new status quo doesn't keep Europe's wines out of UK stores, but it does throw sand in the wheels of a very efficient system. It will take some time before we can understand the final impact of new trade, regulation, immigration status, and work regimes.

Finally, Tesco itself has changed. Where it once had a substantial footprint in Asia and plans to penetrate the US market, Tesco now focuses on its UK home, plus Ireland, Hungary, Slovakia, and Czech Republic. It is a smaller firm but still a wine-selling powerhouse.

THE CURSE OF THE BLUE NUN

Great Britain may be the center of the wine universe by some important measures, but the German wine market is the center of an important universe of its own. Germans have a reputation as consumers who have high incomes but resist spending too much of it on food and wine. They are frugal, value-conscious, economical, if you will—admirable qualities, to be sure. I'd never call them cheap. So it is perhaps no surprise that Germany is the number 1 importer of bulk wines from around the world.

Germany has two stories to tell that are relevant to the themes of *Wine Wars II*. The first is about its most famous (or maybe infamous) wine brand, Blue Nun. And the second concerns its most important contribution to food and wine retailing, Aldi. Together they add depth and texture to our understanding of globalization and wine.

Blue Nun was by some accounts the first truly global mass-market wine brand, an unexpected distinction for a German wine. Blue Nun's roots go back to 1857, when one Hermann Sichel started a wine business in Mainz, Germany. I know little about the early days of Sichel's firm except that it managed to survive the political and economic chaos of the ensuing years, which in retrospect seems like a considerable achievement. The real story begins with the 1921 vintage, said to be one of the best. Sichel sought to export these wines abroad, especially to Great Britain, and the Blue Nun label was invented to facilitate foreign sales. One source holds that the nun on the label was originally clad in standard-issue brown robes, but a printer's mistake turned them blue, and thus a brand was born.

The brand and the famous vintage it represented found a market in England, selling more than a thousand cases a year in the 1930s (quite a lot for a single brand of wine), according to the official company history. Volumes increased after World War II, rising to 3.5 million bottles in the United Kingdom in the 1970s, before sales collapsed back to 800,000 bottles in the 1980s. The pressure to increase quantity in the boom years inevitably affected quality. Lesser-quality grapes from abundant valley vineyards replaced fruit from lower-yielding hillside vines, and for a while it didn't matter very much because the Blue Nun brand was so popular.

Blue Nun itself was the original victim of the curse of the Blue Nun: The global demand for simple, sweetish wine that makes you will also break you. Globalization, it seems, cuts both ways. As tastes changed and wine drinkers sought to move upmarket, Blue Nun wine fell out of fashion, although such is the power of the brand that it continued to find a market.

It is an overgeneralization to say that the whole of German wine suffered the curse of the Blue Nun, but there is some truth in it. Great wines continued to be produced, of course, and snatched up by the educated wine elites (although not at the high prices they once earned), but Brand Germany was Blue Nun, Black Tower, and their Liebfraumilch shelf-mates. German wine hit its lowest point. Sichel sold the Blue Nun brand to Langguth, another German maker, who upgraded the wines. It is a German brand but no longer just a German wine, as the lineup now includes Merlot and Cabernet sourced from France. There is Riesling, an "authentic white" available in both bottle and bag-in-box, and even a Blue Nun Eiswein ("ice wine" made from grapes frozen on the vine) that I was tempted to buy duty-free in Frankfurt.

My personal favorite (perhaps because I've never had an opportunity to try it) is Blue Nun Sparkling Gold Edition. It's a light, fizzy wine infused with flakes of 22-carat gold leaf that glitter in the glass. Young women seem to be the target market, according to both published sources and the look of the advertising copy. Women buy more wine than men, so this is not a crazy strategy, and young women are the market of the future, although the assumption that they are attracted to floaty, shiny things like gold bits is depressing if true. The idea that the friendly nonthreatening female image of the Blue Nun might appeal to women more than men never occurred to me . . . until now.

GERMANY, WINE, AND THE ALDI EFFECT

Are you familiar with Aldi? You should be. Aldi is Germany's largest wine merchant. Aldi and Lidl, another supermarket powerhouse, define mass-market wine in this crucial market and, increasingly, around the world. The business is named for Karl and Theo Albrecht, who founded Albrecht Discount, or Aldi for short, in Essen, Germany, in 1948. Karl Albrecht died in 2014, but while they were both alive, the brothers were said to be the richest men in Germany. They were, I suppose, the German equivalents of Jeff Bezos and Bill Gates, top dogs in the US wealth league. The irony of this is hard to ignore.

Aldi is a "hard discounter" supermarket chain. Its bare-bones stores are stocked with a very limited selection of private-label necessities. Hard discounters are a niche albeit a growing one in the United States. Walmart is a successful discounter, of course, but not a *hard* discounter because it still features many mainstream branded products, its prices are higher, and its stores are a bit more posh. Aldi and other hard-discount stores drove Walmart out of Germany at one point, but the US market was for a long time a tough nut for the hard discounters to crack. Things changed with the global financial crisis of 2008, however, and Aldi's American operations have grown. Aldi and other hard discounters are dominant powers in German retailing. The fact that so much wine is sold in these stores should come as no surprise.

A typical Aldi stocks fewer items in the whole store than your typical American upscale supermarket might display on the wine wall alone. Altogether, your local store in the United States provides ten times the variety of an Aldi. Most of the products carry one of the store's private labels—there are only a few "famous name" products. The goods are displayed, if that is the right word, in their original cardboard packing boxes. Customers snap up empty boxes to use for carrying their treasures out the door, thus providing free and instant recycling. The stores have minimal staff to go with minimal selection; the checkout lines are long; and empty boxes aside, you better bring your own bag or be prepared to pay for one of theirs.

Aldi stores are more austere than Walmart stores, and they attract customers looking for basic value. At last count, Aldi had 10,000 stores in twenty countries (including the United States), divided into two groups: Aldi Nord (with a red, white, and blue logo) owned by Theo Albrecht, and Aldi Süd, owned by his brother, Karl (with an orange and blue logo). The brothers had a falling-out early on regarding whether they should sell tobacco products and, unable to resolve the issue, they divided operation of the business, one taking the north (Nord) and the other southern Germany (Süd). Later they divided the world market, too. Karl took Austria, Australia, Greece, Hungary, Ireland, Slovenia, and Great Britain, and Theo got Belgium, France, Spain, Luxembourg, Poland, Denmark, and the Netherlands. They share the US market in a unique way that I will reveal shortly.

Aldi found a market for low-cost private-label wine and developed it. It is in part because of the Aldi effect that so much of German wine sales are in the market basement. Aldi would seem to be a wine lover's nightmare, with limited choice of private-label products, and if the future of wine is more and more Aldi, I think many terroirists might consider suicide. But there is reason to doubt that the future (or the present) is quite so grim. When Britain's *Which* magazine (it advises subscribers which cars and which televisions to purchase) rated supermarkets in early 2010, it put Aldi and its hard-discount peer Lidl ahead of Tesco, Sainsbury's, and Asda. Aldi and Lidl and their wine walls remain popular today. British consumers seem to be satisfied with Aldi's value-driven model.

The glass is half full here in the United States, too. The Aldi way of shopping has evolved quite a lot since the first American store, an Aldi Süd affiliate, opened in southeastern Iowa in 1976. The first stores took their hard-discount origins seriously, located in small spaces and stocking only about five hundred house-brand items. This is less choice than a typical convenience store with even fewer amenities. And they were closed on Sunday, which was until recently a standard German retail practice. The prices, of course, were very low, which seems to have been enough to attract a following.

Today, there are about two thousand Aldi Süd stores in thirty-six states. Although the original Aldi concept has been modified somewhat for the American market, the core concept remains: "Incredible Value Every Day." I find it interesting that Aldi has been embraced by American consumers to a considerable extent, while much more upscale Tesco's attempt to enter the market failed to gain traction.

One final point: *Both* German Aldi chains are present in the United States now, although you are probably not aware of them. Aldi Süd operates under the Aldi name, of course, with the same logo as in Germany. The owners of Aldi Nord invested years ago in a different chain, based in California and intentionally tailored for thrifty but upwardly mobile US consumers. It's an upscale version of the Aldi Nord chain, and the stores have been incredibly successful here. Perhaps you've heard of them. They have limited selection, smaller stores, lots of private-label products, and low prices. They even sell a lot of wine. The name? Oh, yes. Trader Joe's!

Trader Joe's, the California-based US grocery chain that caters to upscale customers who are looking for a bargain, is Aldi Nord in surfer shorts. The stores are small (compared to US supermarkets); the selections are narrow; and most of the products are house brands produced by outside suppliers, some of them in Europe. If you can't stop thinking that you are shopping at a European food shop when you visit Trader Joe's, well, it is because you are.

And this explains the influence of the German market on the globalization of wine. Two-Buck Chuck isn't really the revolutionary innovation that most of my friends seem to believe; it is simply Aldi's discount-wine strategy transplanted to

American soil, with low-cost wine from California's Central Valley rather than the low-cost producers in France and the Veneto that Aldi uses in Europe. And it seems to be as popular in the United States as it is in Germany and everywhere else the Albrecht brothers (and the winemakers and retailers who have adopted their strategy) have set up shop.

WINE, AMERICAN STYLE

The United States is the world's largest wine market by total expenditure—an amazing achievement given the long-shadow "hangover" of Prohibition—and so must be included in any discussion of the center of the universe. Costco is the largest wine retailer in the United States and arguably the top fine-wine merchant in the world. Costco's notable success reflects its ability to leverage the methods of Tesco and Aldi to break through the bottlenecks that the US wine market presents.

Costco is a members-only big-box discounter with more than eight hundred warehouse stores in the United States, Canada, Mexico, Puerto Rico, France, Iceland, Spain, Great Britain, China, Japan, Korea, Australia, and Taiwan. Its 58 million household and business members pay $60 to $120 per year (in the United States, depending on membership category) to get access to Costco's low prices, good service, and private-label products. The stores are large and relatively austere. They look more like factory floors than retail sales areas. In fact, they *are* factories in a way, where the customers do much of the work (in the same happy spirit as Aldi shoppers) and are happy with the bargain, especially if they score a tasty snack sample along the way.

The merchandise is stacked in ground-level boxes and crates, and inventory is stored on industrial shelves that reach toward the roof. Shoppers push oversize trolleys and flat-bed carts through the aisles, loading up on economy-size packages of irresistible material goods. Although Costco is in many ways a temple of consumer excess, its low prices, Spartan shelves, and humble stacks make you feel almost virtuous when you walk out with a fully loaded cart.

You won't find everything in a Costco; there are far fewer product lines (or SKUs) than in a typical Walmart store, for example, or a big French Carrefour *hypermarché* and usually only one or two product choices in each category. Some of the products are packed in humongous sizes intended for business or restaurant use, but the prices are famously low, and the reputation for quality is unquestioned. Consumers seem to have adjusted to Costco by turning their homes and apartments into soft-goods storage units.

The wine aisle at Costco doesn't look much like the wine aisle in your local upscale supermarket. Most supermarkets provide a surprisingly large selection of wines—hundreds or even thousands of different wines are constantly on offer. A typical Costco store, however, has a rolling inventory of only 100–150 wines at any given time. This is only about a tenth of the number of brands that your supermarket stocks, although it is perhaps ten times the number of choices of any other product category in a typical Costco warehouse.

Selection is obviously much narrower at Costco, so value and quantity sales are the key. If you've shopped for wine at Costco, then you already know that you can spend as little as about five dollars or less for a bottle of simple table wine and as much as . . . well, as much as you want, really. I have seen Dom Pérignon on the Costco rack as well as a Heitz Cellar Martha's Vineyard Cabernet Sauvignon a few years ago.

One way that Costco reflects wine globalization is obvious: They bring global wines to the American market by offering products from France, Italy, Spain, Chile, South Africa, Germany, Portugal, Australia, and New Zealand. But Costco's global connections run deeper than just the origins of the wine.

You would think that Costco's wine strategy would be based on the German discount model because Costco is a high-volume, low-price warehouse operation, and that's the way most wine is sold in Germany. The maximum markup on wine is just 14 percent above wholesale price generally and 15 percent for Kirkland Signature private-label products. This is much less than the standard rule of thumb of 30–50 percent for retail wine and 150 percent or more for restaurant sales.

Costco's wine aisle in the stores I have visited looks a bit like Aldi, with volume wines stacked in their cardboard cases. But Costco's cheapest wines are much more expensive than the Aldi standard. These wines are meant to be good-value famous-brand wines for upscale shoppers, not rock-bottom private-label bargains. These value wines are positioned just down the aisle from carefully arranged wooden cases that display selected fine wines with prices that start at around ten dollars and go steadily upward from there.

Some of the big sellers in the $10.99-plus "fine-wine category" are brands you will readily recognize, large-volume premium producers who can reliably fill Costco's huge pipeline. That's wine marketing the American way. These may not be the wines that customers would select in a grocery store, with more choices at more price points, but they buy them up at Costco knowing that they are getting good value for the money.

Interestingly, however, Costco also stocks wine from many much smaller producers—wines that are likely to sell out and not be replaced as limited inventories are used up. A team of regional wine buyers customizes the selection for each local area. This idea runs exactly opposite of the American model, which supposes that buyers seek consistent, reliable supply and that retailers want to deal with a small number of producers with many brands each. Costco aims to create what it calls a "treasure-hunt" atmosphere in the fine-wine aisle, where buyers will not always know exactly what to expect. It's almost a game, and who doesn't like games—especially when the prize is wine?

TESCO ON STEROIDS?

The use of private-label wine has been the signature tactic of British supermarkets, and it is probably not an accident that Costco has followed suit. A good example is the Kirkland Signature Marlborough Sauvignon Blanc that I found on a recent Costco expedition. The label listed the Kiwi maker of the wine: Ti Point Wines. It had an appealing, sharp, tropical fruit flavor, and it was priced well below the Kim Crawford Marlborough Sauvignon Blanc (a Constellation Brands product) on the adjacent shelf. The Kirkland Signature label first appeared in 2003 and has developed into a robust program of domestic and international wines. I have noticed that some Kirkland Signature wines seem to be available pretty much all the time (the Ti Point Sauvignon Blanc is a good example), while others appear and then disappear when the relatively small production run is sold out. Costco wine shoppers soon learn that if you see something you like, buy it now because it might not be there the next time you visit. This lesson applies to wine generally and not just Costco's private-label products.

Now we can begin to appreciate why Costco is so successful as a wine retailer. Their list of wines is not large compared to other retailers, but they provide a rolling selection of pretty interesting and sometimes unexpected wines (at good prices, but that goes without saying). Costco buyers suspect that it must be a good value to get on the Costco shelves and know that any particular wine might not still be there next week or next month. Better run back and buy more now if you want it. So people keep coming back.

The fact that the Costco system bears a striking resemblance to the British wine model is not an accident. The original Costco wine program was created by David Andrew, a Scot who began his career selling wine in London. After working as a fashion model in Europe and a literary agent in Los Angeles, Andrew returned to London and to wine, studying at the Institute of Masters of Wine. He approached Costco with the idea of building a wine trade at the warehouse store in 1998. The British model, transplanted to the American warehouse, was a quick success.

The fact that the Costco system works in the United States is not surprising; it is an American company, after all. But it is significant because as globalization brings more and more countries and their consumers into the wine market, the ability to overcome the sort of obstacles and bottlenecks that define American wine will be increasingly important.

The future of wine? Aldi, Tesco, and Costco are part of the global story, but wine is too complex to be reduced to retail-market strategy. There is much still to be done in our investigation of the future of wine. But first it's time for another wine tasting. What does globalization taste like? Let's see if we can find out.

GLOBALIZATION
TASTING

For the "Globalization Tasting," I would like you to taste through a flight of Sauvignon Blanc wines. I chose Sauvignon Blanc because it is truly a global variety—it shows up in many corners of the wine world, from France to New Zealand, Chile to California, India to Israel. Maybe it's because the grape variety is so adaptable.

Buy three or four bottles of Sauvignon Blanc, call up some friends, taste the different wines, and talk about how the world of wine has expanded since you started drinking wine. What wines should you pick? Here are my suggestions, inspired by the chapters you've just read.

Start with France. Sauvignon Blanc is grown in several French regions, but it is generally not labeled as such because of the Da Vino Code: The French think of wine as geography (places), not horticulture (types of grapes). When in doubt, choose Sancerre, the Sauvignon Blanc wines made in the eastern part of the Loire Valley.

Now follow the missionaries, migrants, and market reformers to New Zealand, and sample a Marlborough Sauvignon Blanc. Choose the most recent vintage you can find because freshness is often a good thing with these wines. If you can afford it, try Cloudy Bay because it was one of the first Kiwi wines to hit world markets or a Brancott Estate because that's where the first Marlborough Sauvignon Blanc vineyard was planted. But don't worry if you cannot find a particular wine—any one will do to start.

I think you should look to California for the third wine. Get the Robert Mondavi Fumé Blanc if you can or another Napa Valley Fumé Blanc or Sauvignon Blanc if you can't. Robert Mondavi's Fumé Blanc wines are distinctive and historically significant and established Sauvignon Blanc as the white grape that makes the quick-to-market cash-flow wines that helped Napa Valley winemakers finance their more expensive Cabernet Sauvignon projects. Mondavi actually makes several levels of Fumé Blanc wines, culminating with wines from the iconic To Kalon vineyard.

If you are ambitious and have any money left, add a fourth wine. Choose a Sauvignon Blanc from an unlikely or unexpected place. South Africa would be appropriate because we've talked about its wine history, and according to my friends, Sauvignon Blanc is the most popular white wine down there. We particular enjoy the wine from Durbanville Hills.

Sauvignon Blanc wines from Chile have both quality and value in their favor. From a stylistic standpoint, you can often sense the influence that French winemakers have had on the wine industry in Chile. A cross between Old World and New World? You be the judge. You cannot go wrong with the Los Vascos Sauvignon Blanc. Los Vascos is owned by the iconic French winemaking firm Domaines Barons de Rothschild-Lafite.

Whichever wines you select, I think you will find them interestingly different from one another despite being made from the same type of grape. As you enjoy the colors and aromas, tastes and textures, consider the miracle of globalization that has brought all these wines to your table. And ponder a bit the puzzle that cornucopia of choice presents.

Cheers!

FLIGHT 2
NAVIGATING
THE WINE WALL

6

MARTIANS VERSUS
WAGNERIANS

Thomas Pinney devotes the last few pages of *A History of Wine in America: From Prohibition to the Present* to what he sees as a fundamental battle for the *idea* of wine in America. It is a conflict between Martians and Wagnerians, he says. Martians and Wagnerians? Little green men versus opera-singing Rhine maidens (or maybe *wine* maidens)? No, it's even stranger than that.

The Wagnerians are inspired by the ideas of Philip Wagner (not the opera-writing Richard), a Baltimore journalist, viticulturist, and winemaker especially active in the years that bracket World War II, when America's Prohibition hangover was especially severe. Wagner believed that wine should be an affordable part of ordinary life and a constant companion at mealtime. Pinney writes,

> Wagnerians are always delighted to have a bottle of superlative wine, but their happiness does not depend on it, nor are they so foolish as to think that only the superlative is fit to drink. Their happiness *does* depend upon wine each day. . . . [G]ood sound wine will not only suffice. It is a necessary part of the daily regimen.[1]

Wagnerians sing an appealing but fundamentally radical song in the American context, where wine is just one of many beverages and not always the cheapest or most convenient to purchase. Regulations that treat wine as a controlled substance are very anti-Wagnerian.

Wagner founded Boordy Vineyards in Maryland and was well regarded by wine people from coast to coast. He is an important figure in the history of American wine, according to Pinney, and one whose idea of wine lives on in many forms. I guess you could say that Two-Buck Chuck is a Wagnerian wine, for example, although I think there's a lot more to Wagner's idea of wine than just low price.

Wagner promulgated his populist vision by promoting the so-called French hybrid grape varieties on the East Coast and elsewhere. I think he wanted America to be Vineland (the name chosen by the Viking explorers), a country covered with grapevines and abundant with honest wine. This is easier said than done, however, as Pinney's history makes clear.

Martians are inspired by Martin Ray's idea of wine. Whereas Wagner was disappointed that America lacked a mainstream wine culture, Martin Ray was upset that the standard was so low in the years following the repeal of Prohibition. He persuaded Paul Masson to sell him his once-great winery in 1935 and proceeded to try to restore its quality with a personal drive that Pinney terms fanatical. He did it, too, making wines of true distinction—wines that earned the highest prices in California at the time. His achievement was short-lived, however. A winery fire slowed Ray's momentum, and he finally sold out to Seagram, which used a loophole in wartime price control regulations to make a fortune from the Paul Masson brand and its premium price points, starting a trend of destructive corporate exploitation that forms a central theme in Pinney's book. The Martian view, according to Pinney, is that "anything less than superlative was unworthy, that no price could be too high, and that the enjoyment of wine required rigorous preparation."[2]

Ray's history is therefore especially tragic because his attempt to take California wine to the heights through Paul Masson ended so badly. Paul Masson degenerated into an undistinguished mass-market wine brand that was sold to Constellation Brands, which eventually passed it along to the Wine Group (makers of Franzia bag-in-a-box wines, among other products), which quietly withdrew the spent brand from the market. Paul Masson brandy still exists as part of the Gallo portfolio.

When wine enthusiasts of my generation think of Paul Masson, it is often because of film icon Orson Welles's classic television ads, where he, straight-faced, compared cheap California fizz to fine French Champagne and proclaimed, "Paul Masson will sell no wine before its time." "What time is it?" my wine-drinking friends used to joke. "Oh . . . it's time!"

Martians and Wagnerians have two very different ideas of wine, and it is a shame that one needs to choose between them. It seems to me that wine could and should be *both* a daily pleasure and an opportunity for exceptional expression. The good isn't *always* the enemy of the great. But many people see it that way, including Pinney, who reveals himself to be a Wagnerian and expresses concern that the Martians have won the battle for wine in America:

The tendency of all this folderol is to exclude wine from a place in everyday life and to isolate it in a special sphere open only to a privileged elite, or, worse, to tourists on a spree. . . . The people who write about wine in the popular press largely appear to be Martians who take for granted that anything under $20 a bottle is a "bargain" wine and who routinely review for their middle-class readership wines costing $30, $40, $50 and up. Even in affluent America such wines can hardly be part of a daily supper. They enforce the idea that wine must be something special—a matter of display, or of costly indulgence. That idea is strongly reinforced by the price of wine in restaurants, where a not particularly distinguished bottle routinely costs two or three times the price of the most expensive entrée on the menu. No wonder that the ordinary American, unable to understand how a natural fruit product (as wine undoubtedly is) can be sold for $50 or more a bottle, sensibly decides to have nothing to do with the mystery.[3]

I guess I am a Wagnerian, too, if I have to choose, but I'm not as pessimistic as Pinney. Can wine be both common and great? Why not? Wine isn't one thing; it is many things to many people. No purpose is served, in my view, by monolithic thinking.

WHAT ARE WINE DRINKERS LOOKING FOR?

Americans (or at least many of them) have unexpectedly come to love wine, something that seemed impossible just a few years ago. The wine wall has been transformed from a sad little product patch to a selection of global proportions. But have we embraced wine in our peculiar American way and, by loving it, destroyed it? And is Two-Buck Chuck the shaft of our deadly Cupid arrow? Only one way to find out. Away we go!

Here we are again, back at the wine wall of your neighborhood upscale supermarket, but this time I want you to look at the people, not the wine, because we are interested in the mainstream market for wine. Hang around a while and see if you can draw any conclusions about the "typical" wine buyer. Young or old? Male or female? Rich or poor? Expert or novice? Do they reach up to the more expensive bottles on the top shelf or stoop down for the economy-size boxes and bottles at the bottom?

It is actually pretty interesting to be an amateur wine wall anthropologist, so I hope you give it a try. The first thing that most people notice is also the most important: There doesn't seem to be a single, typical wine customer, although there are several types of ritualized behaviors. Some people launch surgical strikes, efficiently plucking bottles from the wine wall and disappearing into Meat or Fish or Produce. Others linger in particular areas, reading the tags that are affixed to the racks, which are called "shelf talkers," and sometimes picking up bottles to read the label more closely. Other buyers seem to be lost: They wander around like a driver looking for a house number on an unfamiliar street until finally grabbing a bottle or just walking away empty-handed.

Does your supermarket have a wine steward or someone who lingers in the neighborhood of the wine wall to offer assistance? This is an increasingly common feature of upscale grocery stores. If so, you might note how many customers ask for advice, how many accept help when it is offered, and how many prefer to confront the wall one-on-one.

The anthropology of the native wine wall culture is an interesting study, but it has its limits, too. To get a better understanding of what is driving wine buyers and their behavior, you would need to do more detailed research, to know more about the people and their motivations, and to take into account all the market factors, like income and ethnicity, that affect demand for any consumer good.

SEQUENCING WINE DRINKER DNA

Fortunately, we don't have to go to the trouble of designing a research methodology to sequence wine buyer DNA in the United States because multinational wine giant Constellation Brands has already done it. They call their study Project Genome, and the results that have been released to the public go a long way toward helping us understand both the people who come to the wine wall and how the wall has adapted in response.

The first phase of Project Genome was released in 2005. A bank of one hundred questions was administered to a panel of 3,500 US wine consumers in the largest organized study of wine buyers at the time. A further study, released in 2008, tracked the behavior of 10,000 wine consumers using Nielsen Homescan data. The Nielsen market research company (now named NielsenIQ to differentiate it from Nielsen, the media-ratings company) created a "mini-USA" consumer panel, according to their website, where participants fill out surveys and scan the barcodes of their purchases. A final report was released in 2014, which seems to have formed the basis for Constellation Brands' wine-market strategies.

So what are wine buyers really looking for? Well, according to Project Genome, your amateur anthropology was on the money: There really isn't a single, typical kind of wine buyer. Wine drinkers come in all sizes, shapes, and colors. It is, however, possible to identify six wine-market segments, which Constellation has named enthusiast, image seeker, engaged newcomer, everyday loyal, price driven, and overwhelmed.

Price-driven consumers were the largest (21 percent) group of wine shoppers in the Project Genome study; they paid the lowest average bottle price of eight dollars and generated just 14 percent of wine-market profits. The size of the price-driven group increased during Project Genome's evolution, possibly as a result of the 2008 recession. Price-driven consumers look for discounts and low prices. I'd guess that they are a good market for private-label wines. They want to buy an eight-dollar wine that tastes like a twelve- or fifteen-dollar wine—irrespective of the fact that wines don't taste like price points. They seek satisfaction from a good wine value; because I have friends in this category, I know that they are sometimes even happier with the bargain price than they are with the wine itself. They are treasure hunters looking for a deal.

Everyday loyals were the second-largest consumer group (20 percent of all shoppers), accounting for 22 percent of profit, with a ten-dollar average bottle price. Everyday-loyal wine drinkers, more women than men, according to the study, are frequent buyers who stick with tried-and-true favorite wines. Looking at the Constellation Brands portfolio, I'd guess they might tend toward the Robert Mondavi Woodbridge or Mondavi Private Selection brands. Given all the options available, it is kind of sad that someone could become so completely uncurious about all the wines on the wall. However, it is even sadder that so few people are so happy with wine that they see no reason to change.

Overwhelmed consumers were 19 percent of the wine-shopper group but generated only 9 percent of profits because of both their low purchase rate and their low eight-dollar average bottle price. The first phase of Project Genome seems to have concluded that overwhelmed consumers have pretty unsophisticated tastes. When asked what kind of wine they bought, many said "blush wine"—White Zinfandel. But the Nielsen scanners revealed that in fact their purchases were much more varied that this. The reason they said White Zin was that they couldn't remember what they bought, a fact that shows just how confusing they find the wine wall (or a restaurant wine list) to be. I suspect that this market segment accounts for the popularity of so-called critter wines—wines with pictures of cute little animals on the label, such as penguins and kangaroos, dogs and cats, birds, fish, and even horses.

Image seekers, though, were found to be a highly profitable market segment. Although they represented only 18 percent of all shoppers, they generated 26 percent of profits, with a twelve-dollar average bottle price. Wines with high critic scores or prestigious brand names appeal to this group, who see wine purchases as identity statements to a certain degree.

Engaged newcomers were a new group in the 2014 report and an important one. Although comprising 12 percent of all shoppers, they produced 14 percent of profits. They didn't always buy wine, but when they did, they seemed to pick from the top part of the wine wall, hence their thirteen-dollar average bottle price. Young, new to wine, and keen to learn more, engaged newcomers were identified as a key market segment to develop.

The final group were the enthusiasts, who accounted for 15 percent of wine profits despite being the smallest (10 percent) market segment. They had the same thirteen-dollar average bottle price as the engaged newcomers but were more wine-focused. Wine accounted for 40 percent of beverage alcohol purchases for enthusiasts, for example, but only 24 percent for engaged newcomers, who were less likely to drink wine exclusively and more likely to mix it up with beer and spirits.

Enthusiasts are at the opposite end of the spectrum from their overwhelmed friends. They are looking for more than wine; they want a "wine experience," which I take to mean wine . . . and a story about the wine. So they are looking for sophisticated information about wine of the sort that causes overwhelmed consumers to bolt for the exit. Wine is a lifestyle choice for enthusiasts, who are likely to read wine publications, make wine an important part of socializing, and take wine-related trips and vacations. They are more likely to live in affluent or cosmopolitan areas, according to the study, but I have found enthusiasts pretty much everywhere.

I think that technology and changing buying behavior will soon shake up the Project Genome wine buyer taxonomy. Direct-to-consumers internet wine sales were growing steadily before the coronavirus pandemic and surged during it. It is interesting to consider how web sales might impact wine. Purchasing online takes away some of the experience that enthusiasts crave—they like holding the bottle, feeling its weight, reading the label. But for a lot of people, the online experience is more familiar than the confusing wine wall and takes away some of the pressure. Price comparisons are more convenient, critic scores and consumer ratings are more readily available, and there is room for many layers of information, which can either be probed or ignored as desired. No doubt about it, online sales have potential to draw more consumers into wine, especially by individualizing the experience using Amazon-type algorithms.

PROJECT GENOME IN THEORY AND PRACTICE

Project Genome and consumer market research projects like it are very interesting because they help us think about wine in terms of the people who drink it and why as opposed to the usual wine book focus, which is on the people who produce it and how. It's the demand side that you need to understand alongside supply.

But there's more to consider. Constellation Brands commissioned the studies and then did the unthinkable: They actually rethought their whole business strategy with these consumer trends in mind. Once the largest wine company in the world, Constellation Brands adopted and then executed a radical strategy to be both smaller and different from before. It is interesting to ponder Constellation's new look.

The first move was to shed down-market wine brands in order to focus on only a few key higher-growth, higher-profit demographic groups. The final element of this downsizing involved the sale of dozens of wine brands to Gallo in 2020–2021. Suddenly Constellation Brands went from 39 million cases of total wine production to just 19 million cases. The brand count fell from 106 to 64. Total SKUs (individual products) went from 515 to 443. The bottom half of Constellation's wine wall disappeared, indicating that the future of wine in the American market, in the company's view, didn't have much of a place for price-driven or overwhelmed wine shoppers.

Constellation's streamlined wine business puts more emphasis on its other lines of business, especially Mexican beer (Corona Extra and Modelo) and maybe even cannabis-based products (Constellation has invested in a Canadian cannabis company called Canopy Growth). It would be easy to read these actions as a no-confidence vote for wine, but perhaps it is best to see it as a "know thyself" moment, and Constellation Brands has done research to know what it wants to be.

The Gallo company knows itself, too, and its deal with Constellation shows that it aims to have wide penetration in the wine market. Already the world's largest wine producer, Gallo's acquisition of Constellation's brands resulted in some truly spectacular numbers. Gallo now produces 96 million cases of wine each year in 17 wineries for 163 brands. Its SKU count: 1,544. Incredible. Gallo has achieved truly Wagnerian proportions!

BOOMERS AND MILLENNIALS

Martians and Wagnerians, enthusiasts and image seekers—there are lots of different ways to divide up wine consumers, and each one reveals something and obscures something else. These days, one of the divisions that is getting the most attention within the wine industry (and causing more than a few sleepless nights) is baby boomers versus millennials.

The baby boomer generation was born between 1946 and 1964, the early post–World War II years, and it has almost magical status in the wine world. They are a big demographic bulge (hence the *boom*) who came into drinking age in the 1970s, give or take a year or two. It is not a coincidence that this was the time when interest in and sales of wine started a boom of their own. *Wine Spectator* magazine was founded in the United States at this time, and *Decanter* magazine in Great Britain started its run then, too. They and the rest of the wine press were guidebooks that enthusiastic boomers used to navigate the rapidly growing wine wall. The growth that the boomers provoked with their interest and disposable income produced perhaps the greatest wine-market surge in history. Incredible. Hey boomers—thanks a lot for kick-starting wine's golden age. But what happens when boomers move on?

Well, that's the problem, because the first baby boomers are in their midseventies now. They are starting to drink less, and well, their numbers will eventually decline even if wine really does increase longevity, as many of them hope. If today's wine market is to be sustained, then someone is going to have to take the boomers' place. But who?

Eyes fall on the next generation coming up to bat after the baby boomers—Generation X. They seem to like wine well enough, but there are not many of them compared to the vast baby boomer crowd. They can't fill the gap by themselves. So attention turns to the millennial generation (aka Generation Y), who were born from 1981 to about 1995 and therefore came of age around 2000. There are lots of them, which is good, but so far, they haven't taken to wine in the numbers and with the enthusiasm that worried wine industry leaders want. Is it because they are poorer than their boomer predecessors at the same age or face diminished economic prospects? Yes, that could be the answer, especially because wine is not the least-expensive alcoholic beverage. Wine is often seen as an "occasion-driven" product: You buy and drink wine for specific occasions in many cases. Are the occasions that smartphone-equipped millennials create different in some way that leaves wine out of the equation? Maybe. Are they are just young, as some argue, and will grow into wine the way other generations have? It's a complicated situation that gives us one more dimension to consider as we think about who drinks wine, how, and why.

AWAKEN BACCHUS!

Many of the world's new wine consumers in the next fifty years will be located in countries that lack a well-defined idea of wine. They will be in China, India, South Korea, and Japan. So I spent two weeks watching a nine-part Japanese television miniseries that is based on a twenty-plus-volume Japanese manga (graphic novel) called *Kami no Shizuku* (*Drops of God*). Have you heard of it? No? Then read on because *Kami no Shizuku* seems to have changed how millions of people outside the traditional wine enthusiast core are thinking about wine. Maybe, just maybe, it is a clue to the future of wine.

Wine geeks like to think of wine as a very serious subject, all vintages and terroir and malolactic fermentation and so on. It is hard for us to accept that something as sacred as wine could be influenced by popular culture. But we know that it happens. The 2004 film *Sideways*, for example, is said to have set off the Pinot Noir boom in the United States and brought to an end a previous Merlot bubble. It also romanticized wine in a way that cannot have hurt wine sales overall. No wonder wine tourists come to the Santa Barbara area to drink the same wines, eat the same foods, and visit the same wineries as the film characters Miles and Jack (played by actors Paul Giamatti and Thomas Haden Church).

Sideways had a big effect on the wine world. The *Kami no Shizuku* effect may be several orders of magnitude larger. The reason you may not have heard about it is that this wine-quake is centered in Tokyo, not New York, Los Angeles, or London. The ongoing comic book series, written by Shin and Yuko Kibayashi, first appeared in 2004 and has sold more than half a million copies in Japan alone. The Nippon television series that I've been watching on DVD premiered in January 2009 and reached millions more. The Kibayashis were ranked number 50 in *Decanter* magazine's July 2009 "Power List" of the wine industry's individuals of influence. *Kami no Shizuku* is arguably the most influential wine publication for the past twenty years, according to *Decanter*.

Kami no Shizuku set off a wine boom in Asia, where, much as with *Sideways*, enthusiasts rush to taste the fine wines (mainly from France, mostly Burgundies and Bordeaux) that are featured in each storyline. The rising sales of these iconic wines have been good for these particular producers, but I think the larger effect has been to draw millions of Asian consumers into the market and help them to develop a personal sense of wine.

I've been trying to decide how to explain *Kami no Shizuku* and why I think it has had such a profound effect on wine in Asia and perhaps around the world. One reason is that it is a good story, and that is always important. The Nippon TV series is pretty much a soap opera, and you know how addictive those are! But I think the real factor is that *Kami no Shizuku* presents a different idea of wine. Wine is presented as a sort of mysterious but not impenetrable secret society (think *Da Vinci Code*), with its own history, geography, rituals, language, and traditions. It is a mystery waiting to be solved. The reward for mastering its intricacies is a kind of divine communication (hence *Drops of God*). Wine can communicate a time and place, an emotion, or an experience. Tasting wine even allows the living to talk with the dead, in a way that the story makes clear but I won't reveal here.

The story's handsome young protagonist is upset with his wine-obsessed father for never leaving flowers on his mother's grave. He always leaves wine—Domaine de la Romanée Conti Richebourg 1990, if you are interested. Later, as he begins to learn the language of wine and unlock its secrets, he discovers that this Burgundy is the truest expression of the love that flowers are meant to represent—not a dozen flowers but a field of them. "Awaken, Bacchus," he says, when he wants to move beyond the physical senses to taste the memories and emotions that lie hidden in the wineglass. Who wouldn't want to have such a transformative experience? Who wouldn't want to see what mysteries wine can reveal?

Kami no Shizuku seems to have unleashed two forces in Japan and perhaps eventually around the world. One is the competition for status and self-esteem through the conspicuous consumption of the trophy wines featured in the comics and television series. This materialistic competition is even part of the plot! It is nothing new, although I'll bet French wine producers were thankful for it during the economic crisis. It is a sort of Martian vision of wine: fanatical but not exactly what Martin Ray had in mind. The other force is a more Wagnerian sort of quest—this one for meaning and fulfillment—with unruly Bacchus an unlikely guide. The competition here is more subtle and inward-looking, but the rewards are much greater (another lesson of the story). Both quests are important from an economic standpoint, but it is only the second one that has the potential to awaken a new kind of audience for the pleasures of wine by waking up the Bacchus inside us all.

THEY ALWAYS BUY THE
TEN-CENT WINE

When Tyler Colman (aka the internet's Dr. Vino) organized a competition for Wine Person of the Decade, I nominated Fred Franzia. No one (with the possible exception of Jesus Christ, who turned water into wine—a miracle!) has done more to bring inexpensive wine to the masses.

Two-Buck Chuck (TBC; aka Charles Shaw wine) is the brand of inexpensive wines that Fred Franzia's Bronco Wine Company makes for exclusive distribution through the Trader Joe's chain. The wines sell for $1.99 in California, hence the *two-buck* nickname, although the prices are sometimes higher in other states. In 2016, TBC sold its one-billionth bottle (stop for a moment and imagine a billion bottles of wine) since its introduction in 2002. It is an amazing achievement, especially considering that the wine is basically only available in one grocery chain. And sales are still rising; you cannot miss the huge haystack display of Two-Buck Chuck wines when you visit a Trader Joe's store.

TBC as we know it today was initially made possible by a worldwide glut of wine grapes in the early years of the twenty-first century. There was a lot more wine made than people would buy. Franzia himself was part of the glut, with around 40,000 acres of vines in California's Central Valley, where yields are high and production costs are low. Bronco is the largest vineyard owner in the United States. Bulk prices fell, creating a profitable opportunity for someone like Franzia, a nephew of Ernest Gallo, who understands how to make wine in industrial quantities. Franzia's wineries have storage capacity for 100 million gallons of wine, according to *Wine Business Monthly*. He partnered with the Trader Joe's people, who know how to distribute and market it efficiently, and

Two-Buck Chuck was born.[1] TBC aimed to find a big demand for a big supply, and it did.

People think that the miracle of Two-Buck Chuck is that they can make and sell a wine so cheaply, but that's really not so hard. I have seen wine in Germany that sold for a euro per liter—that's *one buck*, Chuck! The trick isn't making an inexpensive wine—that's very doable; it's getting people to overcome their beliefs about price and quality and buy it. Once you have made a decent wine that you can sell for less, you need to get buyers to look down from their accustomed layer of the wine wall and try it—and to serve it to their friends without fear of humiliation.

THE PRICE OF EVERYTHING

Oscar Wilde observed that some people know the price of everything but the value of nothing, and I suppose this problem applies to wine. Wine's value is particularly uncertain because of the impossibility of knowing what's really in a bottle until it is opened, combined with rather great differences in taste (and ability *to* taste) from person to person. Price is relatively easy to discover in wine; its value . . . well, that's another matter.

The problem of reconciling price and value—and what to do about it—has brought us back to the wine wall to see what role price plays in the wine-buying decision. Students learn the law of demand in Econ 101—lower price, higher sales. But this assumes that quality is both certain and uniform, which isn't the case with wine, as an examination of the wine wall's vertical layers demonstrates.

When we think about the geography of the wine wall, we usually focus on its horizontal layout rather than its vertical arrangement. Horizontally, the wine wall moves from international wines through domestic wines to sweet and fortified wines in a number of more or less standard patterns. The Old World wines are arranged by region (Chianti, Burgundy, Rioja), and New World wines, by varietal name (Chardonnay, Merlot) and so on. A walk down the wall's horizontal axis in a good store is a quick tour of the wine world's best-known landmarks, the famous names and places that attract our attention. But it is the vertical arrangement that pays the bills.

Have you ever noticed how the wine wall seems to be arranged according to price? Where do you find the most expensive wines on the wall? I think you know—they are usually on the top shelf (a term that signifies high quality) so that you reach up to get them. The most expensive wines stand prominently on top of the wall; buying them may be a reach, something you do for special occasions only, but it is an uplifting experience nonetheless.

Where do you find the least expensive wines? Although it isn't a hard and fast rule, the cheapest wines tend to congregate at the bottom of the wall, where you have to bend or stoop to find them, thus uniting the physical act with its psychological result, unless you think of yourself as a treasure hunter, in which case you'd be looking to find overlooked gems lying on the ground. The rest of the wines on the wall are layered almost like the geological strata that you some-times see in riverbanks or road cuts, only the layers don't run oldest to newest as in nature; on the wine wall it is cheap to expensive.

If you stand at the wine wall and stare straight ahead, you will discover your wine merchant's target audience. All along the wall, from New World back to Old, the price range at eye level will be about the same. If this is where you nor-mally look for wine, then congratulations, you've found your place on the wall.

FINDING THE WINE PRICE COMFORT ZONE

Wine buyers are complicated people with complex tastes, but in one respect, we are simple folks: We tend to buy most of our wines of whatever vintage or variety within a fairly narrow "comfort zone" of price, which corresponds to one or two vertical shelf "strata" on the wine wall. The price points that divide the layers vary from country to country (you can imagine that Germany is different from Britain, for example) and depend on the type of store and its clientele, but here's the basic pattern, running from bottom to top.

Wine people use a special vocabulary to discuss price points. There is no such thing as "cheap wine," for example, just as there apparently is no such thing as "small" canned black olives. The smallest-size olives I've seen is extra-large. Value wines, which sell for $3.99 or less per 750-milliliter bottle equiva-lent, anchor the wine wall.[2] I say "bottle equivalent" because sometimes these wines are sold in larger-format glass jugs, for example, which requires adjust-ment. Once upon a time, the value wine segment was where the action was on the wine wall, but those days are gone, which makes the success of Two-Buck Chuck even more noteworthy. Less than 4 percent of all bottled wine in the US sales vectors measured by NielsenIQ fell into the value category. With a few exceptions, I guess, value wine is all over.

Popular-price wines ($4.00 to $7.99) and premium-price wines ($8.00 to $10.99) are important market segments, accounting for 21.1 percent and 24.4 percent of bottled wine sales, respectively. If you are good at math, you've already figured out that taken together, all wines selling for less than eleven dollars per bottle account for about half the market. These days, eleven dollars is a fault line. As I show in a few pages, the market above eleven dollars behaves very differently from below.

Superpremium wines sell for $11.00 to $14.99 and account for nearly 25.0 percent of all sales. Ultrapremium ($15.00 to $19.99) wines add another 12.7 percent of sales. Luxury wines ($20.00 to $24.99) and superluxury wines ($25 and up) top out the wine wall, with 5.0 percent and 8.4 percent of sales, respectively.

Although NielsenIQ doesn't have a category for them, the very top of the wine wall holds what you might call the icon wines, which cost more than €150 in Europe, or, say, $200 in the United States. These "Martian" wines make up a tiny fraction of all wine sales, but they get disproportionate attention in the wine press and among wine enthusiasts. Do not expect to find these wines in your upscale grocery store. I have sometimes seen them in good wine shops—always sitting on the topmost shelf, of course—there less to sell than to show that the shop owner has style, taste, and good connections in the industry.

Some icon wines are famous for being impossible to buy—you have to get on the winery's exclusive list. This makes them even more desirable, of course. Having the wine—and the wine club membership that goes with it—is a powerful status symbol for certain iconic wines. Some wineries will go to great lengths to cultivate a cultlike status. I know one winery, for example, that has a tasting room that never seems to be open. Whenever I have walked past it, there was always a sign in the window: "sold out." That's bound to make the lucky folks on the allocation list feel good about themselves and make many others want the wine even more.

The wine wall's vertical stratification, value to popular and on up the wall, is convenient because it makes it easy for you to know where to look for wines in a certain price range. But there is more than convenience at work here. Many wine buyers, no matter what they say about their tastes and preferences, fundamentally choose wines based on their price. Even wine buyers who are comfortable experimenting with new varieties from new locations seem to return again and again to a price comfort zone.

Suppose, for example, you are a twelve-dollar wine buyer. This means that you are pretty comfortable paying about twelve dollars for a bottle of wine. You may think that fifteen-dollar wine is better (and buy it for the weekend) and that eight-dollar wine isn't quite as good (you buy it for parties to save a little money), so you stick pretty close to your comfort zone as a rule.

The wine wall's organization is therefore intended to be convenient, to make you comfortable, and to provide a little psychological feedback—you really should reach up to that more expensive brand rather than stooping for the cheaper stuff. This isn't the only way to organize a wine wall, of course, so it is interesting that it is so nearly ubiquitous.

THE ERNEST GALLO EFFECT

The built-in assumption of the wine wall is that more expensive wines are better wines and worth reaching up for. Some people (you know who you are) are always looking for a ten-dollar wine that tastes like twenty dollars, and wine critics and marketers rather boldly reinforce this idea. People often say that they like Two-Buck Chuck because it doesn't taste like it costs two or three bucks. It may not be distinctive, but it tastes better than you'd expect for the price.

It's pretty easy to tell that price isn't a very good indicator of quality in wine. Because you seem to be spending so much time hanging around the wine wall, pick up one of the wine magazines that are often displayed there, and turn to the back for the wine ratings to see if the most expensive wines get the highest scores. I picked a magazine randomly and found this information in a review of red wines from Australia. The highest score (92 points) went to an expensive wine ($70), but the next two wines varied in price a good deal—$152 and $20— and both received 91 points.

The problem of judging a wine by its price reminds me of an old story about the early days of the Gallo winery. Ernest and Julio Gallo built their business in the years after the repeal of Prohibition according to a strict division of labor: Julio made the wines, and Ernest sold them. The story is told of a sales call that Ernest made to a New York customer in the dark days of the Depression. He offered sample glasses of two red wines: one costing five cents per bottle, and the other, ten cents. The buyer tasted both and pronounced, "I'll take the ten-cent one." The wine in the two glasses was exactly the same. Clearly, the customer wanted to buy an identity—the image of someone who wouldn't drink that five-cent rotgut—even if he couldn't actually taste the difference. "They always buy the ten-cent wine," Ernest said. I wonder how much things have changed since the days when Ernest Gallo made his calls? Two recent studies provoke this question.

The first study, which has been widely reported, was published in the *Proceedings of the National Academy of Sciences* and showed that test subjects displayed the Ernest Gallo effect.[3] Their ratings of wines changed when they were given price information—even bogus price information. Identical wines received different ratings depending on price information provided. "Expensive" wines, naturally, were rated higher than their inexpensive twins. This shows how strong the psychological effect of price can be. Consumers want to believe that higher-priced wines taste better, even if they can't themselves appreciate the difference. Pulling the cork transforms desire into belief.

A second study, released by the American Association of Wine Economists, answers the question, Do more expensive wines taste better than cheaper ones? The answer, based on a large sample of blind tastings, is that there is no correlation between price and wine evaluation (or maybe a modestly negative one due to the fact that more expensive wines are often tannic in their youth and unpleasant to the untrained palate). This will be no surprise to readers of wine publications like *Wine Spectator*, as noted earlier. *Sure*, the top wines are usually expensive, but there are also a lot of costly wines that get low ratings.[4]

This brings us back to the miracle of Two-Buck Chuck. If you put an equally cheap Two-Buck Chuck clone in your typical upscale supermarket, it's entirely possible that no one would buy it because they would assume low quality based on the low price. That's where Trader Joe's comes in. Trader Joe's has a reputation for selling upscale products for a bit less—for providing *relative* value. Cheap wine at Safeway? How can it be any good? The same cheap wine at Trader Joe's? How *bad* can it be? That tiny difference (like Ernest Gallo's ten-cent price) makes all the difference. Only Nixon could go to China, as the old Vulcan proverb goes, and only Trader Joe's could sell Two-Buck Chuck—for two bucks. Reputation is key here on the wine wall. Let's see how it is made.

CLIMBING THE PREMIUMIZATION LADDER

The first edition of *Wine Wars* appeared just as the world was recovering from the global financial crisis of 2008. The deep recession that the crisis triggered hit wine very hard, and it seemed like the top tiers of the wine wall would be most affected. "Trading down" to lower price points and abandoning wine for less-expensive beverages—that was the sort of consumer behavior at the center of wine industry anxiety. And, because the wine world is a complicated place, that's what happened in many international markets. But not in the United States, which was just then in the final stages of its rise to world's largest wine market.

While some buyers traded down and others traded over to other products, the most important trend turned out to be what is now called premiumization.[5] As *Wine Wars II* is being prepared, the dominant pattern on the American wine wall is this. Every price category below the ten- to eleven-dollar midpoint has declined, especially at the value wine level. And every price category above center has grown, with the quickest growth sometimes coming from the highest tiers.

"What is wrong with Americans?" my European wine friends ask me. "Do they really want to pay more for wine?" This has been a frequent question over the years just because American wine prices are higher on average that those in most other parts of the world. "But Americans don't *want* to pay more," I tell them. "They just have to because of the complex regulatory structure and of multitier taxation of wine in the United States."

So why premiumization and why now? There is no widely agreed answer; you are welcome to form your own theory. Demographic shifts are likely part of the story. Baby boomers bought a lot of value wine, and as they grow older and drink less wine, they undercut that part of the market.

Some of my industry friends speculate that the quality of lower-priced wine enters into the equation, too. Costs have risen at every stage in grape growing and wine production over the years, but consumers on the lower shelves of the wine wall resisted price increases for finished products. This put a big squeeze on growers and producers. Did they cut corners (and quality) to save costs and protect margins?

There has been an explosion of wine brands in the last few years, and it is tempting to speculate that the new wines were meant to draw buyers to higher price points. There is not much indication that consumers want to pay more for the same wine they have purchased in the past. But they might pay more for something new and different. By introducing new products at slightly higher points, sophisticated wine sellers can lead buyers higher and higher on the wine wall.

UP THE DOWN STAIRCASE

Whatever explanation you prefer for the American premiumization phenomenon, it was unlikely to prepare you for what happened during the coronavirus pandemic of 2020–2021. As the world entered the worst recession months since, well, the Great Depression, American consumers didn't just trade down as you might expect due to tight budgets. They actually traded *up* to an unthinkable extent. The fastest-growing price segment in wine was at the very top—twenty-five dollars and up on the NielsenIQ scale. Incredible. How did that happen? It seems that American wine consumers traded down by buying more expensive wines. That's what I mean by "up the down staircase." Got that? No—I guess I need to be clearer.

The coronavirus pandemic was a complicated set of events. Incomes fell as workplaces shut down due the disease threat. This, by itself, would direct consumers to lower-priced products. But shortages of some important products (toilet tissue, for example) caused buyers to stockpile vital commodities—and apparently wine fell into the "vital" category for many people.

Bars and restaurants were some of the businesses most affected by pandemic shutdowns. These "on-premise" establishments sell a lot of wine in the United States and even more in some European countries. The sudden closure of the on-premise sector pushed wine drinkers from their local restaurants to the local supermarkets or shops, where they found similar types of wine to the ones they had been ordering available at much lower prices. They found themselves reaching up the wine wall for a thirty-dollar bottle of wine to replace, in a way, the seventy-five-dollar bottle they would have ordered at a restaurant. Up is down.

Online wine sales reinforced the up-and-down price pattern. Many wineries, especially smaller wineries making premium products, count on restaurant sales to make ends meet. What happened to all the cases of wine that were earmarked for restaurant sales? Many wineries quietly offered them to wine club members and others at lower—sometimes much lower—prices. High-priced wine but at discount prices. One Napa Valley winery that I won't name was selling cases of Cabernet Sauvignon for the normal price of one or two bottles. Buyers lined up to fill their SUVs with wine until it ran out. Which, of course, it did.

THE SECOND-CHEAPEST WINE SYNDROME

Restaurant wine sales are very important. In some regions where travel and tourism are major market drivers, as much as half of all wine is sold in bars and restaurants. Many high-end wineries focus on upscale restaurants where staff can hand sell their unusual or distinctive wines. Guided to a new discovery, the diner hopefully becomes an ambassador as well as a customer.

Price is a persistent issue in restaurant wine sales. It is not unusual for wine in a restaurant setting to be priced at double its retail cost and maybe three times the wholesale price. Now that smartphone apps make it easy to compare prices, many diners balk at the on-premise surcharge, opting for wine by the glass instead of paying the bottle price or drinking beer, cocktails, or just water instead. The wine-by-the-glass pivot is understandable, but there is still a problem. The rule of thumb is that the restaurant's price per glass is what they paid at wholesale for the entire bottle. When you put it that way, wine by the glass doesn't seem like a great value, either.

Does restaurant wine have to be so expensive? Master Sommelier Andrea Robinson, speaking at the Napa Valley Professional Wine Writers Symposium, argued that some restaurants would be wise to cut prices and sell more wine. Robinson's goal was to have happy diners with a bottle of wine on every table. Because she is a student of economics, she rooted her argument in theory. If the demand for restaurant wine is elastic or price-sensitive, then lowering the price will increase the quantity sold by a proportionately greater amount, increasing total revenue. Win, win, winner!

When I wrote about Robinson's proposal on *The Wine Economist*, I got a lot of favorable comments from consumers but not so much from the restaurants. One European restaurant owner said that he marked up his wine by the same amount as he marked up the food. The difference was that diners didn't seem to pull out their smartphones to compare the finished price of food with its raw ingredient cost the same way that they researched wine markups. Given this, it is perhaps not surprising that private-label restaurant wines are a growth industry. Many wineries produce brands that are sold only in restaurants, which makes retail price comparisons difficult, and some restaurants commission wines that only they serve.

But there's another side to the story. I was speaking at a wine-industry conference in New York City a few years ago when I attended a panel discussion among sommeliers who worked at big-name restaurants. One of the somms explained that his mission was to make his customers happy, and when they came to his famous restaurant, one of the things they most enjoyed was spending a lot of money—sometimes hundreds of dollars—on wine. It made them feel good to drink wine so costly and presumably exclusive. So he focused on big-buck wines that his diners would enjoy. Yes, apparently money can buy happiness when it comes to restaurant wine.

So what is a wine lover of modest means to do? Well, there is a popular notion that the best deal on the wine list is the second-cheapest wine. The cheapest wine is a rip-off, the theory suggests, placed there to extract revenue from suckers. The second-cheapest wine is the sweet spot; you can't go wrong. I didn't realize how pervasive the second-cheapest wine idea was until it came time to select a wine at a Syrian restaurant during a speaking trip to London. I wanted advice—"What do you recommend?" I asked the waiter. "Here, get this wine," he said pointing to a spot on the wine list. "It's the second cheapest!" QED. I don't know if it was the best wine or even the best-value wine, but our waiter knew that it was the most popular.

Maybe the second-cheapest theory works in practice, but there are problems in theory. The whole idea seems to be based on restaurant wine as a zero-sum game, where the restaurants are out to gain at the expense of their customers. That's not a recipe for repeat visits. Worse, it assumes that restaurant managers are dumb and don't react when their customers figure out that the cheapest wine is a terrible deal. If the second-cheapest theory is well known and if restaurants are as evil as it supposes, then they would certainly shift strategies and make the second-cheapest wine a rip-off to restore their margins.

Once diners notice how bad the second-cheapest wine is from a value stand-point, it makes sense that they would adopt the third-cheapest wine strategy, which would force restaurants to revise their wine lists once again. Before you know it, the only good value wine left will be the most expensive wine on the list. Argh! Clearly, price alone is a terrible guide to restaurant wines.

THE CONFIDENCE GAME: BRANDS

The wine wall is huge, as we have seen, and price is not a very reliable guide to quality. Wines taste different from each other, obviously; they taste different from year to year because of nature's unpredictability, they taste different over time as they develop and eventually decline in the bottle, and they taste different to different people based on both sensory skills and preferences. You might say that wine's defining attribute is uncertainty. Some people love to take risks: They buy lottery tickets and recklessly purchase wines based on label art. The chance of winning is almost the same. Other people are so intimidated that they walk away from the wine wall with empty hands and hearts. The rest of us? Well, we try to cut the odds as best we can.

As the wine wall has become more crowded with more domestic wines and more international choices, wine brands have grown in importance. Brands are one successful strategy in the confidence game. The idea of a brand is to inspire confidence through consistency. People go to McDonald's because they know what they will get in terms of choice, quality, and value. There is little chance that they will have an unexpectedly excellent, transformative culinary experience, but there's not much chance that they will be badly disappointed, either. They get what they expect to get. That's what makes McDonald's such a powerful brand: its consistent reliability.

Wine branding is not a new phenomenon. Although people tend to associate the branding trend with New World wine, especially US and Australian, the Europeans, in fact, invented the system and in some respects are still masters of it. The French traditionally define their wines by place, not grape—the *appellation* identifies the wine first, and private producer brands are often secondary.

Their AOP (*appellation d'origine protégée*) system began as a simple geographic designation, like America's AVAs (American viticultural areas), but developed into something more complicated and, well, more French. Originally appellations were all about fraud prevention—protecting the reputation of honest Champagne winegrowers, for example, by making it illegal to put the Champagne label on a wine made mainly from grapes grown in other regions. This assurance, it was believed, would give the Champagne regional "brand" greater value.

And it did, but this led to a different kind of fraud. Some producers cut corners and overcropped, making cheaper, poorer wine that could legally wear the geographic designation because of the grapes' origins. The only way to protect the region's reputation (and the value of its brand) was to regulate both *where* the grapes were grown and *how* the wines were made. And so the contemporary AOP system was born.

It seems to me that the French, who famously reject the idea of branded products in their popular antiglobalization rhetoric, are in fact the world's most successful practitioners of the branding art. If you think of Champagne and Beaujolais as brands, which they are, and not just regions or styles of wine, then this becomes instantly clear. Beaujolais Nouveau, the ultimate Coca-Cola wine, was purposefully developed as a global brand. And of course, such French firms as Möet Hennessy Louis Vuitton are the most successful purveyors of branded luxury products, including wine, in the world. (Möet & Chandon Champagne, Cloudy Bay Marlborough Sauvignon Blanc, and Terrazas de los Andes Argentinean Malbec are all LVMH brands.)

Globalization has been part of the shift in brand strategy. As the global market expands and brings in new consumers, the company-based branding system is simply more successful than the old geography-based grower-driven branding system because it is easier to understand and promote. It brings wine to consumers who are accustomed to purchasing branded products in a format that they can easily comprehend.

THE MARKET FOR LEMONS (AND WINE)

Brands are nothing new, and they are more than just a marketing tool. Brands can serve a very useful economic purpose because of wine's inherent uncertain nature. The Nobel Prize–winning economist George Akerlof wrote about the difficulty of making a purchase under uncertain conditions in a famous paper on the "market for lemons."[6] Buying a used car, for example, is difficult because it is hard to tell if a particular vehicle is a lemon. Some cars, even those made by reliable manufacturers, are simply plagued by problems. Lemons happen. It is not in the seller's interest to disclose this fact, so when you buy a used car, you have to accept the risk that you might be buying a lemon. This uncertainty drives down the price of *all* used cars, according to Akerlof, even the good ones. In the worst-case scenario, people with good used cars are discouraged from putting them on the market because the price is low, so pretty soon the only cars you can find are lemons. What a mess! There are a variety of solutions to this problem, many of which are techniques for the seller of a nonlemon to communicate this fact to buyers, thus differentiating good cars from bad and gaining a higher price.

Do you see where this is going? Although I have never tasted wine made from lemons, I have drunk a lot of lemon wine in my time. The fact is that some wines or some vintages are lemons, and you cannot be sure if you have a lemon until you open the bottle. Solution? Well, the whole wine-rating industry exists because of the lemon-wine problem, doesn't it? *Decanter* and *Wine Spectator* play the same role for wine that *Consumer Reports* does for cars and washing machines.

Brands are another solution to the lemon problem. If brands represent a reliable indicator of quality or consistency (these are not always the same thing), then they communicate valuable information to buyers who are seeking that knowledge. Result (if successful): more confidence among wine drinkers and a higher overall demand for wine. With the market demand for wine growing and becoming more complex in the New World, the value of brands has increased correspondingly.

Brands address the lemon issue, and portfolios of brands are necessary to provide wines in different categories at each crucial price point and to create the breadth and scale that retailers seek. The winemakers who can do this the best will become the leading wine companies of the future. Given the rising importance of wine brands, it makes sense that we should look more closely at a few specific cases to see what lessons can be learned. That's what you will find when you turn the page.

8

OUTLAWS, PRISONERS, AND THE GREAT ESCAPE

Sometimes I think that wine can almost make itself. The yeasts that cling to the grapes in the vineyard are just waiting for an opportunity to start fermenting. My winemaker friends assure me, however, that I wouldn't want to drink what would result from extreme laissez-faire winemaking. "Wine won't make itself," they tell me, and it won't sell itself, either.

Yes, I have heard winemakers proclaim that their supply creates its own demand—make it and they will come. And maybe that's true for some wineries. But the reality for most is this: No one needs to buy their wines; there are thousands and thousands of other wine choices that globalization has brought to the market. In fact, no one needs to buy wine at all, and here in the United States, more people abstain from alcohol in general than drink wine on a regular basis.

How do you stand out in the crowded marketplace? Quality and value are key, of course, but more and more attention is given to branding. At its best, a brand is a way to establish reputation, which is always and everywhere important in wine. At worst, brands are marketing gimmicks, designed to grab buyers' attention for quick sales before—squirrel!—fleeting attention shifts again.

Successful wine brands can teach us something about how the wine world is changing in this era of global wine. Herewith a collection of tales from the wine branding vault. Why is this chapter titled "Outlaws, Prisoners, and the Great Escape"? Read on to find out.

A TALE OF TWO BRANDS

Blue Nun and Mouton Cadet are two of the oldest and most successful global wine brands, and they show us that there is no single path to building a brand. We've already looked at Blue Nun in a previous chapter, but its story merits review. We are in Germany in 1921—hard post–World War I times, for sure, but a great year for wine. The vintage was so abundant and of such high quality that one wine in particular found export success in Great Britain. (Stop and consider for a moment how unlikely the British were to embrace German wine or, well, German anything in the aftermath of World War I!)

The wine was so good that it found a market, and buyers remembered what they'd purchased because of a printer's error on the label. The label was supposed to show nuns in their distinctive brown habits picking grapes in a sunny vineyard—a nice peaceful scene. But the printer accidentally mixed up sky blue and habit brown, and some of the nuns were dressed in blue. Blue Nun. An even more memorable scene, and pretty soon all the nuns were dressed in blue, and Blue Nun was perhaps the world's first global wine brand. High quality plus a stupid mistake equals a brand that continues to sell well around the world today, having survived ups and downs in wine quality and a change of ownership.

Mouton Cadet is Bordeaux's most successful wine brand, even though it isn't one of the high-priced, famous wines that sell for hundreds and even thousands of dollars at auction. Mouton Cadet is modestly priced, made in vast volumes, and sold around the world. It is so ubiquitous, in fact, that it was once used as the reference wine in a study of global wine prices. Richard Hemming, MW, wanted to understand how wine prices differ in different countries, and he needed a specific wine on which to base comparisons.[1] A basket of different wines would have been better from a technical economic standpoint, but one wine had to do, and he picked Mouton Cadet because, as he said, it was a "150-million bottle, 150-country brand distributed from Andorra to Zimbabwe."[2]

Mouton Cadet exists because 1930 was a horrible wine year in Bordeaux and Baron Philippe de Rothschild didn't want to put his prestigious Chateau Mouton Rothschild label on the mediocre wines that were made. So they made up a new brand, Mouton Cadet, which is more or less "Mouton Junior" (*cadet* means *youngest son*). The junior wine wasn't up to the icon Mouton Rothschild standards, but it didn't cost as much either and found a ready market. The new brand had no reputation of its own, of course, but obviously leaned on the prestige of its famous maker.

Quality returned with the 1931 vintage, so there was no need to divert estate grapes to the Mouton Cadet label. But demand for Cadet was there, so the baron bought grapes from other Bordeaux winegrowers to make the popular wine. Mouton Cadet eventually found markets in the United States and Great Britain, where good-value Bordeaux wine was very welcome and then, well, from Andorra to Zimbabwe, as Hemming said.

A WINE WITH NO SHOES

Mouton Cadet shows what can happen when a wine brand is backed by a world-famous name. Association with celebrities from either inside the wine world or outside it is an obvious advantage. But it is neither necessary nor sufficient for a successful wine brand, as the story of Barefoot Cellars shows.

Barefoot Cellars is the best-selling wine brand in the United States and probably in the world. It got its start in 1965, when California winemaker Davis Bynum whipped up some wine in his garage, calling the result Barefoot Bynum Burgundy. Barefoot? Well, the grapes were crushed the old-fashioned way, with bare feet. You could say it was traditional or hand-made, I suppose, but barefoot is more fun.

Zoom ahead to 1986, when marketers Michael Houlihan and Bonnie Harvey acquired the brand, rechristened it Barefoot Cellars, and created the label with its distinctive grape-stained footprint logo. Houlihan and Harvey were obviously attracted to the wine's casual, friendly image, and they saw in it an opportunity to exploit a new idea that they called Worthy Cause Marketing. Lacking the promotion budget that big wineries deploy, they took a grassroots approach, partnering with local nonprofit groups and charitable events rather than taking out ads in glossy wine magazines. Barefoot wine built from the ground up, its laid-back ethos appealing to younger wine drinkers and its association with nonprofit groups burnishing its image.

And then there are the medals. Every bottle of Barefoot Cellars wine featured a medal or award from one wine competition or another. It isn't always clear how significant the honor was, but the external recognition must have given buyers confidence that the wine inside the bottle is good enough to drink. I'm having fun, supporting good projects, and drinking decent wine. What could be better?

Now zoom ahead to 2005, when Gallo bought Barefoot Cellars and began building the brand into the giant we know today. The "kick off your shoes" feeling is still there, but the product lineup has expended enormously. There are red, white, and rosé wines, to be sure, and Barefoot Bubbly, too, plus spritzer and hard-seltzer products. The wines, made to appeal to a broad consumer audience, come in drier, sweeter, and fruit-flavored styles packed in full bottles, mini bottles, cans, bag-in-a-box, and little "wine-to-go" Tetra Pak containers that slip easily into your backpack or picnic basket.

I haven't tasted all the Barefoot wines yet, and I doubt that I ever will because new wines seem to appear regularly as consumer demand shifts. But Barefoot's success isn't entirely about how the wine tastes; I think it is more about how it makes you feel, which is an important insight. Most wine drinkers are puzzled when confronted by detailed tasting notes with their list of esoteric flavor terms, but they can easily relate to positive feelings associated with an affordable product that, unlike a lot of things in wine, doesn't take itself too seriously.

EINSTEIN'S LAW OF WINE

Albert Einstein is said to have declared that everything should be as simple as possible but no simpler. I think he was talking about scientific theories, where it is useful to strip ideas down to the essence in order to uncover underlying forces but without going so far as to lose the connection between the abstraction and the reality it was meant to describe. I don't think Einstein was thinking about wine at all when he uttered what I call Einstein's law, but it holds lessons for anyone interested in wine brands.

Wine brands, like brands generally, are tools that simplify life for consumers. Once you've decided that you like, understand, trust, or even just recognize a brand, life becomes a little bit easier. This is especially true when you are faced with the wine wall's seemingly overwhelming sea of choices. Having brand stars to guide you as you navigate the wine wall can make a lot of difference.

So brands are useful and, as we have seen, powerful, too. Strong brands can keep wine businesses going during troubled times, and sometimes brands can do good (by supporting worthy causes) while they do well for themselves by building a loyal customer base. But there's that Einstein's law risk that brands can simplify too much and something essential is lost. It is a slippery slope, as the case of Martin Ray's Paul Masson wine brand shows, from quality wine to meaningless wine brand to . . . oblivion. It is the sort of thing you might worry about with wine brands like Yellow Tail.

Yellow Tail is a brand of Australian wine that more or less defined the Australian wine category in the United States, and it is easy to see why. It was for a time the best-selling imported wine in the United States—not the best-selling Australian wine but best-selling imported wine, period. In 2009, when depressed market conditions caused Australian wine exports to plummet,

Yellow Tail sales stayed strong in part by cleverly promoting sales in such non-traditional locations as drugstores. Incredibly, at one point, Yellow Tail sold more wine in the United States than all French producers combined.[3]

The winery is located in a small village called Yenda in the Riverina region of southeast Australia. It's a big operation. The warehouse can store nearly a million cases of wine at a time, and the bottling line next door is the fastest and loudest in the world.

Why was Yellow Tail so successful? Some business analysts argue that it's because the Casella family, who owns Yellow Tail, have created something that is new. They tell the Yellow Tail story in terms of blue ocean versus red ocean. The oceans in question are markets. Blue oceans are markets for new products. Red oceans are markets for existing products. Why are they red? I don't really know, but based on what I saw last summer on the Discovery Channel's Shark Week, I'm willing to guess that existing markets are a tough environment to enter. You've got to compete with well-adapted predators who will cut you up badly if you aren't strong (red ocean = bloody ocean—get it?). A blue ocean, however, is uncontested open water. You've got a much better chance of profit if you can stake out the market for a new product before the competition gets there.

So how is Yellow Tale a blue-ocean product?[4] According to one study, it is because Yellow Tail isn't wine as we know it; it's a whole new thing. People don't really like wine, the theory suggests. Even the Casellas don't like it. (Is this possible? They are an Italian winemaking family who emigrated to Australia in the 1950s, planting their own vineyards in the 1990s.) It's very tannic and acidic, and people aren't used to those qualities except in tea. Who wants to pay ten dollars a bottle for something that is bitter and sour? The key to Yellow Tail was the realization that wine without tannin and acid could be very appealing, especially to the majority of Americans who don't really like wine or at least don't drink it very often. (It was designed to appeal to the 85 percent of non-wine-drinkers, according to the theory, while not offending the 15 percent who already like wine. That's 100 percent, if my math is correct. No wonder it is so popular.)

The red ocean, then, is the intensely competitive market for wine, and the blue ocean is the wide-open market for wine that doesn't taste like wine. (You might call it the Blue Nun Ocean in honor of that popular wine brand, which is also easy to drink.) If this analysis is correct, then you can see why Yellow Tail was such a success. But the blue ocean of semiwine was quickly populated by competing predator species. There were dozens and dozens of copycat critter wines out there. Fred Franzia even created a $2.99 Australian wine called Down Under to compete directly with Yellow Tail.

Yellow Tail is still a popular wine brand, but like Blue Nun, the wine's continuing success masks certain problems. Yellow Tail's brand is still strong, but Brand Australia, which it defined for a period, is weak in the United States because Australian wine came to be defined by these popular but relatively simple products. The plan (because Australian wine adopted a plan in 1996 called Strategy 2025) was to first conquer the world markets for entry-level wines and then, from that foundation, to move up the wine wall to more distinctive, expensive, and profitable shelves.

Powered by Yellow Tail and similar products, Australian wine achieved its initial wine-wall objective more quickly and more completely than anyone could have imagined. The time was just right for these wines, as millions of new wine drinkers entered the market. But the next step proved to be more difficult than planned. Once Brand Australia was established in consumers' minds, it was difficult to move upmarket. Australia's share of wine-wall territory declined, and wines closely associated with Australia—especially Shiraz/Syrah—were difficult to sell no matter where they were produced.

So Australian wine producers shifted focus to a new blue ocean, a market where Australian wine was not so clearly associated with a particular type or style: China. And it worked. Penfolds and other premium Australian producers redefined their brands for the Chinese market, and with much investment and hard work, China became Australia's top export market, bigger than the United States and the United Kingdom in terms of wine sales and at a higher average bottle price, too. But the success didn't last, as I explain later in this book, as international politics put a lid on Australia's successful Chinese branding effort.

The Australian wine industry has a new plan and new strategy, which I think of as "brand no brand." Australian winemakers are free to make the best wine they can in the best way they can, the story goes, without a lot of artificial constraints. Australian winemakers aren't prisoners of rules, regulations, oppressive traditions (or out-of-date notions of what Brand Australia wine really is). I don't know if the new plan will work, but at least, by emphasizing the complexity of Australian wine, it should avoid violating Einstein's law.

OUTLAW WINE: BREAKING ALL THE RULES

Just when you think you understand wine brands, they ambush you with something you would never imagine, and you have to figure out if it makes sense. That's the case particularly with an "outlaw wine" that breaks all the rules and yet is still wildly popular: 19 Crimes. What makes 19 Crimes an outlaw wine?

Well, to start with, it is an Australian wine sold in the US market, where Australian wines have weak standing. You have to be a little stir-crazy to imagine that millions of consumers are going to look at a new Australian wine brand and get excited. Second, the foundation of the 19 Crimes lineup is Shiraz, a wine that American consumers think is all over. Maybe not as passé as post-*Sideways* Merlot but nothing to get excited about.

Third, the brand name is a reference to Australian history—who wants to drink a *history* wine? Australia, as you may know, was home to a British penal colony in its early days, and there were nineteen different crimes that were sure to get you sent to serve time down under. I am told that enough time has passed that many people in Australia think it is kind of cool to be descended from one of the early outlaws, but not many folks in the United States are likely to see the connection. If you have to *explain* the history, then it is hard to see how the brand is working for you.

A popular wine brand in America's hangover days was called Virginia Dare, named for the first English baby born in the American colonies in 1587. Virginia Dare is a famous figure; kids learn about her in school and probably remember her, too, because kids seldom get a chance to learn about other kids. That history, better matched with buyer historical experience, worked pretty well as a wine brand in its day. Hard to see how the 19 Crimes history would connect in the same way.

The fourth and final problem with 19 Crimes is its label. The label of each wine in the lineup features a reproduction photo of a prisoner sent to Australia. Do I have to explain that these are not happy men? Caught, convicted, and sent to the end of the earth, they are sad faces, indeed. Who wants to drink Sad Man wine? Who indeed?

Well, that's the interesting part. Despite having four strikes against it, 19 Crimes is a roaring success, selling hundreds of thousands of cases in the US market each year. The brand 19 Crimes seems to have been rather precisely engineered to appeal to an important demographic: millennial men, especially those who see themselves as a bit of a rogue. Outlaws, if you know what I mean, who identify with others who defy convention. Outlaw wine for self-styled renegades? Now you are beginning to see the 19 Crimes logic.

I bought a bottle of the red blend, and after I stared at the sad man for a while, I tasted it. Sweet and tannic was my reaction, and better chilled, sangria-style, than straight up. Not to my taste, but I am not the target audience. Some of the most popular brands on the market today totally succeed with tannic sweet red blends pitched at a particular market segment. A friend who seems to have some inside information told me that the 19 Crimes flavor profile is no accident but rather the result of lots of careful research and consumer testing. No surprise there!

Every bit of the package is carefully linked to the brand identity, and I'd encourage you to take a close look the next time you buy wine. But you will have to purchase and open the bottle to see my favorite part of the branding system—the cork! The cork? Well, that breaks another stereotype, of course, because we sometimes think of Australia and New Zealand wines being topped by screw caps. But there are many reasons cork is so popular today, and 19 Crimes cleverly adds a new advantage to the list: collectability! You see, each cork is printed with one of the nineteen crimes—my cork is number 11: stealing roots, trees, or plants or destroying them. That seems like a pretty petty crime to get my sad guy shipped to Australia, but it might be just the thing to get someone more into it to buy bottles and pull corks relentlessly until all nineteen crime corks are captured.

The brand 19 Crimes is a story wine designed to appeal to a particular consumer category, and Treasury (the owner of the brand) has taken the next logical step by creating a virtual-reality app that animates the sad men (and the sad woman on the Chardonnay label), so that they can tell their own sad stories. Bringing the inanimate to life is a feat with a long artistic tradition; think Pygmalion, Pinocchio, or—especially relevant in this context—the scene in Gilbert and Sullivan's comic opera *Ruddygore*, where somber-painted figures step out of their frames to deliver a stern musical warning. The 19 Crimes figures tell their stories, humanizing their identities, and then step back onto the label. Art may be served by this, but marketing in the form of consumer engagement is the clear intent.

The brand 19 Crimes provides many lessons for anyone trying to understand today's wine market, but perhaps the most important is that it is dangerous to generalize about generations when it comes to such specific products as wine. Many have written that millennials seek authenticity in products and experiences, and this is an important trend. But one size doesn't necessarily fit all, and some millennials (and probably consumers in other generational categories, too) obviously see themselves in a different light.

Identity trumps authenticity. Outlaw! You don't need no stinking badges. And now there is a wine for you.

ART, LIFE, AND THE PRISONER

Wine with a bit of outlaw in its DNA isn't limited to 19 Crimes. In April 2016, Constellation Brands, the company that commissioned the Project Genome study to analyze wine-drinker behavior, announced that it was taking action on its plan to move up the wine wall to higher prices, prestige, and profit by paying $285 million for a Napa Valley red wine brand called the Prisoner.

What did Constellation get for its big-bucks outlay? No vineyards. The Prisoner was made from purchased grapes. No winery either because the wine was produced by a custom-crush winery working under contract (one of wine's best-kept secrets is that what's in the bottle isn't always actually made by the name on the label). Constellation essentially purchased the Prisoner's intellectual property and the right to market wine with it. The brand (and pretty much nothing but the brand) was worth more than a quarter-billion dollars. Wow!

How can just a brand be worth so much? Well, obviously its value depends on what you do with it, and Constellation had a plan to boost the Prisoner's value even higher, which they have done already by expanding the brand portfolio and opening a supercool prison-theme tasting room in Napa Valley. Yes, but $285 million? Well, everyone knows that Apple is the most valuable company in the world. Its total stock market valuation is higher than any other company. But—and I don't want to push this too far—to a certain extent, it is the Prisoner of technology. Apple doesn't manufacture most of its own products. When you invest in Apple, you invest in its intellectual property and ability to market its supercool gadgets especially well.

The Prisoner's Steve Jobs, the guy who got the supercool inspiration, is Dave Phinney, and he is something of a legend within the wine industry because of his ability to craft fine wines and build strong brands. When Sue and I were visiting Roussillon, near France's border with Catalunya, for example, we came across a terrific wine called Department 66—one of Dave Phinney's many global projects. The story goes that when Phinney was twelve, his parents gave him a mildly disturbing print of a Francisco de Goya etching. It showed a contorted prisoner shackled and chained. It's a dark scene, both literally and figuratively, and it is called *The Little Prisoner*. It makes the sad men of 19 Crimes labels seem positively cheerful.

Incredibly, Phinney remembered *The Little Prisoner* when he produced a small batch of Napa Valley red wine in 2000. The wine, a Zinfandel-forward blend, was very good, as Phinney's wines generally are, and received a lot of recognition, including three *Wine Spectator* Top 100 Awards. By 2010, production had grown to 70,000 cases and attracted the attention of the Huneeus family, whose Huneeus Vintners owns Quintessa in Napa Valley and Veramonte in Chile. Huneeus bought the Prisoner and a second brand called Saldo for an undisclosed price, with Phinney staying on to supervise winemaking at the custom-crush facilities in use.

Constellation bought the brand from Huneeus in 2016, presumably to develop further, but perhaps at some point it will flip the brand to someone else. Brands can be very valuable, but strong brands are not easy to create and develop. Our small survey of wine brands in this chapter hasn't revealed any set path or magic formula. So there is a choice to be made: Do you develop your own brand, or do you buy an already successful one from another wine company and try to make it even stronger? And when a brand is worn out, is it better to sell or to hold? These are the sorts of questions that professional soccer managers ask about their players: Develop or buy? Sell or hold? Inevitably there are many answers—and experts to help make the choice.

WELCOME TO THE BRAND FACTORY

Wine is a global business, so it is no surprise that there are global brands and global wine companies that make them. There are flying winemakers who consult for sometimes dozens of different wineries around the world, lending their experience, expertise, and brand-name cachet to the local product. (I introduce Michel Rolland in the next chapter. He is perhaps the world's most famous flying winemaker.) There are also what I call "flying interns," young people looking for careers in the wine business who shuttle between wineries in the Northern and Southern Hemispheres according to the season, building professional networks and getting harvest experience twice as fast as they otherwise could if they had stayed in the same place.

Because wine brands are such an important part of the business, there are also "flying brand makers" who consult on label design, brand development, and even supply-chain structures for wineries all around the world. To give just one example, a friend of mine in Washington State makes a wine called Secret Squirrel that's popular among millennials. If you do an internet search, you'll see an unlikely label: the mischievous face of a squirrel wearing a big red party mask to hide its identity. Who doesn't like secrets, and what could be more fun than a squirrel? It is a distinctive label, and it must be said that the wine is very good indeed and priced just where millennials, who buy wine less often but are willing to spend a little more, might feel at home. Gauge Branding, a Chicago firm that specializes in wine projects, is responsible for Secret Squirrel's look and feel. According to their website, they worked on the brand's strategy, name, brand and label design, shipping-box design, original photography, and website design and execution.

Secret Squirrel? Who would have guessed that it would be a good name for a wine brand? But as I was working on this chapter, I was contacted about a global wine brand with an equally unexpected name: Tussock Jumper. A tussock is a clump of grass, and a jumper is either someone or something that jumps or a name that I heard a lot in England for what we here in the United States call a sweater. Tussock Jumper wine?

Yes. Tussock Jumper is a portfolio of wines sourced from eleven different wine regions around the world (plus a sake from Japan). The wines are sold in the United States and sixty-four other countries, so this is a global brand on both the supply and demand sides of the equation. The wines have a distinctive label design. Each wine features a drawing of an animal that represents the country or region of origin. For example, there's a rhinoceros for the South African Chenin Blanc, a bison for the Zinfandel from the United States, and a llama for the Carmenère from Chile. Each critter is wearing a symbolic sweater (or jumper, I guess), red for most of the wines and green for the wines made with organic grapes. The wines are priced around fourteen dollars for the organic products and about twelve dollars for the rest.

The labels stand out on wine-wall shelves, that's for sure. The name, according to the producers, comes from the fact that the wines are rooted in nature (like tussocks), and the brand is your guide to jump around and try different wines from different regions. If you download the app, you can take advantage of augmented-reality functions. The animals come to life and tell you their stories.

Tussock Jumper is a partnership between a US importer, Tri-Vin Imports, and WineForces, a French-based firm that consults on wine projects like Tussock Jumper and also operates its own brand portfolio. With WineForces' help, you can have your own wine brand without needing to purchase vineyards or build a winery. WineForces can help you design your label and register your trademark and source bottles, corks, and capsules. They'll help you source your wine though their connections with independent wine producers around the world who actually make the wine. And they help with logistics: bottling, transportation, and developing marketing tools like the augmented-reality app. It is a one-stop shop for wine branding, don't you think? And a natural evolution of the wine industry as globalization presents global branding opportunities.

THE GREAT ESCAPE

A final note on the growing power of wine brands. It is easy to come to the conclusion that wine brands are a recent phenomenon rooted in New World commercialization, but clearly that's not the full story. The Prisoner and 19 Crimes fit the stereotype, but remember that their success was built in a way on Blue Nun and Mouton Cadet, older brands from Old World producers. And then there is this: The most successful brands in the world are the Champagnes from France.

Appellations are brands, too, and inevitably, some appellations developed more market power than others. In Tuscany, for example, Chianti Classico is a very strong brand that overshadows to some degree other Chianti subregions and also such neighboring appellations as Vino Nobile di Montepulciano. Vino Nobile wines can be terrific, but they are a hard sell with Chianti Classico nearby, both in geographic terms and on wine-wall placement. And then, of course, there are thousands of wines from other parts of Italy and around the world to compete with. The appellation rules limit how much wineries can do to innovate to get attention and still wear the appellation designation.

One reaction in Italy and elsewhere in Europe has been the boom in what the Italians call IGT wines—wines that eschew their prestigious appellation designation in favor of just a broad geographic identity, which comes with fewer restrictions. IGT wines and their equivalents are a way for winemakers to escape appellation restrictions and create their own proprietary brands. The so-called Super-Tuscans, which broke with tradition by blending forbidden Cabernet Sauvignon with native Sangiovese, were the leaders in this movement. Antinori's Tignanello, a blend of Sangiovese, Cabernet Sauvignon, and Cabernet Franc, was introduced in 1971 and, well, changed everything. If appellation rules made winemakers prisoners to the past, then Tignanello was the great escape.

Sue and I recently tasted wines made by Avignonesi, a Vino Nobile di Montepulciano winery that is Italy's largest biodynamic producer. Their Vino Nobile DOCG wine was terrific and also a good value because the Vino Nobile brand just doesn't have the market power of Chianti Classico. We also tasted three Avignonesi IGT "outlaw" wines. A Super-Tuscan blend of about half-and-half Sangiovese and Cabernet had power and finesse. A Merlot was remarkable, with a finish that went on for days. And then there was a Sangiovese that was fermented in vessels made of clay similar to the soil that nurtured the grapevines. It was a crazy wine—dynamic, exciting, unexpected. Wines like these compete in a different league and can fetch higher prices than their traditional counterparts. Without a collective appellation brand for identification, regional-designation IGT-type wines rely on private brands to make an impression. Some of the most interesting Old World wines you will find today represent this new way of thinking about—and branding—wine.

So what have we learned about wine brands? They are powerful tools in selling wine, that's for sure. Are they also a threat to wine's soul? Do they violate Einstein's law? I leave that question for you to answer for now.

A BLIND BRAND
TASTING

For this tasting, I'd like you to experiment with some of the ideas you've read about in this flight of chapters, especially the power of wine brands and the influence of price on wine-drinker behavior. To do this, I want you to organize a blind tasting of some branded wines.

Blind tasting? If you haven't done this before, then the idea might sound confusing. You don't have to blindfold yourself, although I have seen that done; rather you should put all the bottles to be tasted in bags or wrap them in paper so you cannot see what's what. Sometimes professional tasters also use special black wine glasses so they cannot see the wines themselves. They say that you eat and drink first with your eyes, so it is important to hide this vital bit of information if you want to be guided by taste and aroma alone. But for our purposes, all we need to do is to make it impossible to read the label or guess the wine type by seeing the bottle.

I don't really enjoy blind tasting when the purpose is to identify a mystery wine. My taste memory isn't well trained, and I almost always fail at these games. But I do like blind tasting when the purpose is to take away information that might introduce a bias about the wine one way or another so that you are forced to think for yourself about how the wine tastes and whether you like it.

Here's the plan. Brands are very important in wine today, as we have seen, and many medium- and large-scale wine companies offer wines at a number of price points, sometimes ranging from Wagnerian to Martian prices and quality levels. I propose that you buy three wines at different price points within a particular brand's portfolio and then taste them blind. Which one do you like best?

Which do you think is the least or most expensive? Then remove the bottle covers, and see how your perceptions match up with wine-wall price strata.

This is a fun tasting for a small group of friends in part because there is usually a wide range of opinions that might not have been expressed if the labels had been visible. Some people get the "right" answer every time, but there is always a fairly significant group who prefer the cheapest wine in the flight. They usually aren't embarrassed at getting the "wrong" answer (there is no wrong answer in matters of taste) because they now feel they have permission to drink the less expensive wine that they prefer. A liberating experience!

Which wines should you choose for your tasting? Well, it depends on what kinds of wines you like and what is available in your market. I suggest three flights from around the world. You can go with one of them or make up your own experimental tasting along the same lines.

AN ANTINORI FLIGHT

The Antinori family has been in the wine business for twenty-six generations. Giovanni di Piero Antinori became a member of the Florentine wine guild in 1365. The Antinori family has wine investments in Tuscany, of course, and in other parts of the wine world. In the United States, for example, they are partners with Ste. Michelle Wine Estates in three ventures: Stag's Leap Wine Cellars and Antico Napa in California and Col Solare in Washington State.

A very pleasing tasting can be made with the Antinori Tuscan wines. Start with Villa Antinori Chianti Classico or Santa Cristina by Antinori Chianti Superiore; then add Villa Antinori Chianti Classico Riserva, which costs about twice as much. Finish your flight with any of the more limited-production wines, such as the Antinori Badia a Passignano Chianti Classico DOCG Gran Selezione. You can taste the famous Antinori Tignatello if you like—it is delicious, but it is an IGT Super-Tuscan, not a Chianti, with a different recipe, so it won't be a real apples-to-apples comparison. But do it anyway if you want to and can afford it. It will be interesting to see if you can pick it out in the blind-tasting lineup.

A PENFOLDS TASTING

Penfolds is an Australian brand owned by Treasury Wine Estates. Its Penfolds Grange Shiraz is one of the most famous wines in the world and among the most expensive New World wines you can find. Assuming that you can't afford to taste the Grange, here are Penfolds wines to experiment using the blind-tasting format.

The Penfolds Koonunga Hill Shiraz is a good place to begin. Next in line is Penfolds Max's Shiraz, named for Max Shubert, the winemaker who created the iconic Grange. Penfolds Kalimna Big 28 Shiraz completes the tasting flight, but you might want to randomize the tasting order so that the progression from low- to higher-price wines is not obvious. It would be to okay to toss in a ringer wine, too, a wine by a different Australian producer or perhaps one of the distinctive Penfolds Shiraz–Cabernet Sauvignon blends, just to see if your tasters can spot the difference.

A GALLO TASTING

It is time for a white wine, and Chardonnay is a good choice, and the E. & J. Gallo company, my suggested supplier. Gallo is the largest wine company in the world and very likely the largest producer of Chardonnay wines, too. But these facts won't be obvious when you visit the wine wall because most of the wines made by the Gallo company have a different brand name on the label. Gallo has more than 150 different brands in its portfolio and more than 1,500 individual products. You could very easily fill an entire wine wall from the Gallo catalog.

So how can you tell the Gallo products from the rest? One trick is to turn the bottle around and look at the back label. If it says Modesto, California, then it likely comes from Gallo. But look closely at the universal product code (UPC). If the code begins with 085000, then you've got a wine that is either made by Gallo or distributed by Gallo in partnership with an international producer. La Marca Prosecco is an Italian partner, for example, and Catena partners with Gallo for the Alamos Malbec brand. Once you start looking for Gallo's 085000 UPC "zip code," you will begin to understand Gallo's huge wine-wall presence.

So, with the UPC as your guide, pick out three Gallo Chardonnay wines at different price points. Here's one possibility: Barefoot Cellars Chardonnay is a good place to begin, and it won't cost you much, either. Note that Barefoot makes both a regular Chardonnay and a Buttery Chardonnay, which doesn't actually contain butter at all; it is just a popular style. (Jam Cellars makes a brand of Chardonnay called Butter). Edna Valley is another Gallo brand, and its Chardonnay (and Buttery Chardonnay) cost a bit more than the Barefoot and so make a good addition to the flight. Finally, add William Hill Napa Valley Chardonnay to your list. It is more expensive than the first two wines but quite surprisingly affordable for a Napa Valley wine. Many people are surprised when they learn that this is a Gallo product, but obviously there isn't any monolithic definition of Gallo any more than there is of wine itself.

My friends Pierre and Cynthia sometimes play an interesting game. They blind-taste wines and then decide how much they would be willing to pay for each one. If the actual price is less, then it is a good deal. If, as is often the case, the market price is higher, well, that's a wine to avoid. I call this the "Is it worth it (to me)?" test. You shouldn't base your decision on price alone, of course, but it enters into everyone's consumer calculus in one way or another, and at least this makes a fun game out of it.

These are my suggestions, but feel free to improvise by simply choosing a type of wine you enjoy and then doing a blind tasting of wines from different makers at different price points. Whatever you do, it is an opportunity to enjoy the wines and think about how much price matters when you are standing at the wine wall or studying a restaurant wine list—which is why these wineries offer products at so many price levels. You can also focus on how fundamentally unimportant it can be when you don't know the price and instead simply enjoy the wine itself.

Cheers!

FLIGHT 3
REVENGE OF THE
TERROIRISTS

9

MONDOVINO AND THE REVENGE OF THE TERROIRISTS

If you want to understand how globalization is changing the world of wine, then a good place to begin is to watch *Mondovino*, filmmaker Jonathan Nossiter's 2004 documentary about markets, globalization, and wine. *Mondovino* is a classic tale of good and evil and the tension that exists between these forces in the world of wine. Good wine, according to *Mondovino*, is wine that reflects local land, climate, culture, and traditions. It embodies its *terroir*, to use the unavoidable French term. It is wine with somewhere-ness.[1]

Evil wine, however, cannot hide its nowhere-ness. It is a reflection of the industrial process that produced it and the unselfconsciously commercial motivations of its makers. It may be free of technical imperfection, as precision industrial products often are, but it has no soul. This wine isn't evil in itself; its evilness derives from the economic threat it poses to terroir. *Mondovino* fears that nowhere wine is here to stay but hopes that soulful winemakers, the *terroirists*, can persevere and perhaps even triumph.

Films about *things* are boring, but films about people and places can be fascinating, so *Mondovino* travels through the world of wine (to France, Italy, Britain, America, Argentina, and even Brazil) to meet people who cast themselves into various roles in this drama. Three famous Americans represent the forces of evil that threaten good wine and its makers: Robert Mondavi, the California corporate winemaker (who died in 2008); Robert Parker, the Maryland wine-rating guru; and Michel Rolland, the micro-oxygenating multinational wine consultant (the king of the flying winemakers). Michel Rolland is really French, not American, but he numbers Americans among his many global clients, and as an emissary of evil in the film, he thinks and acts like an American is supposed to—talking too loud, dropping names, privileging market values over traditional values, and generally treating wine as processed industrial output rather than a handcrafted product of sun and soil.[2]

There are many heroes in *Mondovino*, and they are mainly French. First among them is bleary-eyed, tweedy old Hubert de Montille, the Burgundian winemaker of ancient tradition who stands for everything that is good and true and noble about wine—in stark contrast to Mondavi, Parker, and the turncoat Rolland. Bemused, outraged Aimé Guibert, owner of the famous Mas de Daumas Gassac in Aniane, is a *Mondovino* hero, too. When Mondavi sought to purchase vineyards in France and set up operations there, Aimé Guibert led the noble vignerons of Languedoc into battle like a modern-day Astérix the Gaul and repelled the foreign invaders. The wine war between Guibert and Mondavi is immortalized in France as *La guerre des vins: L'affaire Mondavi.*[3]

Everything seems black and white in *Mondovino*, on first viewing at least, even the dogs, who play an unexpectedly important part in the film.[4] Aimé Guibert's dog is good and faithful, as a dog should be, for example. Robert Parker's bulldog, George, farts extravagantly. This is significant, apparently, because according to Nossiter, dogs resemble their masters' wines.[5] Old World wines, like its dogs, are faithful and true, while New World wines are enthusiastically vulgar.

Everything about *Mondovino* makes clear the filmmaker's opinion of how globalization and branded commercial wine are reshaping the world of wine. New replaces old, tradition is destroyed, and taste is debased. Even the noble dog is disgraced. It isn't a simple process; it's not really as black and white as I may have made it seem here. Not all the Americans in the film are evil industrialists, for example, and not all the French are sons and daughters of the soil, but the message comes through pretty clearly. A new world of wine is assaulting the old one, and the soul of one of the world's oldest and most revered cultural products is in jeopardy.

I think that *Mondovino* is a terrific film, but is the story that it tells about globalization and wine the whole truth? Well, of course not! How could it be? How can anyone explain what is happening to the world of wine today in a 135-minute video?[6] To find out what is really happening, you need to dig a little deeper, both into the story that *Mondovino* so effectively tells and into the counterstory, as well, because there isn't just one answer; there are many. Each story is like a bottle of wine itself: a mystery, really, until you pull the cork and see, smell, and taste what's inside. Let's pull some corks and see what we find.

GLOBALIZATION AND WINE IN THE LANGUEDOC

The French are suspicious of globalization, just like the rest of us. They are simultaneously pulled by its opulent appeal and appalled by its frightening, disruptive potential—just like the rest of us. It is no wonder, then, that the prospect of Robert Mondavi, the human face of global wine, bringing an American idea of wine to France would produce strong reactions, as *Mondovino* makes clear. Some, like Andrè Ruiz, the prodevelopment socialist former mayor of Aniane, welcomed the Mondavi investment enthusiastically. Others, like Manuel Diaz, the militant communist mayor, and Aimé Guibert, the outraged winemaker, couldn't wait to drive the Americans out. Many, perhaps most, were simply torn between the two poles, unwilling to commit to one or the other.

Aniane, the location of the drama of *L'affaire Mondavi*, is a wine town in the South of France, a couple hours' drive southwest of Avignon. It lies in the Languedoc, the place that lays claim to the title of world's largest vineyard. It is the largest winegrowing region in the largest winegrowing country on earth. Perhaps as much as a third of all the wine grapes in France come from this arc of land that reaches from Provence to the Spanish border.[7]

Languedoc has had an uncomfortable experience of markets and globalization in its history. Wine markets are to Languedoc, I think, like Lucy and her football are to Charlie Brown in the *Peanuts* cartoon. The market for wine has tantalizingly promised prosperity and sometimes even delivered it, only to jerk it away again and again. You would have mixed feelings about markets, too, if you made your living from wine in Languedoc.

Wine and the wine trade came early to Languedoc, perhaps as early as the sixth century BC, when Greek and Etruscan settlers planted vines. Wine became big business, however, with the Roman invasion of Gaul around 125 BC. Wine grapes thrived on the broad alluvial plains of the Roman province of Narbonne in today's Languedoc, and soon its wines were being exported to Rome and elsewhere in the empire. The Languedoc vignerons connected to the "global" market for wine, as it were, and apparently profited greatly from it.

In fact, they were too successful for their own good. Rising production from Languedoc threatened the livelihood of Roman winegrowers, so Emperor Domitius issued an edict in 92 AD that ended Languedoc's boom. No more vines were to be planted in the Roman Empire, the order proclaimed, and half of all existing vines in the provinces were to be uprooted. Languedoc's great vineyards were suddenly empty fields. The subsequent collapse of the Roman Empire and its well-organized market for wine effectively finished off what was left of the Languedoc industry—no more demand, no more supply. Kaput!

Wine survived on a limited scale mainly due to the influence of the abbeys in the region, which made wine for their own consumption and for religious purposes. The biggest vineyard in the world sat barren because of politics and foreign competition.

The wine industry was revived as a major force in the seventeenth century in response to rising demand in growing north European cities. The Canal du Midi was completed in 1681, connecting the Mediterranean port of Sète with the inland city of Toulouse. Goods could ride the canal northwest from the sea to Toulouse and then move on to the Atlantic via the Garonne River. The Canal du Midi cut a month of transportation time between southern France and the thriving northern markets in Britain and Holland. A new era of prosperity seemed ready to bloom. But politics and competition got in the way again. Languedoc's main rival for the northern trade was Bordeaux, and the Garonne, the Canal du Midi's natural extension, meets the sea at the port of . . . Bordeaux! Apparently, the burghers of Bordeaux, seeing clearly their self-interest in the matter, erected no end of barriers and obstructions to trade, which favored Bordeaux wines over those of the south. Bordeaux protectionism prevailed until 1776, when the "Bordeaux preference" was removed and freer competition prevailed. Languedoc prospered from 1776 to the middle of the next century. Its wines enjoyed a good reputation (the American oenophile and future president Thomas Jefferson visited in 1787, drawn by the wine's renown) and as wide a market as sea trade would allow.

The fall of Languedoc wines from this high plateau is easy to trace. It is due to an excess of prosperity of the type that only markets can create. To be specific, it was due to the railroad and the effects and reactions that came with it. To an economist, the arrival of the railroad in the nineteenth century is much like globalization and the internet today: It was a disruptive innovation that lowered costs, shrank time, and thereby made the world more interconnected. If this analogy holds, then we can say, without doing too much damage to the truth, that the fall of the Languedoc wine industry was due to nineteenth-century globalization.

The railroad reached the Languedoc in about 1845, connecting it with the large and growing urban centers in Paris and Lyon with their thirsty wine-drinking worker populations. Wine could be loaded into huge vats called *tuns* or pumped into specialized tank cars and sent by rail to Paris at a lower cost (and with less damage to the wine) than ever before. The railroad vastly expanded the market for Languedoc wine and set in motion a chain of events that transformed the wine market in France over the course of the next seventy-five years.

Urban factory workers were interested in strong, cheap wine, and the wines of the south were certainly cheap. In fact, they were cheaper than wines from other parts of France, and the first effect of the railroad was on the northern winemakers, whose market had previously been protected by high transportation costs. The advent of cheaper southern wines put many of these winemakers out of business, as they could not match the price and strength of the southern wines. The winemakers who remained evolved to fill niche markets based on quality or distinctive appeal. If today the Languedoc winemakers are fearful of competition from cheaper New World wines, then they are perhaps motivated by the knowledge that once they were that cheaper source themselves.

As late nineteenth-century industrialization gained pace, urban centers grew, and the market for cheap wine increased dramatically. You would think this would be music to the ears of the Languedoc vignerons, but in the end, it created a problem because of the asymmetrical structure of the wine business. Wine distribution in Paris, Lyon, and elsewhere was big business, with efficient, large-scale wine wholesalers. They built what I think of as big pipelines that they needed to fill with cheap wine of consistent, if not high, quality. (They weren't real pipelines, of course; wine was delivered in barrels by cart.) Wine production, however, was badly fragmented. Most wine was produced by family farms (or by families working on a sort of sharecropping arrangement). There were literally thousands of small producers of uneven-quality wine. The structure of supply and the structure of demand just didn't line up. Unless and until the wholesalers could find reliable bulk suppliers, they would not be able to fully exploit their distribution efficiencies.

The solution to this mismatch came in the form of an intermediary called a *négociant*, a merchant who bought up new wine from individual producers, blended and aged it, and filled the pipelines that the urban markets created. The wine blended by a good *négociant* would necessarily be more consistent than wines from perhaps hundreds of individual small-scale producers and cost less too, once scale economies were taken into account. *Négociant* wines were also sometimes better because these merchants didn't hesitate to import even stronger wines from Algeria and the south of Italy to beef up their blends and better match their customers' requirements. More to the point, *négociant* wines had a broad market because they were supplied in quantities and styles that matched the market structure. The market for a small lot of wine by an individual producer of uncertain reputation was very limited by comparison.

Market power shifted from the individual producers (supply) to the *négociants* (demand), particularly as the *négociants* developed brand-like reputations. They used this market power to squeeze the growers, offering lower prices for the new wine and sometimes refusing to buy it at all if it lacked quality or during periods of excess supply. The *négociants* had what economists call *monopsony* power—the power that comes with control over demand. Demand for Languedoc wine was surging in the cities, but the growers found themselves on the wrong end of the market. The profits increasingly went to the merchants—the *négociants*.

Cooperatives—or *caves coopératives* as they are called in France—were the producers' response to this imbalance in market power. Groups of growers formed cooperative cellars and signed contracts to supply their grapes (in some cases, they committed their entire crop; in other cases, the contribution was variable). Large wineries were built, subsidized by the French government (due to the political clout of the winegrowers) and financed with cheap loans from the Crédit Agricole. New vats and equipment were purchased, and a professional winemaker was hired. Winegrowers brought their grapes to the cooperative and were paid according to crop weight, sometimes in cash and in other cases in a share of the wine itself when it was ready, which they could sell on their own.

Cooperatives in general have a socialist smell, but you would be wrong to think of the Languedoc cooperatives that way. The vignerons were stubbornly independent and did not feel any strong proletarian solidarity. The cooperatives were a defensive measure, a way to gain concentrated market power over supply to match *négociants'* demand power. And it worked. The cooperative wines were more consistent than the wines of individual growers and easier to market, too. It must also be said that the new vats and equipment were generally cleaner and more up-to-date than the sometimes worn and moldy cellars of the vignerons. The *caves coopératives* were an effective institutional reaction to the new "global" wine market.

Cooperatives remain an unexpectedly important component of the wine business. It is easy to imagine that wine production today is basically cold corporations versus noble family growers, but the cooperatives still dominate in many regions, especially in Europe. More than half the vineyard area in France today is owned by cooperative members, and the *caves coopératives* produce more than half of all French wine! Two-thirds of German winegrowers are cooperative members. More than 60 percent of Italian wine is made by their cooperatives, called *cantina sociale*. The cooperatives are similarly strong in Spain and Portugal. Much of the inexpensive bulk wine made in Europe is the product of these cooperative cellars. An increasing number have managed to establish reputations for high quality, however, and charge a premium price. We have been stunned by the excellent wines we have tasted on visits to cooperatives in northern Italy, for example, but you can also find mediocre wine—unable to hold a candle to inexpensive wines from Chile, Australia, and elsewhere. Why?

The problem is the age-old trade-off between quantity and quality. The cooperatives were designed to provide consistency, not quality, and individual growers were rewarded based on the quantity of grapes they delivered, not the quality of the wine that was produced. This created predictably unfortunate incentives that have undermined the cooperative cellar system.

Where growers were not required to sell all their grapes to the local cooperative, they would naturally reserve the best grapes for themselves for their own wine production or for sale to quality-conscious buyers—and dump the rest in the cooperative vats. Where growers must sell all their grapes to the cooperative, their incentive is to produce the greatest possible tonnage of grapes at the lowest possible cost, resulting in weak, characterless wines. I am tempted to call it McWine because that's the sort of term we usually apply to least-common-denominator products, which is what the worst of the cooperative wine was and still is, but I don't want to offend French readers any more than I have to!

The choice of quantity over quality even extended to the types of grapes grown. Most wine drinkers are familiar with the names of the famous French grape varieties: Cabernet Sauvignon, Merlot, Chardonnay, and Sauvignon Blanc. These are the names that you see most commonly on labels in the supermarket, so you might reasonably assume that these would be the most commonly grown grape varieties in Languedoc, the world's largest vineyard. But you would be wrong.

Carignan was the typical grape of the Languedoc cooperatives for many years. Have you heard of it? Because French wines are mainly identified by region rather than grape variety, you may have drunk wine made from Carignan grapes without knowing it. Carignan can produce stunningly good wines—I can't forget the Carignano del Sulcis wines we tasted in Sardinia, for example. But the advantage of Carignan is its great productivity. Carignan makes wine that is strong and deeply colored, which has made it useful to French growers in the years since Algerian independence, when the supply of blending wine from North Africa dried up, but it can also be acidic, bitter, and tannic. It is, at its worst, according to experts, notable for being too harsh to drink young and not worth aging. Only a merchant (or her banker) could love it—for its low cost. And so the market-driven cooperatives fell in love with bad wine.

The situation of the Languedoc vignerons in the *Mondovino* drama is thus a complicated one. We would like to think that they represent a tradition of good wine, soulful and reflecting a distinctive terroir. This would make their battle against the forces of industrial science (Michel Rolland) and terroir-free multinational corporation (Robert Mondavi) a noble one. Who wouldn't root for them to prevail?

But the situation on the ground was far different. The Languedoc cooperatives are creatures of the market as much as Mondavi is—more perhaps because Mondavi (and the forces he represents here) at least could sometimes shape the market to a certain extent, whereas the history of the cooperatives is mainly that they react to the market. Mondavi and the large-scale commercial winemakers that he represents in *Mondovino* must make better wines because of competition. Who will buy cheap bad wine when, in today's global market, there is always the option of better, cheaper wine?

The truth is that many of the Languedoc cooperatives were and some still are dinosaurs—creatures of a previous era when quality mattered little, quantity counted for a lot, and French wine consumption was high. In today's world, with per capita wine consumption in a free fall in France and other Old World markets and global competition heating up, the Languedoc cooperatives and the world's largest vineyards are threatened. Does the world really need them and their wines anymore? No. Not unless they change—adapt to changing market conditions.

And many of the cooperatives have indeed adapted by investing in new techniques and equipment, replanting vineyards with dense rows (to reduce vigor and improve quality) of quality grapes, and hiring one of the flying winemakers like Michel Rolland to introduce modern winemaking techniques. Some would say that the wine that results has been McDonald-ized or Mondavi-ized because it has more in common with wines from Chile, California, and Australia than it does with the harsh and bitter Carignan-based wines of recent tradition.

But resistance to change is strong, and it is easy to understand why. At one time, the Languedoc vignerons saw a vast market before them, only to find themselves under the thumb of the merchants who controlled access to that market, the *négociants*. The only way they could escape that dilemma was to form cooperatives, which gave them supply power to match the demand power of the other side. But now that supply power has slipped away again, what are they to do? An alliance with Mondavi would formalize the pressure to change. Better access to global markets, which Mondavi could provide, would come with a loss in power and independence. It would be the railroad story all over again.

And so the real story is revealed. It is not about tradition and terroir. It is about power and autonomy. Having been powerless once, the growers of the Languedoc fear they will become powerless again. So they cling to the false security of their cooperative and hope, falsely again, that mediocre wine will come back into style. They are terrorists in *Mondovino*, but their motivation is less a noble principle than it is power.

ASTÉRIX THE GAUL VERSUS MONDAVI THE AMERICAN

The terroirists' leader, who died in 2016, was Aimé Guibert, or so the film suggests. This makes a good story because Guibert is such a colorful character, a sort of winemaking Astérix the Gaul (a popular French cartoon character); he lacks only the extravagant mustache to complete the picture. Except that where Astérix opposes Roman imperialism, Guibert seems to think of himself as leader of the resistance to imperialism of the foreign corporate kind. This image, which is easy to take from *Mondovino*, is filled with irony. Aimé Guibert is an unlikely terroirist, and the enemy that he opposes is not as foreign as it seems. The battle we see in parts of *Mondovino* is less about wine than it is about gloves.

Aimé Guibert's family business wasn't wine; it was gloves. The Guiberts were a major Parisian manufacturer of gloves until globalization in the form of cheaper gloves from Asia put them out of business. The property that is now their wine estate, Mas de Daumas Gassac, was purchased as a vacation retreat with no thought of making wine. This changed when a professor of oenology from the University of Bordeaux who happened to visit recognized the outstanding potential of the soil and site for making fine wine. (I suspect that the site wasn't previously developed as a vineyard because its higher elevation made it unsuitable for high-volume heat-loving Carignan grapes.)

The first vines were planted in 1974, but they weren't the grapes of local tradition; they were high-quality "international" varieties, fitting for an enterprise that aspired to an international reputation. Today the vineyard includes grapes traditionally associated with Bordeaux (Cabernet Sauvignon, Merlot); Burgundy (Pinot Noir, Chardonnay); and the Italian Piedmont (Nebbiolo, Barbera), as well as a number of quality varieties historically associated with the Languedoc. The first vintage was made in 1978 under the supervision of Emile Peynaud. Peynaud was a famous oenologist at the University of Bordeaux and one of the first internationally famous winemaking consultants. The villainous Michel Rolland was his pupil! Peynaud shook up the wine world in the postwar era by putting taste above tradition (demand above supply, to use my terms). He advocated strict control of all elements of winemaking, from vine to bottle, and introduced many of the vineyard and cellar techniques that are standard practice in quality winemaking today.

Under Peynaud's influence, Mas de Daumas Gassac produced really excellent wines that were nothing like the cheap plonk that flooded the Languedoc plains in those days. Of course, it was different: different grapes, low yields, stressed vines, no fertilizers, modern winemaking techniques, and an aim to exploit the potential of an exceptional vineyard site. Daumas Gassac wines are built to be aged—decades are required for the wine to achieve its full potential, according to Guibert, unlike the ready-to-drink Chateau Cash Flow wine of the region. The wine expresses its terroir, but I have to think that it does so not because this is natural but because it is the intentional consequence of cold calculation. Daumas Gassac is often called the "Grand Cru of Languedoc," which is meant as a compliment, comparing the wines to the best of Bordeaux, but the real truth is that they are Bordeaux wines made in Languedoc and therefore are selling at lower prices.

Although I am sure that he would object to this comparison, I think you might call Aimé Guibert the Robert Mondavi of the Midi. Mondavi built his famous Napa Valley winery at roughly the same time that Guibert built his. Both operations were driven by a strategy of quality instead of quantity, which ran counter to the prevailing pattern. Both based their best wines on Bordeaux grape varieties. Both were successful but in different ways—Mondavi in the big American way and Guibert in the cunning French way. Of course, there are differences, but they only add to the irony. The Mondavi family business was wine, not gloves, for example, and the Mondavi Napa project was an intentional business risk, not the happy accident of a well-placed vacation home. Guibert was a victim of globalization because global competition ruined his glove business. Mondavi was a victim in a different way. His attempts to harness globalization and expand his business weakened his control of it until finally it was bought up by one of the world's biggest wine producers, Constellation Brands. Probably Guibert feared that the same could happen to him.

It seems to me that Aimé Guibert doesn't really have much in common with the Languedoc vignerons he appears to champion and represent in *Mondovino*. Well, he does share one thing: fear of foreign competition, and it is a legitimate concern for anyone at the margin of an industry. Guibert is on the margin in the sense that he cannot overcome the fact that he is a Languedoc producer and will never be able to get top dollar (or top euro, I suppose) for his wine. If Guibert makes the best wine in Languedoc, then this will not pay as well (or provide as much prestige, which is important, too) as making, say, the thirtieth-best wine in Bordeaux. Guibert's wines sell for less than some of Mondavi's. The Languedoc growers and their cooperatives are on the margin, too, but in a different sense. They need to make better wine, not more wine, and they need to do it in a market where demand is falling and foreign supply is on the rise. They have the largest vineyard in the world, but that doesn't mean a thing if no one wants to buy their wine.

WE HAVE MET THE ENEMY . . . AND HE IS US!

Who is the enemy? It is easy to say that it is Robert Mondavi, the American invader with the Italian-sounding name who is not the enemy himself but represents the enemy: the global wine market and the need for supply to adapt to demand in that market. But really, I think the greater threat is closer to home. A better symbol of the global market and how to succeed in it, which is what the Languedoc cooperatives must confront, is a Frenchman with an Italian-sounding name: Robert Skalli.

Robert Skalli founded the Skalli Group, a holding company that was at one time one of the largest producers of wines in the Languedoc. The Skalli conglomerate made branded varietal wines, just like Mondavi, and sold them in France and around the world, just like Mondavi. Skalli's story provides us with a particularly French image of wine and globalization. Robert Skalli's parents were *pieds noirs*, French migrants to Algeria. Many *pieds noirs* emigrated to Algeria starting in the 1870s, when phylloxera wiped out vineyards and grower incomes in the Languedoc. The Skallis left France in the 1930s, presumably in search of greater opportunity in North Africa—and they found it. Robert-Elle Skalli, Robert Skalli's grandfather, built an empire on grain and wine. By the time that Francis Skalli took over from his father after World War II, the family business included a huge grain operation, Rivoire et Carré, with a mill in Marseilles; the number 2 pasta company in France, Lustucru; a vineyard in Corsica; a rice producer, Taureau Aile; and of course vineyards in Algeria. By 1964, the Skalli vineyards in Algeria spread over 600,000 acres, which is nearly as large as all the vineyards in Languedoc. This was the wine that the French *négociants* blended with the weaker Languedoc product to make industrial-strength *vin du jour*, and they made vast quantities of it.

Like many other *pieds noirs* families, the Skallis eventually fled to France because of the Algerian war and Algeria's independence in 1962. They settled in the Languedoc and went about rebuilding their business. Robert Skalli entered his father's and grandfather's business in the 1970s and, as part of his education, studied and worked (as a flying intern) with winemakers in Australia and the United States. Significantly, according to the official company history, he worked with Robert Mondavi, who introduced him to the idea of branded varietals and opened his eyes to a different vision of the wine business, one based not on the condition of supply (and the traditional practices and regulations governing production) but on demand and the development of vineyard, cellar, and marketing techniques that would provide buyers with wine that they could understand and appreciate and that they would buy.

Skalli returned to France and began to organize a business to make the clean, consistent, midrange varietal wines that he saw in California and Australia. He established partnerships with growers and cooperatives in the Languedoc, providing financing for the process of pulling out their tough old vines and replanting with market-friendly varieties like Merlot and Chardonnay. Replanting is expensive, both in direct outlays and in lost production while the vines mature. I suppose having the backing of the profitable Skalli grain business was useful in this transformation process.

The main Skalli brand, Fortant de France, was established in 1983 to produce and market these wines both in France and around the world. A premium brand called simply F. (for Francis Skalli, Robert's father) was a Languedoc wine that "dares" to approach Bordeaux "Grand Cru perfection," according to the marketing literature. It was made from the best grapes from the best sites in the Skalli portfolio, blended under the watchful eye of Michel Rolland and sold for about the same as Aimé Guibert's Daumas Gassac, the other famous Bordeaux wine made in the Languedoc.

The Skalli family eventually concentrated on wine—the grain and pasta businesses were sold or spun off. They had wine interests in Languedoc; the Rhône Valley; Corsica, where they owned the largest private vineyard; and California. Skalli bought what is now the St. Supery winery in Napa Valley in 1982. St. Supery is best known for its Sauvignon Blanc and Cabernet Sauvignon. Skalli credited Mondavi with helping him make this investment. And in return, Skalli supported Mondavi's aborted attempt to invest in the Languedoc on the logic, I believe, that Mondavi would draw favorable attention to the Languedoc, which would benefit both family businesses.

In 2011, Skalli sold most of its wine interests to Boisset, the Burgundy-based French wine multinational that also owns Raymond in Napa Valley and DeLoach and Buena Vista in Sonoma. St. Supery was sold separately to Chanel, the French fashion house.[8] Robert Skalli owned vineyards, of course, but he wasn't a vigneron. He was really a *négociant*. Most of his wines were made from grapes supplied under long-term contract and subject to strict control. Some of the wine was made by local winegrowers and cooperatives, too, also under tight control. The resulting wines were frequently criticized for being soulless—for lacking terroir. But I can't help but observe that this might sometimes have been a good thing, in the context of the Languedoc, where the wines of recent memory have been acidic, bitter, and thin and often produced in such excess supply that they ended up being distilled to make industrial alcohol.

I can also appreciate how Skalli's success must have felt to many of the local growers and cooperatives who were not part of his network. The battle in the twentieth century was cooperatives versus *négociants*—supply versus demand—and the suppliers were able to hold their own, or so it seemed. And now, the twenty-first century seems already to belong to Skalli (a *pied noir!*) and his like, and this means that power has shifted to them, and the French cooperatives have lost. Mondavi's arrival in Languedoc would not have changed the balance between supply and demand. The balance had already shifted. Mondavi was only a symbol of the change and, because he was an American, a useful target in a country that loves to bash America even as it embraces all things American.

SHARP EDGES AND THE TASTE OF PLACE

As I was revising a draft of this chapter for the first edition of *Wine Wars*, I came into possession of a book by Jonathan Nossiter, *Mondovino*'s creator.[9] Although *Liquid Memory: Why Wine Matters* is not intended to be a supplement to or continuation of *Mondovino*, I certainly learned quite a bit about the making of the film, its characters, and Nossiter, too. Indeed, the book is really about Nossiter and how wine inspires his memories and provokes his emotions, just as a small cake, a madeleine, famously provoked Marcel Proust. It's not my favorite book because I guess I'm not that interested in Nossiter's memories or at least not as interested as he is, but I did find things to like in it.

In one of my favorite scenes from the book, Nossiter and a filmmaking colleague are driving back from a day of *Mondovino* preshoot research in Burgundy, and they talk about why they are so attracted to terroir—why they have become terroirists in the way that I use the word. Members of a somewhat rootless transnational artistic class, they recognize that perhaps terroir is so precious to them because it is something they feel they have lost. Nossiter, the American raised in Paris, now lives in Brazil; well, you can see how he would feel nostalgic for the authentic home terroir he maybe never had. That's an emotion many of us can appreciate.

Another passage subtly probes this same feeling in a different context. Why is terroir and regional identity so important now? Because sharp divisions have caused so much pain and hardship in the past (think Europe and the two World Wars). Suppressing differences and rounding off sharp corners to create a more peaceful whole has been the agenda of the last fifty years. Now we find that universalism has gone pretty far, creating the terroir-free transnational world of the European Union, and we start to value what we have lost. Sharp edges seem pretty desirable now that we've lost them, even if they sometimes bruise or cut.

I tasted both sides of this problem when we visited Friuli in the Italian northeast a few years ago. We stayed outside Cormons with the Venica family at their winery estate and visited the Sirk family at La Subida. The land and people of this area were brutalized by the two wars, and so when postwar peace appeared, they gathered grape varieties from around the world and planted them all together in one serene vineyard. The wine from these grapes, *Vino Della Pace* (wine of peace), isn't especially distinctive on the palate as I recall but is memorable nonetheless for its optimistic symbolism.

We longed for the taste of peace when we didn't have it. Now that we do, we find it a little bland. So we seek out terroir, even if it threatens to divide us once again. Interesting, isn't it? Even in Friuli it is the intensely distinctive local wine of long memory—Pignolo, Schioppettino, Ribolla Gialla—that attracts our attention today, not the wine of peace.

Although Nossiter's book is about cultural politics (if you believe the French title, *Le Goût et le Pouvoir—Taste and Power*) and social philosophy (if you consider the American one), it seems to me that a great deal of space is actually given over to wine economics. The business of wine with its commercial pressures, and especially the ethics of wine pricing, is discussed at length. "It occurs to me," Nossiter writes, "that it is impossible to talk about wine without talking about money"; I think he is right. He elaborates, "Wine is inextricably linked to money like all objects of desire in a capital-driven world." He continues,

> Though a given bottle's price varies even more peculiarly than the price of fine arts, a given bottle's price is supposed to be a reflection of its intrinsic values. Whether it is the producer who sets the initial price, or the importer, distributor, or end seller, each time the price of the wine is set an ethical decision has been made in relation to the wine's origins and contents.[10]

Nossiter is disgusted by the religion of money, but in this passage, he seems instead to be seduced by it, to accept the premise that market prices are moral judgments, even as he protests their verdict. I think the premise is wrong and that intrinsic worth is measured by a different scale. It isn't easy being a terroirist.

I was pretty hard on terroirists in this chapter. My defense is classic Astérix: They provoked me (or at least *Mondovino* did)! But that doesn't mean I don't respect their ideas and accept that they have a point. In fact, I think they will play a crucial role in the future of wine. But, as I said, it isn't easy being a terroirist.

WE ARE ALL
TERROIRISTS NOW

The crime was typically French, an *assemblage* of politics, viticulture, and vigilante violence:

> On March 6 [2006], more than 120 masked men armed with crowbars descended on the Mediterranean port city of Sète in France's Languedoc region. They targeted two wine merchants' warehouses, dumping thousands of gallons of wine onto the ground.[1]

The masked men, fashionably dressed in black with balaclavas disguising their identities, were not anarchist protesters of the sort who typically attack McDonald's restaurants and Starbucks stores at meetings of the World Trade Organization. Nor were they the radical Arab terrorists who once inhabited the nightmares of paranoid National Front voters in the South of France. Some of them drove tractors:

> More *vignerons* formed a roadblock on the highway between Montpellier and Béziers, blocking traffic and setting a police car on fire. When the police arrested nine of the men and brought them to trial, the court simply released them. Charges were dropped against five, while four received suspended one-month jail terms.

It was easy to tell who was behind the attack. A press photo shows "CRAV" scrawled on the wall next to a now-empty wine tank that was previously full of cheap Spanish wine destined for French supermarket shelves. CRAV terroirists fight fire with fire. Each bottle of foreign wine is a "bomb targeted at the heart of our rich European culture."[2] No wonder they feel it necessary to respond in kind, with explosives and guerrilla raids. And no wonder their destructive acts are tolerated, apparently even by the courts. They are the resistance, like during the German occupation, not criminals. They resist the occupation of France by the unsophisticated wines (and cultures) of Mondavi's world.

CRAV stands for Comité Régional d'Action Viticole (Regional Committee for Viticultural Action), a group of about a thousand protesters and activists who are outraged at . . . at what? Well, at everything, really. Everything that threatens their idea of *terroir*, their notion of French wine. So they are mad at the hypermarkets, who sell cheap imported wine in cardboard Tetra Paks for a euro a liter, undercutting French producers. They are mad at the European Union for kicking the Common Agricultural Policy (CAP) subsidy stool out from under them and forcing them to compete with foreign producers in a game increasingly played by international, not French, rules. They are mad at their fellow Frenchmen and women, too, for seemingly abandoning wine as the beverage of choice and drinking more beer, soda, and water.

CRAV has a lot to be angry about, and it all got worse in 2009 as the continuing effects of the economic crisis added to the pressures facing Languedoc vignerons. No wonder they threatened that "blood will flow" if French president Nicolas Sarkozy did not find a way to push French wine prices higher.[3] CRAV struck again, vandalizing equipment and burning barrels at a *négociant* facility near Béziers and at a cooperative in Clermont l'Herault. The war goes on; the resistance will not yield.

THE WAR ON TERROIR

Terroirists have an important role to play in the future of wine, even the black-clad activists of CRAV (although I admit that I don't see them as *especially* important, not unless Jonathan Nossiter decides to make *Mondovino 2: CRAV Strikes Back*). Globalization and commodification are agents of change, and change is very disruptive. It threatens vested interests and embedded values. You can't expect such change to go unopposed. Two of my favorite political economists explained how and why.

Joseph Schumpeter was perhaps the first political economist after Marx to take change seriously as an economic force.[4] He compared the economy to a living organism with two interdependent types of systems. One, which you can compare to the circulatory system, is meant to sustain the organism, while a second governs growth and development. The sustaining system needs to be constant and consistent, but the growth system operates in fits and starts; we call them growth spurts in young people. Both systems need to work well to sustain people through their lives and societies over time.

Growth spurts and the punctuated equilibria of personal development are disruptive—you surely know this lesson if you have ever had to buy shoes for or give relationship advice to a teenager. Schumpeter coined the term *creative destruction* for periods of disruptive economic change. New products, processes, and opportunities are created, but they threaten or replace older elements of the economy. Schumpeter was thinking about the first industrial revolution (change due to the introduction of steam power) and the second industrial revolution (electrical and chemical innovations), but his ideas apply pretty well to the information-driven postindustrial revolution of today, as well.

Karl Polanyi went beyond Schumpeter and created the theory of the "double movement."[5] Creative destruction does more than open some doors and close others, disrupting profits, income, and investment opportunities; it also challenges fundamental values and shreds the fabric of social relations. You cannot expect society to sit quietly while this destruction takes place, so a dialectic is unleashed, which is the heart of the double movement. Economic change (the first movement) provokes social resistance and reaction (the second movement), and the combination of the two pushes economy and society forward. The future is not just one movement but both in a continuing dynamic interaction. Resistance, in this context, isn't futile as in the *Star Trek* films about the Borg collective. Resistance is inevitable, although just what form it will take and how it will alter the dynamic path is unclear.

I first thought seriously about the double movement when I was asked to edit a book about globalization in the twentieth century for a series the *New York Times* was putting out.[6] I was given one hundred years of the *Times* to work with—all the news articles, book reviews, editorials and op-eds, obituaries, photos, and cartoons—and asked to tell the story of the rise of the global economy in the twentieth century. I think the publisher expected me to tell a simple story of globalization's rise and rise, but that's not how I read the history. Instead, I drew on Schumpeter and Polanyi and found articles in the *Times* that underlined the disruptive nature of globalization (easy to do, especially with the financial crises of the late twentieth century) and the social and political reactions (easy to do, both in the 1930s and at the end of the century, with the anti–World Trade Organization protests in Seattle).

You can't understand the past without taking into account both disruptive change and the political and social reactions to it. You can't understand the future without taking both forces into account, either. The future of wine will be the story of globalization, which brings new products, producers, and consumers into the market; the rationalizing and commercializing force that I associate with brands; and the reaction of those whose interests and values are threatened—the revenge of the terroirists.

SECOND THOUGHTS ABOUT TERROIR

I'm optimisic that thoughtful terroirists will complete the double movement and prevent the wine industry from being drawn into the self-destructive—Einstein's law violating race-to-the-bottom competition that terrorist *terroirists* fear—but I admit that it isn't a sure thing. Wine lovers like to sniff and swirl (and sometimes spit!) as they rhapsodize about the local characteristics that they find in their glass, but the fact is that terroir is a contested idea. Not everyone takes terroir as seriously as the terroirists themselves do.

And it is easy to see why. Most products and services we buy and use today are pretty terroir-free—they could come from anywhere and go to anywhere. When the particular local attributes of a product—its somewhere-ness—are stressed, we wonder if it is real or just hype. I see this all the time on restaurant menus, where it seems like each additional adjective pushes the cost up a few bucks. A grilled chicken breast is usually a good deal cheaper than a grilled free-range product from a particular farm and region. Is it real or just marketing hype? Some of both, I suppose.

Voices inside the wine business argue that it is possible to make great wine almost anywhere if the right choices are made in the vineyard and the cellar. Michel Rolland, the devil in *Mondovino*, is often linked with this view—a fair association, I suppose, because he makes wine on several continents. Is terroir just an excuse for bad wine? Sometimes, I think, it is! Sometimes attacks on terroir come from unexpected sources. In his 2008 book *Bordeaux/Burgundy: A Vintage Rivalry*, French cultural critic Jean-Robert Pitte argues that although terroir is real, the character of fine wine is often much more determined by other factors.[7] One argument is that the association between terroir and great wine is a self-sustaining virtuous cycle.

If your wine was identified as great in the famous Bordeaux Classification of 1855, for example, then it is natural that the vineyards and winemaking have received enormous attention and investment over the years, and this extra effort alone may be responsible for its exceptional quality (as compared to a wine that was omitted in the 1855 rankings and so has languished in terms of both input and output all these years). I'm sure that the idea of virtuous and vicious cycles in wine is true to at least some extent. Wine becomes great because it is said to be great, just as some celebrities are famous for being famous. The fact that the Classification of 1855 was based on market prices and not critical assessment reinforces the argument.

Pitte also asserts that market terroir is as important as vineyard qualities. Wine evolves, he argues, to suit the tastes and requirements of the people who buy it. So Burgundy, for example, is different from Bordeaux not just because of climate and geography but also because historically Burgundy was the wine of the French court and Bordeaux was the wine of British aristocracy. Because these two groups were so different in many ways (and shipping the wine to them involved such different challenges), it is unsurprising that the wines themselves are so different.

I appreciate the importance of market terroir. It is hard to make a living selling bad wine to a sophisticated clientele and perhaps even harder to profit from selling good wine to undemanding customers. The former won't buy if they have better choices, while the latter will balk at the required price. Great art requires both great artists and an appreciative (and hopefully affluent) audience. Supply and demand.

WE ARE ALL TERROIRISTS NOW

Terroir is contested territory, and I am not sure that all terroirists would agree on a working definition of the term, much less a practical checklist for terroirists to follow. I title this chapter "We Are All Terroirists Now," but I don't want to suggest we are all CRAV-class activists or vine-hugging naturalists, either. In fact, there are lots of people who aren't terroirists at all. It isn't that they oppose terroirism and favor some harshly soulless idea of wine. It's just that they don't think about it.

So the title isn't really true, but there's a reason for it. I am inspired by a quote from Richard Nixon, of all people. (Nixon was a wine lover, so it is not completely ridiculous that his name would appear in a wine book, but it isn't exactly expected, either.) Nixon famously proclaimed, "We are all Keynesians now." What Nixon meant was that there was a sudden consensus that government action was necessary to stabilize the economy and that just letting markets work on their own wasn't the best policy. That, in very simple terms, was the message that the British economist John Maynard Keynes broadcast during the Great Depression when, eventually, everyone became Keynesians for the first time.

In fact, there were lots of non-Keynesians and anti-Keynesians when Nixon made his declaration. It was mainly meant to provide political cover, I think, because some of Nixon's economic policies were radical departures from the status quo. On August 15, 1971, he broke the Bretton Woods link between the US dollar and gold (a legacy of Keynes's international economic diplomacy work, as it happens) and imposed wage and price controls on the US economy. Not what you'd expect from a free-market Republican president, but they were all Keynesians then, I guess.

While everyone's not a terroirist in a philosophical sense, there are lots of wine people who act like terroirists or support terroirist ideals for reasons of their own. That, I hope, gives me as much cover as Nixon had in his day. There are lots of little reasons that I see a terroirist movement gathering force and one big one. The big one—which is so important that it gets a chapter of its own later in this book—is climate change. Climate change is poised to change everything about the wine industry, and in the process, it will force us all to think seriously about terroirist issues. In the meantime, is it realistic to think that wine companies, especially the biggest ones, share terroirist concerns?

CORPORATE VERSUS FAMILY WINERIES[8]

Take huge multinational wine businesses, for example, the ones that fill the wine wall with millions of bottles, boxes, and cans each year. It is hard to imagine that these industrial wine producers can have terroirist hearts, isn't it? The scale of such operations is breathtaking. Use Google Earth or Google Maps to take you to Modesto, California, the home of E. & J. Gallo. You won't have too much trouble locating the main Gallo production facility; warehouses; and the forest of huge, stainless-steel tanks that store millions of gallons of wine. The picture you get here doesn't have much in common with the sunny vineyard scene you imagine when talking about wine.

But looks can be deceiving. Large wine businesses are not all the same. For one thing, only a surprisingly small proportion of wine businesses are public corporations with professional managements that have to answer to investors with constantly rising quarterly profits and share prices. A great many wine businesses, even the largest of them (think Gallo!) are family firms that think in generational terms more than quarterly reports. This long-term thinking doesn't guarantee a terroirist attitude, but it at least sometimes points in that direction.

The family-ownership structure is supposed to limit access to capital and make expansion and effective management difficult. And yet some of the most famous names in the wine industry are family-owned firms, and some are both large and quite dynamic. Some, like the Gallos of California and the Ruperts of South Africa, have kept ownership closely held for years. Others, like the Antinoris of Italy, have experimented with outside capital only to return, at considerable expense, to the family model. Why are family-owned wineries so vibrant despite their structural economic limitations? The conventional answer to this question (and there is in fact substantial academic literature dealing with family businesses and even family wine businesses)—stresses the ways that family businesses take a multigenerational approach and are able to negotiate the trade-off between short-run returns and long-run value. Corporations, it is said, are sometimes driven too much by quarterly returns and end up sacrificing long-term interests to achieve immediate financial goals. When business requires a long-run vision, families gain an advantage. Wine is certainly a business where it is necessary to look into the future, if only because vines are perennials, not annuals like corn or soybeans, and successful brands aspire to be perennials, too.

LEVERAGE

But maybe the question isn't why family-owned wine businesses are so robust and instead why corporate-owned wine businesses are sometimes so fragile. Is there something about wine that turns smart corporate brains to mush (not all of them, of course, but maybe some of them)? One difference that I have noticed about family wine businesses versus some of the corporations is the role of such key assets as brand and reputation. Many family wineries seem to see their role as protecting brand and reputation so that they will continue to provide benefits well into the future. Some corporations, however, seem to focus on leveraging brand and reputation in order to increase short-run returns.

What's the problem with leveraging a brand? Leverage has the potential to increase returns in any business, but it also increases risk. And one risk is that the integrity of key assets can be undermined by the leverage process itself. An example? Well, I hate to pick on Treasury Wine Estates, which is based in Australia, but one of my readers e-mailed me in dismay about a news story on a Treasury market strategy. I'll use this as an example, but Treasury isn't the only wine corporation that I could pick on and maybe not even the best example.[9]

One element of Treasury's plan was to develop brands for the "masstige" market segment, which means taking a prestige brand and leveraging it by introducing a cheaper mass-market product that rides on the iconic brand's reputation. Masstige? Sounds like something from a Dilbert cartoon, which means of course that it is a totally authentic contemporary business term. Prestige fashion house Versace, for example, developed a masstige product line for mass-market retailer H&M. The line was launched in 2011, and I'm not sure where it stands today. Maybe it was a big success? If masstige worked for shoes and dresses, then how could it be a bad idea for wine?

The bottom line is that a lot of family wine businesses, even very large ones, are different in ways that make them a bit terroiristic (if that's a word), and this difference might be one reason for their sustained success. Indeed, a number of important wine businesses are benefit corporations (B Corps). Oregon's A to Z Wineworks was the first in this growing group, and Portugal's Symington Family Estates is one of the most internationally recognized. Fetzer, the California winery long known for its environmental focus, was the world's largest B-Corp wine company until its parent company, Viña Concha y Toro, announced that all its global operations had received B-Corp certification. Amazing!

B Corps make no specific commitment to winegrowing terroir, of course, which is natural because these companies can be found in all sorts of industries (the little coffee shop on the corner hereabouts is part of a regional B-Corp operation). But the social, environmental, and governance values that B Corps commit themselves to supporting are different from those of the stereotypical corporate behemoth and lean into terroirist territory.

A TERROIRIST CRITIQUE

We aren't all really terroirists now, but in my enthusiasm to make the terroirist movement seem broad and growing, have I sacrificed depth and commitment? Would a *real* terroirist agree that the battle is being won? Or am I just covering up wine business as usual with a coat of green (or should it be brown for the color of the earth) paint?

These are good questions, and I think it is important to take the terroirist greenwashing critique seriously. One way to probe this issue deeper is to draw on the work of the Slow Food movement, which I wrote about in my book *Globaloney 2.0.* Founded in Italy and now spanning the globe, Slow Food is a grassroots counterpoint to industrial food and agriculture. It doesn't confront global corporations directly by, for example, bombing McDonald's restaurants the way French antiglobalization protesters used to do. Slow Food instead works to identify products and practices of tradition and terroir and then seeks to promote and preserve them using the very tools of media and markets that we usually associate with industry. Slow Food uses the weapons of global capitalism against itself, an elegant irony, don't you think?

It is not a foolproof process, however. I note in *Globaloney 2.0* that some proponents of the very values and practices that Slow Food promotes are actually opposed to its activities. Shining a light on a traditional product or process can help preserve it, they acknowledge, but the attention also puts commercial pressure on producers, who may be forced to cut corners or make compromises to keep up with demand. I suppose Slow Food recognition also encourages knockoffs and counterfeits that exploit the opportunity while diluting the intent and debasing the product. Real tradition is slowly replaced by the sort of cheap faux tradition that you see at tourist traps of all types. So while the Slow Food movement may be part of the terroirist revenge that I'm seeking, it is a problematic situation.

What would a terroirist manifesto look like? Well, we don't have to wonder because I found "The Slow Food Manifesto for Good, Clear, and Fair Wine" in my copy of *Slow Wine Guide USA 2021*.[10] This obviously isn't *the* terroirist manifesto because there can never be just one, but it will give us something more concrete to work with. The Slow Food wine manifesto sets ten criteria, which I paraphrase here. Wineries should grow at least 70 percent of the grapes they use in winemaking (except in regions where the greater use of purchased grapes is common). No use of chemically synthesized fertilizers, herbicides, or antibotrytis fungicides. Sustainable resource use, including limited use of irrigation.

Winery buildings need to "respect their environmental surroundings" and be operated taking sustainability into account. Avoid manipulation of the wine, such as concentration of the wine using reverse osmosis. Additions, including sugar, are not permitted except in certain circumstances, and forget about using oak chips. Use of sulfites is permitted up to the levels permitted for organic wine by the European Union.

Because the "wines must show terroir and reflect their place of origin," the use of wild or native yeasts is encouraged. The wines must be "free of any winemaking effects" that would mask regional identity. The winery needs to engage with the local agricultural community and promote biodiversity.

Taken together, the ten slow-wine criteria present a stern test, and so it is not surprising that only a relatively few wineries make the grade, and some of those don't satisfy all the rules strictly speaking. Some, for example, purchase all or nearly all their grapes from growers. Presumably they guide the use of water, fertilizer, and so on in the vineyards. Just 285 wineries from California, Oregon, Washington, and New York are recognized, a small share of the roughly 5,500 bonded wineries in these states. It makes my proposal that we are all terroirists seem ludicrous. But then slow wine's aim is to recognize an elite few and encourage others to work to join the club. My purpose is to draw out terroirist attitudes and actions in people and places that would never make the slow-wine cut. It is a messy position to take. I want, for example, to find the link between Aimé Guibert of *Mondovino* fame and a Canadian billionaire named Anthony von Mandl.

AN UNLIKELY TERROIRIST

My realist perspective is that there are many types of wine, including high-volume commercial wines as well as small craft operations. It's all wine, and each category fills a consumer niche or else disappears into market oblivion. What is important to me is that the big doesn't crowd out the small, that terroir wines and the terroir that produces them endures, and that consumers understand the choices they make and their implications.

It's a complicated situation, a fact easily illustrated by the case of Anthony von Mandl. Terroirist or not? You be the judge! Von Mandl doesn't exactly come to mind when you imagine a big-league terroirist. He is in the wine business, but his business isn't just wine. Von Mandl is the head of the company that makes Mike's Hard Lemonade and White Claw hard seltzer. These terroir-free alco-pop beverages are insanely popular, and my market-research friends tell me that they are partly responsible for declining sales of inexpensive (and, it must be said, also relatively terroir-free) commodity wine.

However, von Mandl is the Robert Mondavi of the Okanagan Valley in Canada. He's the founder of the iconic Mission Hill Winery and is a driving force in British Columbia's organic-wine movement. Six wineries in von Mandl's Mark Anthony Group are leading the charge, converting about 1,300 acres to organic viticulture: Mission Hill Family Estate, Cedar Creek Estate Winery, Road 13 Vineyards, Liquidity Wines, Martin's Lane, and Checkmate Artisanal Winery. Do you appreciate the irony here? Big-brand White Claw money funding a terroirist revenge in the beautiful Okanagan Valley.

Whether you think of terroirism as a broad phenomenon or a narrow reaction movement, I hope you can see its importance in the wine wars of today and the battles of tomorrow. Are we all really terroirists now? No, not really. But then I think the wine world has come a long way from the David-versus-Goliath world of *Mondovino*.

We have one last chapter in this flight before our tasting, and I'd like you to pack your bags because we have a long journey ahead of us. We are going to travel the Silk Road from wine's past to its likely future, searching for terroirists along the way. And finding them—but not necessarily in the places you'd expect.

11

SILK ROAD TERROIRISTS

The Silk Road is the name we give to the ancient trade route that connected China and Europe, East and West, as it is often said. The Silk Road is history, romance, and (in its current reincarnation as part of China's Belt and Road Initiative) a source of a certain amount of international controversy. We are here in Tbilisi, Georgia, because the Silk Road has meaning in the wine world. It connects Georgia, the country with the oldest and perhaps deepest wine culture, with China, the wine world's much younger rising wine force. I am interested in exploring the connections between very old and relatively new to see what they reveal about the terroirist revenge.

Because any investigation is best when you have a working hypothesis to test, here is where we begin. I hypothesize that just about everyone in Georgia is a terroirist who resists the intrusion of industrial wine. Georgia might be the one place on earth where it really is true that we are all terroirists now. And I guess that China is just the opposite. Grape wine has been around for a long time, but the wine culture you see today is very recent and influenced by international brands and advertising. Is anyone in China a terroirist? If so, it will be a pleasant surprise.

Working hypotheses are satisfying when the guess is good but most important when they are proven wrong. Let's see what is true in this case.

ANATOMY OF WINE IN GEORGIA

Georgian wine is very old, and the wine culture is strong. I have never been anywhere where wine is so central to the culture. Wine and vine were everywhere we looked during our Georgia visit. Wine grapes were a central element, for example, of a Soviet-era war memorial we saw in Sighnaghi. And grapevines are at the heart of the image of Georgia as a Christian nation. Saint Nino fashioned the first Georgian cross using her own hair to bind two lengths of grapevine. Wine is Georgia's DNA.

But wine in Georgia is not a simple thing, which I guess is what makes Georgia like every other wine country we have visited, but because the importance of wine is greater, the complications are more visible. The event that brought us to Georgia in the first place, for example, was a United Nations conference on wine tourism. Georgia is a poor nation, especially outside of Tbilisi's bright city lights. Mexico's per capita GDP is about $9,000, according to World Bank statistics. Georgia's is about $3,800. So anything that can create employment opportunities (especially rural jobs) and spur economic development is welcome here. Tourism of the nature and adventure varieties is a big contributor to national income. Why not leverage Georgia's rich culture and especially its deep wine traditions to create economic opportunity? So Georgia hosted this global conference to show off its wine-tourism potential and learn from international experts. This is wine as a national economic development strategy.

Wine is also a family matter in Georgia. A great deal of the wine that is consumed is produced by families for their own use and to give to friends and neighbors. Such large family production necessarily shapes the market. Not much imported wine enters Georgia, for example. And a great deal of the commercially produced wine must be exported. Georgians prefer white wines, we were told, and traditional export markets prefer red wines, so the division of red and white has economic significance.

Not all the export markets are the same, either. Russia was for many years the largest export market for Georgian wine, and because of this, the focus was on semisweet red wines made in state-owned factories and often sold in bulk. Quantity was a priority over quality. But then came the Russian embargo of Georgian and Moldovan wines in 2006, and in an instant, the most important market, accounting for perhaps 80 percent of sales, was gone and did not return until 2013.

The Russian embargo was the worst thing that could have happened to the Georgian wine industry in the short term and the best thing in the long run. In retrospect, it is easy to see that such complete reliance on a single foreign market for wine sales was not a healthy situation. The sudden loss of that market forced Georgian producers to develop new markets, improve quality to be competitive in those markets, and find strategies for product differentiation to raise margins and secure market niches.

Georgia's largest export markets in 2019 were Russia, China, Poland, and Belarus, with sales to the United States and United Kingdom smaller in volume but rising quickly. The growth of sales in the Chinese market, which was the original inspiration of this Silk Road theme, has been particularly noteworthy and follows on investments in Georgia-themed wine shops and culinary centers that were established in China. There are ambitious plans to open one hundred Georgian Wine Houses there.

One wine executive we talked with noted a Silk Road connection that works in Georgia's favor. Georgia has negotiated a preferential trade agreement with China and Chinese traders and investors who visit the country taste and enjoy the Georgian wines and learn about the country's eight-thousand-year wine history and its Silk Road connection. Nothing could make more sense than to buy Georgian wine, with its long history and connection to China. Very smart of Georgian producers to leverage this authentic cultural-link advantage!

Here in the United States, much of the buzz about Georgian wines concerns natural wines made using the traditional *qvevri* clay containers to ferment and sometimes age the wines. Alice Feiring is a leading advocate of these wines, and her book *For the Love of Wine* gives a highly personal account of her passion for them.

No one we talked with is sure how much Georgian natural wine is made by families for their own consumption, but commercial production is relatively limited. One producer estimated total output of perhaps 120,000 bottles more or less, with several wineries in the 3,000- to 6,000-bottle capacity range. Little of this wine is sold domestically in Georgia because of its relatively high cost and the existence of family-produced alternatives. So the focus is clearly on export to markets where natural wines have a strong presence, including Italy, France, and Denmark, and developing natural wine markets, such as the United Kingdom, Canada, and the United States.

PAST, PRESENT, AND FUTURE

My mental framework when we left for Georgia was this: The Russian market is the past; now they need to look to the future. But which future? The natural *qvevri* wines are Georgia's key to differentiation in the new markets, but high-quality natural wine is too narrow a category to carry the ambitions of a great wine-producing nation.

My theory, based on the process of elimination, was that the way forward for Georgia is to focus on increasing the quality of their conventional wines, making them in a clean international style and differentiating by stressing a small number of exciting indigenous grape varieties (perhaps red Saperavi, white Rkatsiteli, and various blends) from among the dozens of native Georgia wine grapes. That is a conventional idea, and I am generally suspicious of conventional wisdom. Georgia is an unconventional wine country, so I needed to learn more. I'm still trying to make up my mind, but I think my theory was both right and wrong.

If you want to see what the future of Georgian export wines in the international style might look like, consider a brand called Orovela. But don't look for these wines in Georgia; they are strictly for export and are essentially unknown in their country of origin. You can, however, find them in the United Kingdom at Waitrose stores and Whole Foods and in restaurants, too, where they are possibly the most successful Georgian wine on the market.

The name Orovela comes from a traditional plowing song, but the project is as contemporary as can be. Brothers Giorgi and Vasili Sulkhanishvili saw an opportunity for Georgian wine exports, began investment in 2000, and rolled out the brand in 2004. There is one red wine, an Orovela Saperavi, and Oro Chacha, which is Georgia's signature grape spirit (think grappa). Quality was a key factor right from the start, and this has paid off. Jancis Robinson declared the 2004 Orovela the best Georgian wine she ever tasted, for example. A search of the Waitrose website reveals that the Saperavi is a "buyer's choice," selling for £16.99. Vasili told us that the wine is available in selected markets in the United States and sells for thirty to thirty-five dollars in shops and perhaps one hundred dollars in restaurants. The packaging of both the wine and the Chacha is beautiful and effective in communicating the wine's origin and story. Orovela is a completely professional project, carefully designed and tightly focused, reflecting, I believe, the brothers' international-drinks industry experience.

Orovela isn't the only example of an international-style wine made with Georgian grapes for export markets. We visited both Chateau Mukhrani and Telavi Wine Cellar and were impressed with the substantial investment and obvious commitment to quality. The idea that Georgia could be successful in global markets with wines like these is certainly valid. But is it the best strategy for the industry? These markets are insanely competitive, and effective product differentiation is crucial. Are these wines different enough (there is little room for "me too" products), and can that difference and the quality be communicated effectively as Orovela has done?

I wasn't prepared for what I discovered when we started tasting natural *qvevri* wines and meeting the winemakers. The wines varied a good deal, of course, but many of them were simply stunning and not at all the rustic products that I imagined. Wines from Gotsa Family Wines, Pheasant's Tears, Iago's Wine Cellar, and the Alaverdi Monastery especially stood out. The wines had real tension—they were alive in the glass. No funk, nothing mousy, just great wine. I was really impressed.

I admit that visiting the wineries and meeting the people made a difference, as it always does. I was moved by Iago Bitarishvili's hard work and humility, for example, and excited by Beka Gotsadze's energy and ingenuity. The fact that these people can make natural wines like this using traditional Georgian methods is something to celebrate. The wines and the stories that come with them are the product differentiation I was looking for. The natural *qvevri* wines are a great symbol of Georgia and its wines, but can they open doors for other Georgian wines? Not sure.

My confusion reached a peak when we visited Teliani Valley winery, which is a large, diversified producer. Production is about three million bottles, divided into 30 percent domestic and 70 percent exports. Both semisweet and dry wines are produced here, with about 10 percent made in *qvevri* and the rest using conventional methods. Something for everyone at Teliani Valley winery.

After a brief tour of the big factory-style facility, we were asked to choose wines to taste. "Could we try three red wines?" I asked. "An international-style wine, a *qvevri* product, and one of the semisweet wines popular in Russia and other traditional markets." The wines were produced, and the results were interesting. The oak-aged international Saperavi and the *qvevri* wines were fine but not especially memorable. No electricity here. Well made but not distinctive.

The semisweet wine was different, which caught me by surprise. It was 100 percent Saperavi from the Kindzmarauli vineyard; it was fruity and, well, delicious. To paraphrase my favorite philosopher, Charles Barkley, it tasted like itself: It was good because it wasn't trying to be something else. It was the surprise hit of the tasting. It was the wine that we would want to taste again.

Sweetish red wines enjoy a growing market in the United States (although their sweetness isn't always advertised). High-quality wines like this might have a bright future, not the dim past that I had imagined. In fact, we recently received a sample of a Saperavi-based sweetish red called Lost Eden, which featured a custom bottle crisscrossed by sculpted grapevines and topped with a sketch of Nino's cross. It paired up very well with spicy Asian fare and could well be a distinctive entrant into the US market.

My initial theory was based on the conventional idea that Georgia needed to choose a clear, simple strategy to move forward in the global markets—to decide which of its wines to take the lead. But Georgian wine isn't one thing; it is many things. And I think any attempt to oversimplify—to choose the one wine style to rule them all—is bound to fail. In fact, that's my concern about Lost Eden wine: The packaging is so good and the wine so enjoyable that it might cause consumers to lose focus on the rest of Georgia's wine offerings. International style, natural *qvevri* wines, and the semisweets, too. These are all Georgia wines, and Georgia is all of them and more. My hypothesis was off base, but the journey of discovery it provoked has taught me a lot.

ARE THEY ALL TERROIRISTS NOW?

So are the Georgians all terroirists, as my working hypothesis supposed? The answer came to me during the United Nations conference. We loaded into coaches and headed east toward Kakheti, the main wine region and the location of our first meetings. We stopped at the historic Alaverdi Monastery, were wine has been made using the traditional *qvevri* method since 1011.

We toured the monastery; visited the *marani* cellar, with its *qvevri* vessels; and tasted one of the wines, a complex golden Rkatsiteli. After the tour, we adjourned to a café, where we had coffee and cups of delicious *matsoni* (local yogurt) with local honey and walnuts (a fabulous combination). The wine tourism here was seamlessly integrated into the cultural elements and featured local food products and the opportunity to purchase traditional crafts, too. A great tourist and wine tourist stop. And this is not an accident.

Georgia correctly sees tourism as an economic development opportunity, especially in rural areas like Kakheti. The government has worked to develop tourist infrastructure and marketing strategies in partnership with international development organizations, including the World Bank, the European Bank for Reconstruction and Development, and the US Agency for International Development. The Alaverdi Monastery is an example of how these efforts have come together successfully to leverage history, culture, and wine to create real opportunities for local workers and producers while giving tourists a memorable experience.

Our visit to the Alaverdi Monastery, where wine was clearly at the center of everything, provided just the context I needed. Yes, I do think Georgians are all terroirists—how could they not be? The story of Georgian wine, its rise and fall and now rise again, is the story of Georgia and its people. How can a country of winemakers, because that's who they are, not be terroirists? But that doesn't mean they are all the same. Some are terroirists by habit or tradition. Others are pragmatists, who see terroir as a means to an end. And for some, both inside the church and elsewhere, terroir is like a religion or maybe *is* a religion. Wine isn't just one thing. Why should terroirism be different?

THE TASTE OF CHINESE TERROIR

Each of my books about the wine business, starting with the first edition of *Wine Wars*, includes a chapter on China. A dozen years ago, this was a novel feature. The idea of wine from China was still off the radar of most readers. Not anymore. But China has been a moving target and not always easy to pin down, in terms of both consumer demand and wine production. There is terroir in China, that's for sure. But what about terroirists? Let me frame my investigation in terms of four of the many Chinese wines we've sampled, starting at the beginning and moving toward a conclusion.

My first taste of Chinese wine was exactly what I expected and quite a shock at the same time. Odd combination of reactions, but sometimes, you know what you are in for but just can't believe that it could be true. It was a 1999 Changyu Cabernet Sauvignon that Brian West brought back from his semester abroad in Beijing. Changyu is China's oldest winery (and one of the biggest); it was a good example of a midmarket Chinese red wine at the time. I knew what to expect because I'd found a video review of this wine on the internet that described the wine as being all about ashtray and coffee-ground flavors with aromas of urinal crust. Hard to imagine that wine could taste this way (or that a critic would be so familiar with urinal smells)—until you taste it, that is. The description was right on the money. We passed the bottle around so that everyone could get a little taste. A taste of what? The taste of Chinese terroir? Gosh, I hope not!

Based on that Changyu, you'd have to say China was very far from being an important factor in the world of wine, but it would have been a mistake to rule them out. Wine is a dynamic industry. Fifty or sixty years ago, I don't think that anyone would have predicted that New Zealand would make great wines or that the United States would become a global wine-market leader.

How in the world did a wine so bad get into my glass? And why, you might ask, did I ever try another Chinese wine? The answer to the second question is easy: I'm either nuts or hopelessly optimistic when it comes to wine—I'll let you decide. The answer to the first question is more complicated. You'll need to know a little about the history of wine in China and about the peculiar nature of the product supply chain for Chinese wine that resulted in the Changyu I tasted back then.

Wine has a surprisingly long history in China, reaching back more than two thousand years to the first wine imported from Ferghana in what is now Uzbekistan. It wasn't until the nineteenth century, however, that more than a trickle of wine was produced or consumed. Western missionaries brought grapes and wine to China along with their Bibles, as they did in so many other countries. The real roots of today's industry were planted in the late 1800s, when Changyu and other wineries were founded, mainly to produce wines for the foreign communities in the commercial centers.

The communist government expanded wine production after the 1949 revolution. Wine was promoted as a form of alcohol made from abundant fruit (grapes, including *vitis vinifera* and indigenous varieties and other fruits) in order to reduce use of precious food grains for alcohol production. Wine was meant to replace beer or grain spirits in the diet. Wine was typically made from a combination of grapes and other fruits. I understand that it is still sometimes necessary to specify *grape wine* in China because generic *wine* may be made out of any number of fruits. It is probably not surprising that Chinese who were brought up on these mixed-fruit wines might today mix dry grape wine with fruit juice or Coke to get a more familiar flavor.

China has the third-largest area planted with grape vineyards, according to the OIV's 2020 report, but not all the grapes are for wine (table grapes are an important market in China). China was the world's tenth-largest wine producer in 2020, ranking between Germany and Portugal in volume of production. Both production and consumption of wine in China have increased rapidly in the last twenty years, a fact that is best appreciated in contrast to relatively stagnant global trends.

Per capita wine consumption in China is very small, just 1.3 liters per person in 2020, according to the OIV, although because the population is so large, the total wine market is significant. For perspective, per capita wine consumption in the United States is ten times China's figure; in Portugal, it is nearly fifty times that of China. Only a small part of China's vast population drink wine, and few of those drink it frequently. About a third of the wine Chinese consumers drink is imported, so international wine sellers see China's low per capita figure as both a challenge and an opportunity. Plenty of room for growth.

So why was that glass of Changyu so shocking? Wine is only as good as the grapes that go into it, or so growers tell me, and the grape supply in China back then was, well, difficult. Most of the wine grapes were grown by families who leased about an acre of land from their local agricultural communes. That acre was typically divided into four or five small plots that were planted with different crops so as to minimize risk. One or perhaps two of the plots could be wine grapes in the vineyard regions. So vineyard scale was impossibly small—smaller even than in the South of France.

These small growers insisted on calling the shots, which is natural because they were so dependent on the success of their tiny farms. The wine producers had little or no control over what these thousands of microvineyards produced, how they were cropped, and when the grapes were picked. Researchers suggest that the grapes were chosen and grown to maximize quantity not quality and that the grapes were picked as soon as possible to minimize risk of poor weather that could destroy the crop. So small crops of flavorful, fully ripe grapes—the winemaker's dream—were not going to happen in a typical Chinese vineyard.

Grapes sold for as little as eighty dollars a ton, an indication of their poor quality. The rule of thumb in winemaking in the United States is that the per-ton price divided by one hundred gives you the per-bottle price of the finished wine. So Pinot Noir grapes can sell for three thousand dollars per ton if they have the quality to produce a wine that consumers will pay thirty dollars a bottle for. If the wine isn't good enough to earn thirty dollars per bottle, then buying the grapes for three thousand per ton is a money-losing deal. The US rule of thumb might not apply to China, but it gives you a feeling for the economics of the situation. Chinese grapes at eighty dollars per ton? Well, if the one one-hundredth rule translates accurately into Chinese, then it means that they are only good enough for eighty cents per bottle (or a dollar per liter) of wine.

There was not much incentive for individual growers to sacrifice quantity for quality because their grapes were sold by weight to agents who lumped together fruit from dozens or hundreds of individual growers. Good fruit would quickly get mixed with inferior fruit, so why pay more? The local agents often then resold the fruit to regional agents, who sold again to the large winemakers. You can just imagine the condition of the fruit by the time it finally got to the winemaking facility, having passed through so many hands. This system was worse than even the most uncompetitive European cooperatives (and I didn't think anything could be worse than that).

The bottom line, I wrote in the first edition of *Wine Wars*, is that the future of wine in China is difficult to predict:

> Surely wine consumption will grow as China gets richer and Chinese adopt more Western consumption habits. Wine production will grow, too, and quality will rise as better technology is adopted. But it will be interesting to see how quickly Chinese consumers accept dry Western grape wines after their long experience with mixed-fruit wines. And it will be interesting to see how quickly the quality of grapes can be raised. It seems to me that the biggest barriers to quality wine are

not in the stores or even in the habit of mixing red wine and Coke. The biggest problem remains the sorry state of rural Chinese agriculture—a good reminder that wine is fundamentally a product of the soil.

A TASTE OF THE FUTURE?

Even as I wrote those words, the sort of changes I saw in the future were happening on the ground, and we could taste it in this chapter's second glass of Chinese wine, poured from a bottle of 2003 Grace Vineyard Tasya's Reserve Cabernet Franc. Grace Vineyard was often cited as the most promising winemaker in China, and the contrast between this bottle and the Changyu was night and day. The attention to detail in the winemaking was evident, and the use of estate grapes (rather than the unreliable supply chain cited earlier) was apparent, too. The contrast between the two wines was stunning, mainly because the Changyu was so very bad, of course, but that didn't stop me from finding out more about Grace Vineyard. I wanted to understand how they could make good wine in such unfavorable circumstances.

Here, briefly, is what I learned. Hong Kong businessman C. K. Chan invested $7 million to build a French-style château in Shanxi Province. Most people who see pictures of the winery are fascinated by the château building and the paradox of such an ornate structure in the middle of China. I was more interested in the vineyards, which looked just great. I don't know how Judy Chan, Mr. Chan's daughter, managed to get the resources and necessary permits to plant a private estate vineyard, but somehow she did. A reliable source of first-quality grapes is an obvious advantage if you are trying to produce quality wine.

Grace also drew on international connections. A Bordeaux flying winemaker got the project started, and an Australian made the wine we tasted. Torres, the Spanish giant, handled distribution within China (one of its many successful partnerships). International networks come naturally to Ms. Chan, who is a graduate of the University of Michigan and a veteran of international investment banking at Goldman Sachs. Just as Mondavi was the benchmark when French wine enthusiasts thought about California wine back in the 1970s, Grace was the Chinese standard as the first edition of *Wine Wars* went to press.

How did it taste? We thought our Grace Vineyard Cabernet Franc was a bit light compared with American wines of this type. Writing in the *Wine Economist*, I noted a distinctive "green" taste I associate with wine made from underripe Cab Franc grapes. A problem in the vineyard, I speculated. Maybe the climate's just too contrary to fully ripen these grapes.

A day later, one of my readers lobbed in a counterargument.[1] Maybe, he said, that green flavor is intentional. He had heard that this particular flavor is familiar to Chinese consumers and that some Chinese wineries harvest grapes a bit earlier in order to achieve it. It wasn't a flaw in the wine, he suggested, but a feature. Something that makes it Chinese wine, not a Chinese imitation of someone else's wine. It's the Chinese market terroir, if you will.

A little research turned up more evidence that the judgments of Western critics might be unfair to Chinese wines. Jeannie Cho Lee, Korea's first Master of Wine, argues that Asian food and wine traditions prime consumers to think about wine differently and to appreciate different qualities in it.[2] Why don't Chinese wine drinkers appreciate that a crisp Pinot Gris pairs nicely with their cuisine? Well, Ms. Lee explains, many Asian cultures do not consume beverages (apart from savory soups) with their meals; they drink them before and after. White wines are generally chilled, of course, and most Asian drinks are warm or room temperature. And the sweetness of a Pinot Gris can seem unrefined to palates that are used to more complex sweet-sour flavor profiles.

For a time, the Chinese market was almost defined by its fascination with wines from Bordeaux. What is the attraction? Reputation is obviously important, but it could also be the tannins, Ms. Lee argues, which are appealing to wine drinkers from cultures with a tradition of consuming very tannic teas. Even the basic flavor reference points are different, she explains. Westerners think of Pinot Noir in terms of raspberries and strawberries, for example, but the Asian descriptors would be *yangmei* (bayberries), dried wolfberries, and dried bonito flakes! An Asian description of Sauvignon Blanc would start with pandan leaves and longan and move on to mangosteen—not a familiar flavor or aroma vocabulary for me. But I can relate a bit better to her description of Riesling: Thai white blossoms, lemongrass, and green mangoes.

Wouldn't it be great if the most important qualities of Chinese wines—the ones that Westerners reject—turn out to have been lost in translation and that a true indigenous Chinese wine culture evolves, one that reflects China's history, cuisine, and palate? I hoped so back then because it would support my theory of the future of wine. Suffering just now from the excesses of globalization and commodification, China needed to unlock its inner terroirist soul!

THE WINE FROM SHANGRI-LA

I was able to sample quite a few Chinese wines in the years after the Changyu and Grace Vineyard experience, thanks in part to the generosity of my colleagues and friends Cynthia Howson and Pierre Ly. Cynthia and Pierre have been studying the Chinese wine industry and have brought back dozens of bottles from their research trips, which form the basis of their book *Adventures on the China Wine Trail*.[3] They shared the third wine in this flight, although they didn't have to lug it all the way from China. It was sitting on a store shelf here in the United States.

The wine was called Ao Yun, and I first learned about it when I spoke at the Wine Vision 2014 conference in London. The speaker before me on the program was Jean-Guillaume Prats, then head of the wine division of the LVMH luxury multinational. Prats talked about a crazy project that LVMH was pursuing in China: to make a Bordeaux-style blend of Cabernet Sauvignon and Cabernet Franc in some of the most extreme terroir in the world high in the Himalaya foothills. It was called Ao Yun, or "flying above the clouds," and the vineyards, at 2,600 meters elevation, fit that description. Conditions to grow high-quality grapes and to construct the winery itself were extraordinarily challenging—*hors catégorie* (beyond category), as they say in the Tour de France. At one point, Prats just kind of shook his head. "There are some things that we probably shouldn't do just because we can do them," he said softly. But the 2013 vintage was already in the barrels, aging even as he spoke.

The Ao Yun winery was not really receiving visitors when Pierre and Cynthia put it on their research agenda, but they managed to get there anyway using luck, intuition, determination, and the techniques of what I call guerrilla fieldwork (you can read all about it in their book). It was quite an adventure. How did the wine taste up there high in the Himalaya foothills? No idea. They never had an opportunity to sample the wine they had traveled so far to discover.

So Pierre didn't hesitate a minute when he learned that the wine was on the shelf at a nearby big-box alcohol superstore. Powered by LVMH's global distribution network, this rare wine was surprisingly easy to find. The price ($299 plus state tax per bottle) wasn't as shocking as you might expect because everything about this wine is, well, a bit *hors catégorie*.

Sue and I were indeed surprised when Cynthia and Pierre revealed the Ao Yun at dinner a few weeks later and pulled the cork. The wine? Well, it was very good, as you would expect. It is not likely that LVMH would allow a bad wine or even a mediocre wine to be released as Ao Yun given all the time, talent, and money that went into the project. Ao Yun just had to set a standard for Chinese wine.

Tasting the Ao Yun was a memorable experience, but it left me confused. It is the product of distinctive terroir, that's for sure. And a reviewer for *Decanter* even noted the "strong sense and imprint of place which is partially revealed by its saturated colour, exquisite ripeness, silky, grainy tannins and exciting freshness."[4] But what does it say about Chinese terroirists? Or is it more about the French who conceived its production?

CHINA WINE TODAY

I hesitate to say anything about China wine today because China is changing so fast that whatever I write now will surely to be proved wrong in the few months it takes to turn these pages into a finished book. There has been huge investment in vineyards, wineries, and even wine-tourism experiences, as Cynthia and Pierre make clear in their book. The supply-chain issues that made that first glass of Changyu so foul have been overcome in many regions. The local government in Ningxia, for example, has worked closely with both international and domestic Chinese wine companies to create conditions where world-class wine can be grown and made. Pierre reports that while some wine grapes still sell for as little as 1 yuan per kilo (about $150 per ton), he's heard through the grapevine that prices of 3 to 5 yuan per kilo ($450–$750 per ton) and up to $1,500 per ton are common, depending on specific circumstances. Those prices suggest grapes of good commercial quality, nothing like the fruit I suspect went into the awful first glass of Chinese wine. Things have changed in China very quickly indeed.

The final glass is this flight takes us back to Grace Vineyard; it is the Tasya's Reserve Marselan 2012, a delicious wine that makes me believe that although I can't possibly say for China that "we are all terroirists," the terroirist movement is there and growing.

Why this wine? In part to honor Judy Chan and Grace Vineyard's commitment to pushing Chinese wine ahead in terms of both international reputation and (much more difficult to achieve) domestic recognition. But the choice is even more driven by the grape variety: Marselan. Marselan? I'll bet you've never heard of it. It is a French grape—a cross between Cabernet Sauvignon and Grenache that first appeared in 1961 and is grown mainly in the Languedoc . . . and now China!

Professor Li Demei champions Marselan as a candidate to be China's signature wine grape variety.[5] He cites the grape's productivity, disease resistance, environmental adaptability, and beautiful flavors and aromas. Even more, according to Professor Li, the wines can be made in many styles. Marselan may be a bit of a blank slate in some ways—a canvas where terroirists can paint a distinctly Chinese future for China's wines.

I said at the start that I would be pleasantly surprised to discover Chinese terroirists given the history of wine in China, its intense exposure to global forces, and of course the taste of that first glass of Changyu. Now that I think back, however, that first glass told no lies; it revealed the truth about the state of wine in China at the moment it was made. And I think the final glass in this tasting, the Grace Vineyard Marselan, speaks truth as well, and, along with other wines by other thoughtful producers, is a milestone on the evolving Chinese terroirist path.

And perhaps those Georgian Wine Houses that are sprouting up in China will help Chinese consumers get in touch with their Silk Road terroirist roots. Thus does the revenge of the terroirists proceed, overcoming the bad wine of the past and undermining foreign interests. Vive le Marselan! Vive the Silk Road! Vive terroirists everywhere!

A TERROIRIST TASTING

The theme of the terroirist tasting is resistance because although terroirists are a diverse lot, one thing they have in common is a passion to resist the market forces that threaten wine's soul. As wine has become more global and commercial, it has in some ways also become more homogenized. The enormous diversity of wine grape varieties in nature is undermined by the perceived need to focus on just a few highly marketable "international" wine grape varieties. It is a trend that would make anyone worry about Einstein's law.

Wine Grapes, a thick reference book by Jancis Robinson, Julia Harding, and José Vouillamoz, identifies and analyzes 1,368 unique grape varieties—and it is possible that they didn't get them all.[1] That is the sort of enormous diversity that would make any terroirist happy. But diversity in theory doesn't necessarily translate to diversity in practice on your local wine wall, according to Kym Anderson's 2013 book *Which Winegrape Varieties Are Grown Where?* Anderson and his team found that in 2010, half the world's total vineyard area was planted with just 20 (out of nearly 1,400) wine grape varieties. And the concentration on the top-selling grapes is increasing. When the study was repeated recently using 2016 data, it took only fifteen grape varieties to account for half the world's vineyards. One percent of the grape varietal library covers 50 percent of the world's vineyards. What a waste!

So for this tasting, I challenge you to find, taste, and help preserve some of the wines that are threatened by the march of global markets. These wines are hiding in plain sight on your wine wall—you just need to look for them and not be afraid to give them a try. No Cabernet Sauvignon, Merlot, Pinot Noir, Tempranillo, or Syrah! No Chardonnay, Sauvignon Blanc, or Pinot Grigio!

Here is a story that I hope will inspire you. It is an account of a recent visit to Napa Valley, where market forces are very strong and terroirists are fiercely determined.

BACK TO THE FUTURE IN NAPA VALLEY

Wouldn't it be cool if you could travel back in time and tweak events just a little so that the past's future (our present) would be better? That was the idea behind Steven Spielberg's hit 1985 film *Back to the Future* and its many sequels. Scientists are not optimistic that this time-bending strategy would work. They question whether a souped-up DeLorean sports car is the ideal time-travel vehicle. And they warn of the dangers of changing history even a little. It's dangerous to tinker with the past because of potential unintended consequences further down the road.

These days, Napa Valley is intensely focused on Cabernet Sauvignon, crowding out wine grape varieties like Zinfandel and Petite Sirah that once dominated vineyards here. The prices of Cabernet grapes and the wines they produce are sky high—unsustainably high, in my opinion. I fear a Cabernet bubble that could someday pop. But it is the nature of bubbles that they seem unstoppable while they are inflating, so Cabernet is king. What if we could go back to 1976 and alter the famous Judgment of Paris so that Napa Cabernet wasn't the surprise victor of that France-versus-California taste-off? What would Napa Zinfandel be today if Cabernet Sauvignon didn't so completely overshadow it? Zinfandel, once the *numero uno* wine grape variety in the Napa Valley, now accounts for only about 5 percent of vineyard acreage. Petite Sirah is just 0.5 percent. But some of the wines that are made tell a fascinating "back to the future" story of what could have been.

Sue and I met with two devoted Zinfandel producers, Julie Johnson of Tres Sabores winery in the Rutherford district and Bob Biale of Robert Biale Vineyards in the Oak Knoll district, to learn more about Zinfandel's present and its potential future. Julie Johnson dry farms forty-plus-year-old Zinfandel vines in a foothill vineyard niche that is shaded from the afternoon sun. The wine is aromatic, balanced, and medium-bodied, with delicious fruit and spice. Such wines are not easy to grow or make, Johnson told us, and selling them is also a bit of a problem.

Zinfandel is the eleventh-most popular varietal wine in the United States, according to recent market surveys, wedged between Riesling and Syrah/Shiraz toward the bottom of the table. White Zinfandel outsells Red Zinfandel by a substantial margin in the US market. Ouch! That really hurts. Zinfandel buyers often expect big, ripe, boozy Zin, which is not a style that's on the Tres Sabores radar. Store shelves are peppered with California-appellation Zinfandels that are dark and strong (and sometimes a little sweet, too). They are the market's idea of Zinfandel but not exactly a terroirist treat.

Wines like this sell in part because they can fit into the popular red-blend or dark-red category pretty easily. But the Tres Sabores Zin is a horse of a different color, and many restaurant wine programs hesitate to take on wines like this, despite their quality, because they differ so dramatically from what they think consumers expect from a Zinfandel wine. The idea of Zinfandel with finesse is fading fast.

And so you have to be pretty committed to go all in on Zinfandel as Robert Biale Vineyards has done. Sue and I met with Bob Biale at his beautiful winery and tasting room in the Oak Knoll district. Bob's father, Aldo, and the family's heritage as winegrowers are the inspiration for the business, which makes fifteen different Zinfandel wines, as well as other varietals, including a surprising Greco Bianco we were served directly upon arrival. Bob is devoted to preserving Napa's Zinfandel DNA through many efforts, including especially his work with the Historic Vineyard Society, which seeks to identify and preserve producing vineyards that are fifty or more years old. Tegan Passalaqua, who specializes in single-vineyard old-vine Zinfandel at Turley, is also active in this group.

A few of these historic vineyards provide grapes for Biale's wines, such as the Valsecchi Vineyards Carneros Zinfandel we tasted. There's just an acre or so of one-hundred-year-old vines, Bob told us, and they produce just ninety-five cases of wine. But the wine is very special—elegant and balanced like all the Biale wines. Fantastic. Seriously, some of these old-vine Zinfandel wines made me think of elegant Pinot Noir. I wonder if these wines would age like a fine Burgundy? Hmmm.

Occasionally Biale is able to persuade a grower to plant a bit of Zinfandel when it is time to renew a vineyard rather than the certainly more profitable Cabernet. Maybe the site just isn't right for Cab. Or maybe the winegrower has been influenced by Bob's obvious devotion to the wine and its history. Doesn't matter. With a little luck, these could be the historic vines of the future.

I don't think I can manage the Marty McFly trick and rewrite the past, so the legacy of the Judgment of Paris is safe. Napa is Cabernet Sauvignon territory, and the valley has developed around the production and sale of luxury wines. The history of the pioneers and their Zinfandel and Petite Sirah is there, however, hidden in plain sight and ever threatened by the Cab boom. Maybe it had to be that way, but it is interesting to imagine an alternative universe where

Zinfandel's heritage is honored and celebrated to a greater extent. I am glad that there are people like Julie Johnson and Bob Biale, who are keeping the old vines and their memories of Napa days long past alive for us to taste today.

And I am glad there are readers like you, who will take up the terroirist tasting challenge and keep the souls of the forgotten grapes from disappearing. For this tasting, you don't have to go to Napa Valley and sip Zinfandel, although you can see how interesting that would be. A really committed terroirist would look for field blends, which is what the old Italian immigrants made in Napa. They planted several different grape varieties together, harvested them all together at the same time, and made wine from what nature gave them. I can't pass up field blends because they are a taste of history.

Your terroirist tasting should be guided by your personal tastes and interests and what is available in your market. Start by pushing aside the most popular international varieties and appellations; then dive down into the bottles that remain, looking for overlooked treasures. Try to surprise yourself and discover new favorites. Every bottle that you open helps to keep these grape varieties alive in a world where they are often under siege. Enjoy!

FLIGHT 4
WINE'S TRIPLE CRISIS

⑫

THIS CHANGES
EVERYTHING
Wine's Environmental Crisis

It's all very clear in retrospect. All the clues were there right in front of me as I was writing the first edition of *Wine Wars*; I just didn't connect the dots. Wine's triple crisis isn't a new thing; it is simply more in-your-face immediate now and so easier to see, even if all the implications are still a bit hazy.

The triple crisis is the result of a global environmental crisis combined with wine's seemingly perennial economic crisis, mashed up with wine's particular identity crisis. Each of the crises, if I can be allowed to give them that name, is serious enough. Taken together, they challenge all the givens of global wine: who makes what, where, and how and who drinks it and why. What will wine look like when the storm clouds part? That's what we are here to find out.

ENVIRONMENTAL EXTREMES

This chapter's theme comes from Giuseppe di Lampedusa's famous novel *The Leopard*. Early in the book, young Tancredi warns his aging uncle, the prince, about the storms of change that are sweeping over Italy: "If we want things to stay as they are, things will have to change. D'you understand?"[1] Tancredi's storms are social and political, and the wine storm that is this chapter's focus is environmental: climate change. It is the first element of wine's triple crisis.

We all know the basic facts about climate change; I only briefly summarize them here so that I can focus on the business and economic implications that don't always get the attention they deserve. We often talk about global warming, and indeed the globe's hottest series of years since records have been kept has come in the twenty-first century. But rising temperatures are only part of the story because the global environment is a complex system. Change one element, and you may change them all. So climate change is also an increase in extreme weather events and the magnification of certain weather-sensitive patterns, such as wildfires.

Wine is caught in the climate change crosshairs because wine grapes are sensitive to growing conditions. As average growing-season temperatures rise, some regions find that the grape varieties they have long depended on are no longer best suited to the changing environment. In Bordeaux, to cite an important recent case, climate change is forcing winegrowers to think beyond the Cabernet Sauvignon and Merlot that have been the foundation of their success for centuries. The list of approved red grape varieties was expanded in 2021 to include, among others, Marselan from the sunny Languedoc and Tourega Nacional from Portugal's hot Douro Valley.

Many of the wine industry's efforts when it comes to climate change are basically defensive in nature—adapting the current model to make in through the next few decades. Thus we switch out grape varieties in some cases and alter viticultural practices in others. Vineyards are often planted north-south, for example, so that grapes catch the morning and afternoon sun. That's great when the issue is getting ripeness but problematic as temperatures rise. Replanting on an east-west axis is expensive but can work as a defensive strategy because the canopy shades the grapes from the sun all day long. In extreme cases, it may be necessary to shift vineyard locations to cooler areas, as some Champagne producers have done by planting vineyards in England and some South Australian winemakers have done by moving to Tasmania.

Extreme climate events are so frequent and, well, extreme that they show up, collectively, in global wine production numbers. Violent hail, unseasonable frosts, drought, and accelerated wildfires all take their toll and in 2017 produced the lowest global wine output in a generation (followed in 2018 by just the opposite—extremely large grape harvests). Planning for the future is challenging in such a volatile environment.

CLIMATE CHANGE BEYOND THE VINEYARD

How will climate change impact the wine business? That was the topic I was invited to address for a webinar sponsored by the Institute of Masters of Wine.

It is a hard question because the wine product chain is global and complicated and because climate impacts are foreseen at all the product chain links.

One approach—and a good one—is to develop a taxonomy of effects. Start with nurseries and vineyards (an obvious climate impact point) and move to the cellar, where water availability is key, then through logistics (getting necessary inputs into the production process and the final goods to market), and then distribution, sales, and final consumption. Climate change is a factor, either directly or indirectly, at each and every stage. This is already pretty complicated, but we need to consider direct effects, financial effects, and regulatory responses and their costs. Indirect effects and what we might think of as counterparty impacts add more complexity. You can't really address climate change and wine without taking a broad, deep perspective.

Because the climate change impacts are complex and uncertain, they are properly considered business risks. Businesses confront lots of risks in their operations, some more tangible than others, and they are expected to disclose and analyze them so that investors understand the business implications. (Confession: Reading what firms have to say about risk in their annual reports is one of my guilty pleasures—along with reading really, really negative wine reviews.) Often the risk analysis is hidden in the back pages of annual reports, almost always in fine print. But it is always there because regulators are serious about requiring businesses to reveal to investors the risks that they are taking. You cannot evaluate risks and return if you don't know the risks.

I like to think of these risk disclosure statements as being like the fine print you are given when you get a new prescription drug. Do you worry about possible side effects? If so, be careful about reading drug disclosure statements because it can make your imagination run out of control. Lots of bad things can happen, although the probabilities are low enough relative to the benefits to justify a drug's regulatory approval.

In the United States, the Biden administration's Securities and Exchange Commission has committed to requiring the firms its regulations cover to make their climate change disclosures more comprehensive—in effect to treat climate change as a material risk—a higher-priority category than a financial risk. The era when climate change risks could be overlooked is ending. Analysis of the material-risk sections of corporate annual reports is one way to learn what climate change risks businesses see ahead of them and perhaps also what they are doing to prepare for them. At the very least, it is a way to see if climate change is taken seriously. I admit that this is not deep analysis. The firms might be myopic and not see climate change risks clearly. And there may be differences in the priorities listed in the report and those reflected in their actions. Getting values, priorities, and actions aligned is a universal problem, not limited to just corporations or to climate change.

I've chosen four quite different firms in different parts of the wine business to discuss here. I start with Constellation Brands because it is a very large publicly traded company, which therefore has many investors who will look closely at its analysis of risk. Constellation is an important wine and spirits producer, but it derives much of its income from Mexican beer imports and has cannabis interests, too, and each business is subject to a number of significant risks. Constellation identifies four categories of risk: operational risk; strategic risk; financial risk; and "other risks," which includes risk stemming from the fact that the company has a dual-share class structure and is effectively controlled by the Sands family.

Seven pages of the report are devoted to the operational risks (pandemics are risk number 1 in the 2020 report), and each risk receives relatively detailed analysis. Climate change is next to last on the list, with discussion focusing on risks to wine supply (through the impact of climate change on vineyard production, for example) and the potential costs of environmental regulatory compliance. My key takeaway from the Constellation annual report is perspective. Climate change is a business risk, and environmental advocates would like it to be the top priority. But in practice, there are a great many risks, and although climate change is taken seriously, it must necessarily compete with other risks for attention and resources.

Treasury Wine Estates (TWE) is a large multinational wine business with substantial assets in Australia and the United States and key markets in China, the United Kingdom, and the United States and around the world. Its Penfolds brand is iconic. It published both a summary annual report in 2020 and a supplementary sustainability report, so clearly the importance of environmental issues is recognized. I focused on the main annual report for this summary.

TWE's 2020 annual report identifies twelve categories of material risk. Changing geopolitical risks is number 7 on the list, but I suspect that it was close to the top of the minds of the company's leaders in 2021. Political friction between China and TWE's home country, Australia, resulted in high Chinese "antidumping" tariffs on Aussie wine imports and the collapse of TWE's number 1 export market. That, my friends, is an example of how a seemingly low-probability material risk can strike suddenly and with major impact.

Climate change is listed as the number 1 material risk due to its potential impact on access to and cost of water and energy, TWE's ability to efficiently source grapes and wine, and the inability of third-party suppliers to adapt to and mitigate climate change. In addition, governmental actions to reduce the impacts of climate change, such as packaging, waste, and emission-reduction targets, may also increase production cost. The report lists a number of mitigation strategies. Treasury's report suggests that its management recognizes both the direct and indirect impacts of climate on their business and, like Constellation, also anticipates changing regulatory environments as governments address climate change issues.

Tesco, the big British supermarket chain, is an incredibly important link in the global wine-product chain. But wine is just one of many products and services that Tesco sells. Tesco's 2020 annual report presents what it describes as a "robust approach to risk," with a long list of risks, each assessed according to movement (increasing, decreasing risk) and key controls and mitigating factors. Going through the list, I began to worry when I didn't see a category for climate change. Then I turned the page and discovered that climate is so important to Tesco that it has its own special risk task force.

In addition to general climate risks, Tesco seems to be undertaking specific studies of key product categories and risk areas, which makes sense. Wine is not one of the focus areas in the current report, but it is interesting to look closely at what's there. Some UK stores and distribution centers, for example, are at risk from flooding due to climate change. And supplies of produce from outside the United Kingdom are threatened by climate effects in the countries of origin. South Africa, Egypt, Spain, and Peru are noted as particular concerns. The supply chains for protein (beef, chicken, etc.) are concerns, too. But there are also demand-side impacts. Tesco expects that climate concerns will shift consumers to plant-based proteins that have less environmental impact than animal-based foods, so building those supply chains and anticipating demand is on the agenda. Very interesting.

My final case study is Corticeira Amorim, the world's largest producer of cork closures. Amorim is well known for its commitment to sustainability, so I was sure that climate change would factor into its business plan. Amorim categorizes its business risks as short-term and long-term potential threats. In the short time frame, anything that can affect its two main markets—the world wine industry and the construction sector—will have a major impact on the business. The list of things that Amorim must worry about is thus nearly endless.

Long-run risks include foreign exchange shifts, competition from alternative closures, and of course the environment. The cork forests in southern Europe and Northern Africa that supply Amorin's raw materials are environmentally significant for their ability to take carbon out of the system and lock it away. As climate concerns intensify, the report suggests, the value of the forests for this purpose will grow. But, ironically, the cork forests that help mitigate climate change are also threatened by it, which gives the need to address climate issues a particular urgency, both for Amorim and, I think, for wine more generally.

The question is, What are the climate change risks to the wine industry, and how are wine businesses responding? Inevitably, this brief study uncovered more questions than answers, in part because of its inherent limitations. I've looked at just four firms, examined their material climate change risks through the lens of annual reports, and of course only had space for fairly superficial summaries here. Critical readers would have been suspicious of definitive answers or broad conclusions in the context of these limitations. That said, the actual complexity of the problem starts to show through as you read the reports. And the urgency shows through, too. I think we can expect climate disclosures to be taken even more seriously soon. Much too soon for a victory lap but good news for wine and the environment, nonetheless.

THE PORTO PROTOCOL

Many important global wine industry actors are even more committed to addressing the climate change crisis than these material-risk statements suggest, as I learned when I was invited to speak at a wine and climate change leadership conference in Porto in 2019. The program was a who's who of wine industry leaders who have chosen to have a dog in the climate change fight. The list began with Adrian Bridge, CEO of Taylor's Port, who was instrumental in organizing the event, and continued with Miguel Torres, Cristina Mariani-May, Pau Roca, Antonio Amorim, Greg Jones, Roger Boulton, Jamie Goode, Gerard Bertrand, and on and on. Some guy named Al Gore gave the summit keynote. Anyone heard of him?

There are lots of meetings and conferences about the environment, sustainability, and climate change. Sometimes in the past, they have reminded me of the 1993 film *Groundhog Day*, where the same talk and motions are repeated as if on an endless loop and little of substance seems to change (until, at last, it does). Climate change has reached a crucial moment, however, that demands action over talk.

But then there is the Gulliver problem. Jonathan Swift's Gulliver found himself in Lilliput, where he was vastly larger and more powerful than the tiny citizens. His every action posed a threat to their world, and their only hope was to work together to control the giant. Lacking a massive rope to tie the big guy down, the Lilliputians teamed up with thousands of tiny strands. Climate change is a bit like Gulliver, in that it is a huge force that none of us has the power to control by ourselves. Top-down initiatives like the Paris Agreement are very important but need to have bottom-up support. Grassroots. Tiny strands. Addressing climate change head on requires thousands of small concrete actions that taken together can have real meaning.

So where does the wine industry come in? What is different about wine that makes its Lilliputians think that they can take on Gulliver? There are many reasons wine is particularly responsive to climate change issues (you have probably already thought of a few reasons as you read this sentence), but here is an important one: Climate change is an existential threat to civilization and the natural environment, but it is not taken seriously enough by many people because its impacts are uncertain, uneven, and projected into the future.

But wine really is different. The future is now for climate change and wine, as the combination of higher temperatures and more frequent extreme weather events redraws the world wine map. Wine is fragile, vulnerable. Ultimately there is no escaping the climate change threat to wine.

The highlight of the summit was a presentation by Al Gore, the prominent climate change activist and former US vice president. Gore's presentation was intense, focused, and inspiring. Sue called it a "stem-winder" of a speech—it really got the audience worked up. The Porto gathering promised to break out of the *Groundhog Day* cycle and offer real solutions; I am happy to say that it generally delivered. Starting with Miguel Torres, we were offered concrete examples of determined companies and leaders who backed up their talk with action.

One thing I learned is this: The basic outline for progress on climate change issues is fairly clear. Start with an environmental audit to establish a baseline, set specific quantitative goals to reduce emissions and improve efficiency, evaluate results, then repeat the process. Some of the achievements reported in Porto were startling and show just how much can be accomplished once a serious commitment is made.

UC Davis professor Roger Boulton's presentation "The Winery of the Future" was a fascinating deep dive into what is possible with current technology if you decide to design a winery from scratch to have zero or negative emissions. It is like a Rubik's Cube in a way because each action has many reactions, but Boulton showed that a solution is possible, with a superefficient production facility the result.

You could tell that many in the Porto crowd were still struggling a bit with exactly where to put priorities: Try to make progress everywhere? Or focus on a few big goals, either the ones that would be easiest or cheapest to achieve or perhaps the ones that would have the biggest impact? I do not know what the answer to that question is, but it is better to know what you want to do than to thrash around blindly. Participants were encouraged to sign the Porto Protocol, a platform created in the first iteration of this conference (which featured a keynote by Barack Obama). Those who sign the protocol commit to doing more in the future than they are doing now and to sharing their methods and results with others. The idea is to create an open-source database that will help everyone do more, faster, better.

Interestingly, Sue and I ran into several people who confided that their organizations were having trouble deciding whether to sign up, which was puzzling because each of them has developed a strong program to promote sustainability and confront climate change. What's the problem? One colleague said that his organization was already doing more than the protocol currently requires, so there was a concern that they might not get credit for what they have done. No one said it, but I think it is possible that the transparency requirement could also be an issue. If that's the case, then I hope we can get past it. As Adrian Bridge, the CEO of Taylor's and the driving force behind this initiative, has said, "There is no time and no need to reinvent things. If we share our successes and experiences, we will all benefit." He is certainly right.

I do not recall hearing anyone say that consumers would be willing to pay a premium for climate-change-friendly wine, although some of us talked at dinner about what could be done to draw consumer attention to wineries that are taking climate change action. Does that mean that the costs fall, like a tax burden on the wineries that fight climate change (and not on those that don't)? Yes and no. Some of the defensive costs of mitigating climate change, especially in the vineyard, are going to be unavoidable.

Some positive actions have the potential to pay for themselves, at least in part. Katie Jackson, of Jackson Family Wines, told the story of the decision to move to slightly (one ounce) lighter-weight bottles for some of the millions of cases of wine they sell. The conventional wisdom is that consumers associate lower bottle weight with lower quality, so there was pushback about this method to reduce the firm's carbon footprint. Happily, according to Jackson, consumers didn't notice the difference, and the environmental savings became a cost-reducing part of Jackson's carbon-reducing program. The world is not filled with free lunches like this, but there were several examples of actions that paid for themselves, contributing to both financial and environmental bottom lines.

With this in mind, I'd invite you to weigh the next ten wine bottles you open just to see how big the gap is between the heaviest and lightest bottles. I used to include a bit about wine-bottle weight in one of my *Wine Wars* public talks.

I asked for a couple of volunteers to come forward to heft bottles of different weights. They usually expressed great surprise at the difference and wondered why very heavy bottles are needed when lighter-weight alternatives are available. Good question.

Bottle weight is a frequent topic of conversation at the *Wine Economist* dinner table. Unexpected heavy- and lightweight bottles are swept away to be weighed and recorded at the end of the meal. Just for fun I got out the group of bottles and other containers that I used in the *Wine Wars* talks. Here is the range of weights, from lightest to heaviest:

375 ml wine can: 16 g (× 2 = 32 g)
1 l Tetra Pak wine container: 40 g
750 ml plastic wine bottle: 56 g
750 ml eco wine bottle: 444 g
750 ml midweight wine bottle: 650–750 g
750 ml heavyweight wine bottle: 1,084 g
750 ml superheavyweight wine bottle: 1,198 g
ultraheavyweight bottle from China: 1,218 g

Can you believe that some wine bottles weigh more than a kilo? The 1,084-gram bottle on the list was a Chilean wine, so it is interesting to speculate the size of the carbon footprint it created. The bottle might have been made in China, for example, then shipped to Chile and then on to the United States. Incredible when there are good alternatives.

IS SUSTAINABLE WINEGROWING SUSTAINABLE?

As we saw in Porto, there are many ways to address wine's climate change crisis, and one of the broadest and most dynamic is the drive for sustainable wine production. Winegrowers around the world have united in a general way under the sustainability flag. But there are issues. Sustainability is a powerful movement in northeast Italy, for example, where Sue and I participated in a program sponsored by the Consorzio Collio. I spoke on a roundtable panel on sustainable winegrowing's many sides. One of the other speakers had recently converted his family vineyards to organic viticulture, and he talked about the experience and his commitment to sustainable winegrowing. A hand went up. "Now that you are spending less on chemicals and so forth," a journalist asked, "will you be passing along the cost savings to consumers?"

Wow—I didn't see that question coming. Implicit in the query was the assumption that organic or sustainable wines should be cheaper than other wines, not simply better for the environment. Most winegrowers, however, hope that sustainable practices will be rewarded in the marketplace—that consumers will be willing to pay higher prices for sustainably produced wines, not demand a discount. Environmental sustainability needs to be economically sustainable to survive.

I would like to say that wines that are certified as sustainable, organic, biodynamic, or otherwise proactive regarding climate change command a price premium, but I don't have the data to support this broad conclusion. Wine is a complicated product category, and it isn't easy to make an apples-to-apples comparison of sustainably produced wines with similar wines made using conventional practices in order to extract the existence and size of a general price differential. Much of the research on this subject, therefore, has involved surveys that ask consumers how much they hypothetically would be willing to pay for sustainably produced wines compared to others.

Wine Intelligence released a 2019 study of US wine drinkers that both reinforced a strong willingness to pay and uncovers significant generational diversity among Gen Z, millennial, Gen X, and baby boom consumers.[2] Millennials in the study, for example, were more than twice as likely as baby boomers to say they would be willing to pay a five-dollars-plus sustainability premium, while 43 percent of boomers said they wouldn't pay any extra at all. The study suggests that consumers would be willing to pay about three dollars more per bottle for a sustainably produced wine. What do you think? How much more would you be willing to pay to support sustainability in wine?

Because it is hard to determine if sustainable wine actually receives a price premium in the market, I decided to work backward. If sustainable wine sells for an average three-dollar premium, then sustainably grown grapes should sell for a premium, too. How much? The Law of One Hundred holds that if grapes cost one thousand dollars more per ton, then the wine has to sell for at least ten dollars more per bottle ($1,000/100) to pay the bills. It's a back-of-the-envelope sort of calculation—a long way from rocket science but useful here. Working backward, the Law of One Hundred rule of thumb suggests that a three-dollar higher bottle price should translate into a maximum of three-hundred-dollars-per-ton sustainable grape price premium. That could be a substantial incentive for winegrowers to farm sustainably, depending on the region.

What is the sustainable premium for wine grapes? Once again, it is hard to generalize because there are all sorts of special cases in grape contracts. But I consulted two well-connected California colleagues, and the answers they provided were very consistent. In general, sustainably farmed wine grapes receive a premium of fifteen to twenty-five dollars (average of about twenty dollars) per ton. That's a lot less than I was expecting. It implies a very small potential bottle price premium—nothing like the three-dollar survey result. Some contracts provide a premium up to 7.5 percent, I'm told, which can be valuable depending on the underlying grape price and yield. In many cases, however, the premium is exactly zero. Grape buyers specify sustainably farmed fruit but are not willing to pay extra for it. Bottom line: Growers generally farm sustainably because these are sound practices, not for the money (yet).

Why is the sustainable-grape premium so low? One answer is that premiums are low because it is a buyers' market for some grape categories these days. With surplus grape supplies and wine in tanks from previous vintages, buyers don't pay more because they don't have to. That is bad news for growers in the short run but better news in the long run because the supply-demand imbalance is likely to adjust over time, and perhaps improved prices will follow.

A second answer is that the grape premium is low because the premium for sustainable wines is low—much lower than the three-dollars-per-bottle survey estimate. How can this be? Are the survey takers fibbing? Well, sometimes people do give aspirational answers to survey questions. But there's another answer. Consumers may be willing to pay more for sustainable wines, but they can't tell for sure which ones they are.

Organic and biodynamic are very clearly defined wine terms (although consumers may not fully understand them—especially biodynamic), but sustainable does not have a single meaning or certification standard. Most of the regions we visit have their own sustainability certification programs, each tailored to local conditions. So the term *sustainable* shows up a lot and doesn't always mean the same thing. This is one reason it is hard to calculate the price premium for sustainable wines.

The term *sustainable* is popular in part because of this ambiguity. I found one wine that boasted "Sustainably Dry Farmed" on the front label. On the back label, I learned that this meant that the vines were actually irrigated (which seems like the opposite of dry farming to me)—but only as necessary to sustain the vines themselves. The fluid nature of the term *sustainable* makes all the difference. Does that mean a one-size-fits-all certification program? No. I think that the fact that there are many regional sustainability programs is a good thing, even if it confuses consumers a bit, because it increases the proportion of the industry that adopts sustainable practices.

Sue points out that consumers support sustainable practices in other sectors when they understand them and appreciate their importance. Sustainable fisheries are important, for example, and many retailers and restaurants make a point of featuring sustainably harvested seafood. The existence of different certification programs doesn't seem to diminish the impact. We need to make sustainable wine as transparent and appealing as sustainable fish. Perhaps the key is to focus less on the what and how—what we are doing (certification) and how it is done—and more on the why. The why is pretty clear when it comes to sustainable fisheries. Maybe we can make the why of sustainable wine clearer, too. Sustainability would be more sustainable from an economic standpoint if we could communicate better with wine buyers so that the sustainability premium is greater and trickles down to growers better than it does today. Sustainable sustainability? That's a goal worth pursuing as we confront global wine's triple crisis.

So you can see that wine's environmental crisis really is an "everything must change" dilemma. If nothing is done, then change in the form of adaptive responses will be forced on us as the environment evolves, first gradually and then, I suspect, suddenly. The issue is not just technical because economic incentives are involved and must change. Boulton's Rubik's Cube and Gulliver's collective-action problem all apply. It can seem overwhelming. And of course, the environment is only one part of wine's triple crisis.

13

HOW TO MAKE A
SMALL FORTUNE
Wine's Economic Crisis

It is the oldest joke in the wine business. How do you make a small fortune in wine? Easy. Start with a large one. Growing wine grapes is a challenging endeavor, and making wine from them isn't always easy, either. But selling the wine and making a living from doing it—that's hard work. Over the years, I have talked to many winemakers who confess that they never suspected how much time and effort they'd need to spend on selling the wines that they love to make. Part of the success of the first edition of *Wine Wars* was that it helped these accidental entrepreneurs understand the world of wine markets that they need to uncork in order to pay the bills.

WINE IS A RISKY BUSINESS

Sometimes I think that economic crisis is the wine industry's natural state. Honestly, it seems like the wine world (or at least important parts of it) is always in a crisis, recovering from a crisis, or sliding into a new one. No wonder (this is another wine-industry joke) the only person crazier than a wine-maker is her banker.

From an economic standpoint, it is useful to think of the wine industry as three vertically linked sectors that are all risky and capital intensive. First, there is growing the grapes, which requires long-term thinking because grapevines take several years to bear good fruit and then have a productive life of thirty years or more (some bearing vines today were planted more than one hundred years ago). The initial vineyard investment can be substantial. There's a hill called Cartizze in the Prosecco region where vineyards sell for one million euros a hectare. Needless to say, growing grapes is a risky business because of such natural risks as disease, adverse weather, and smoke taint and such economic risks as unexpected price or market shifts. Agriculture in general is hard, and wine grapes, because of the long wait for new vines to become productive, is especially hard.

Making wine is also capital intensive, which is why custom crush facilities have become popular in many places. It takes less upfront capital to rent or share buildings and costly equipment rather than owning them. Mobile bottling lines can substitute for expensive permanent equipment, too, for small producers. The next time you visit a wine-production facility, count up the investments you see: the tanks, barrels, grape presses, destemmers, sorting tables, lab equipment, and so on. And remember that some of this equipment is used just once a year during harvest. There are risks in the cellar part of the wine business, too, both because things can go wrong and because a lot of choices have to be made in terms of which wines are made, how they are made, and whether they will find willing buyers.

Selling the wine is the final stage, and this of course is where brands enter the story. Brands (or reputation, if you prefer) can be expensive to build and maintain. And there are lots of risks involved in selling wine due to unexpected overall economic conditions, changes in the competitive landscape, and shifting tastes and preferences. A 1991 episode of *60 Minutes* told viewers about the health benefits of red wine, for example, provoking a consumption surge. The 2004 Alexander Payne film *Sideways* convinced its audience that Merlot is lame and Pinot Noir is ethereal. You never know what is going to happen next. Which leads to this chapter's third and final wine-business joke: The Bible says that Jesus turned water into wine. That was easy. For two thousand years, winemakers have been trying to do something much harder: turning wine into money.

Because winegrowing, winemaking, and wine selling are all capital intensive and risky, it is a brave individual who undertakes all three. Yes, I understand and appreciate the romantic image of the noble vigneron who grows the grapes, makes the wines, and sells them to enthusiastic customers at the cellar door, but from an economic standpoint, that's a high-risk play, especially as scale increases. Breaking up the product chain is one way to reduce capital costs and limit risks. In the United States, for example, it is fairly common for winegrowers to specialize in grape production, selling their fruit to other businesses that make and sell the wine. Many important wineries purchase most of or even all their grapes from independent growers.

Cooperatives are very important in the European wine sector. Growers specialize in grape production, then share the cost and risks of winemaking with their cooperative colleagues. The wines are then sold to *négociants*, who specialize in marketing and sales, or even directly to such retailers as Tesco or Costco for their private-label brand portfolio.

Adam Smith argued that the economic benefits of the division of labor are limited by the size of the market, so perhaps we should not be surprised that as the wine market has gone global, the result is greater specialization in one link or another in the product chain. I like to think that Adam Smith's favorite wine, if he were alive today, would come from a California company called Castle Rock Winery. They produce 375,000 cases of wine (that's 4.5 million bottles) each year and do it with only eleven direct employees. How is that possible? They don't grow the grapes or make the wine, but they can contract for those products and services, leaving their lean staff free to focus on making the right choices and building the brand. In fact, they are known for offering Pinot Noir with an unusually strong quality-price ratio, so whatever they are doing works.

WINE'S BOOM-AND-BUST CYCLE

The economic shadow that hangs over the wine industry can be best understood as the result of three patterns that, taken together, create a sometimes-chaotic environment in which to do business. There is a cyclical pattern of the type that is not uncommon in markets for agricultural goods generally. On top of that, there are structural imbalances that can take years or even decades to work themselves out. Then, finally, there are what I call "wild cards," short-term events that punctuate the already-complicated economic pattern and create challenges and opportunities. With so much happening at once, it is no surprise that the wine business can drive you to drink!

Let's start with the cyclical pattern of boom and bust. If you took Econ 101 at university, then you learned that markets are extremely stable—almost boring in a way. The famous British economist Alfred Marshall said that an efficient market was as stable as an apple in a bowl, and that is true if both demanders and suppliers are able to react to market changes in roughly equal time frames. Suppose that there is a shortage in the market for some reason, for example. This makes prices rise, which sends a signal to buyers and sellers. Sellers increase the amount they offer for sale because of higher profitability, while buyers reduce purchases at the higher price. The result slowly (or sometimes quickly) closes the gap between demand and supply until the shortage is gone and the price hits

its stable new level. A similar symmetric, demand-supply adjustment takes place when a surplus causes the price to fall. Market adjustments are as orderly and predictable as an apple settling into the bottom of a bowl.

Now switch things up a bit. Imagine that demand can adjust quickly but that supply has to wait a year or more to respond to changing market signals because, for example, this year's crop has already been harvested, and any substantial change in production will have to wait until next year or even longer. Demand and supply still work but within different time frames. This sets up a dynamic that is different from the classic textbook case.

Suppose an unexpected shortage of Pinot Noir wine appears for some reason (maybe it is a *Sideways* effect that creates a surge in demand). Prices rise, of course, but wineries find their options to satisfy the higher demand limited in the short run. Maybe they have extra Pinot Noir in storage tanks from previous years that they can sell to take advantage of the higher price. Maybe they can buy bulk Pinot Noir from abroad and sell it (clearly labeled by origin) under their brand umbrella. But with the next harvest as long as a year away and three or more years before any newly planted Pinot vines bear quality fruit, the ability to increase production to take advantage of higher prices is limited. Result: Prices will rise much more than in the textbook case, and they will stay high longer.

Many winegrowers will see the booming Pinot prices and plant new vines or graft to replace less-profitable grape varieties with Pinot Noir. As many growers do this at once, the number of nonbearing acres of Pinot increases and then perhaps increases again. A wave of new Pinot builds up like water behind a dam. But is demand rising to match? No, because the higher price of Pinot Noir has discouraged some consumers. So what happens in three or four years, when all those new Pinot Noir vines are harvested, and then, a year or so later, when the wine is released to market? Isn't it obvious? The Pinot boom is replaced with a Pinot bust. Prices fall, and the process of adjustment starts again.

Turrentine Brokerage, a California-based grape and bulk-wine broker with offices around the world, has created what they call the Turrentine Wine Business Wheel of Fortune.[1] It shows how boom becomes bust, which leads to boom again in a permanent wine-crisis cycle. Booms and busts are baked into the cake in the wine industry.

The wine-market cycles are typical of many agricultural markets, where supply responds to market conditions more slowly than does demand. Interestingly, beer doesn't suffer the same problem, but some spirits do. Can you guess why? Beer is made from grains that can be stored for future use, and the production process takes only a few weeks to complete. If demand for a particular beer rises, you can often organize the necessary ingredients and get new batches made relatively quickly—no waiting around for next year's harvest or for newly planted vines to mature. Some spirits are like beer in this sense, but anything that requires aging will be subject to its own wheel of fortune. It is pretty hard to quickly increase the supply of twelve-year-old single-malt Scotch, for example.

One final thing about wine's boom-bust cycles: Usually, the ups and downs get smaller over time, and the market slowly converges (unless it is upset by some other new event). But it is theoretically possible for the surpluses and shortages to get bigger and bigger as each cycle unfolds and as the market spins out of control until finally there is a fatal crash.

I confess that I find these cycles fascinating, and I think they are one reason I became an economist. Apples in bowls are very nice, but I have always been interested in change, and when I discovered these agricultural cycles (which are examples of what is sometimes called "cobweb theory" because of the way the dynamic supply-demand graphs are drawn), I knew I'd found a home. And so, I suppose, it was natural that I'd end up studying wine economics, too.

STRUCTURAL PROBLEMS: THE WINE LAKE

The wine-market cycles make being in the wine business a bit of a roller-coaster ride, but that's agriculture for you, and somehow growers and producers find ways to ride things out. But now we add on top of the cycle the periodic presence of structural features that distort wine markets, sometimes for many years, and can alter the cycle's dynamics in unpredictable ways.

Take, for example, the famous European Wine Lake, which existed in one form or another for nearly thirty years. The figurative lake held unsold wine, which European authorities bought up and distilled into industrial alcohol to get rid of it. Why do this silly thing? Well, politics had something to do with it.

When the European Economic Community (which became the European Community, which is now the European Union) was set in motion in the 1950s, the goal was peace, free trade, and prosperity. But the agriculture sector was a problem because each country's farmers feared that the others would get subsidies and have an unfair advantage. Farmers had enough political clout to keep the European integration train from leaving the station, so an exception was worked out. A system called the Common Agricultural Policy (CAP) was organized to support farmer incomes. Because winegrowing is farming, the wine sector was included in the system as part of the Common Market Organization (CMO), which provided regulations on a range of wine-market issues. The relevant feature, which stayed in effect from 1970 until 2008, was a subsidy scheme to support producers of lower-quality table wine. In effect, inexpensive wines that could not find a market were purchased by the European authority (accumulating in the virtual wine lake) in order to stabilize farmer incomes. The lake was drained through distillation.

Distillation itself can be a useful tool in wine policy. In 2020, for example, several European countries invoked "crisis distillation" to take millions of liters of surplus wine out of markets that were severely stressed by pandemic lockdowns and restrictions. But the CMO system set up incentives that proved its downfall. In some parts of Europe, it was possible to overcrop in the vineyards and produce unmarketable wine at cost below the distillation scale, so that's what crafty producers did. It was profitable to make large quantities of wine that had a guaranteed buyer at the distillery gate. What a waste! Finally, the cost and waste became too much, and the plug was pulled on the wine lake. The distillation price support system has been replaced by a number of programs that encourage the grubbing up of uneconomic vines, focus on grape varieties that have more export potential, and support various marketing and winemaking technology schemes.

The existence for many years of structural surpluses of lower-quality wine in Europe distorted the world wine market. The price-support system meant that the producers of these wines weren't subject to periodic boom and bust to the same extent as winemakers in other parts of the world. But the existence of the wine lake hung ominously over winemakers around the world. Because of the lake, there was also a lower-cost competitor.

OLD WORLD WINE COLLAPSE

The European Union's price-support regime was meant to stabilize winegrower incomes and dampen wine-market cycles, and I guess it did that in the short run. But the incentives it provided for overproduction of low-quality, inexpensive wine led to an inevitable crisis as the cost of the program grew and grew. The problem—too much low-cost wine—was made worse by a second structural shift: the collapse of Old World wine consumption.

They say that wine is food, and although it is easy to forget this fact now, it was certainly true for centuries in many regions. Grapevines are prolific plants, but the berries they produce have a very short shelf life in their natural state. Grapes can be dried to preserve the calories and nutrients, or they can be fermented into wine. Today we take for granted that a bottle of wine will be drinkable for at least several years, but early-modern winemakers were happy if this harvest's wine stayed good until the next harvest season. There is a reason many regions have a tradition of drinking fresh, young wine a month or two after fermentation: best to enjoy it before it starts to go off.

If you think of wine as preserved grapes, full of energy and nutrients, then it makes sense that wine would be an important part of workers' diets in the years before refrigeration made other food products an affordable alternative. Kym Anderson, Signe Nelgen, and Vicente Pinella have compiled historical statistics for wine consumption and much more in their monumental study *Global Wine Markets 1860 to 2016: A Statistical Compendium.*[2] Their data suggests just how much more wine Europeans consumed a few decades ago compared with current levels.

The average per capita consumption of wine in France for 2010–2016 was 44.0 liters, which is a considerable amount given that not everyone uses alcohol, and among those who do, not everyone drinks wine. It is a higher per capita wine consumption than Italy (33.3 liters), for example, or Spain (14.9 liters), and much higher than the United States (10.3 liters) or the United Kingdom (19.7 liters) for the same period. Only Portugal, with a seemingly incredible 49.6 liters of wine per capita, exceeds the French rate of wine consumption.

But as high as some of these wine-consumption figures are, they are dwarfed by the wine-drinking levels of earlier years. In the decade of 1920–1929, for example, French per capita wine consumption was 151.4 liters, and Italy's was 106.0 liters. Today's wine consumption levels in these Old World countries are only about a quarter of the amounts that prevailed a hundred years ago.

Zoom ahead to the 1950s, when European economic growth was just starting to recover from World War II and wine consumption was still much higher than current levels. Average French per capita wine consumption during 1950–1959 was 131.9 liters; in Italy, 108.9 liters; and in Portugal, 90.2 liters. But then a steep secular decline in wine consumption set in. Between the 1960s and 2000, per capita wine consumption in the biggest Old World wine countries fell by half! Incredible. An even greater wine bust occurred in Argentina, which is a New World wine country if you go by geography but is part of Old World wine in terms of history and culture. Argentina's average per capita wine consumption was 83.8 liters in 1960–1969, for example, but just 23.2 liters in 2010–2016. Wine consumption in Chile fell from 53.7 liters per capita in the 1960s to just 16.1 liters in the study's most recent period.

What accounts for the relative collapse of Old World wine consumption? Well, there is no single explanation, but it is not hard to piece together some of the most important factors. Very high levels of alcohol intake are not really sustainable from a health standpoint, for example. And as Europe grew into its postwar economic miracle, the sort of hard labor that would burn off a liter of wine at lunch diminished, and the generation of workers who accounted for this high intake grew older and were replaced in a generational transition by younger consumers with different preferences. Wine became more of a pleasureful beverage than a nutritious food.

The shift away from very high wine consumption levels was a good thing from a health standpoint (wine is best in moderation), but you can appreciate the problems this created for the wine industry. The decline in demand for wine, especially the inexpensive sort that workers might want, both helped create the need for the EU wine price-support regime and then, as things played out, increased the gap between rising supply and falling demand. No wonder the wine lake grew so deep!

WINE GOES GLOBAL

A third structural shift I want to feature is at the core of this book's main argument: the rise of the global wine market. It is convenient to give a date to mark the start of wine's global era, and so I propose January 1, 1973. That is the day when Great Britain entered what is now the European Union (should we call it Brenter?). That's when what became the world's most important wine-import market tied the knot with the world's largest wine-exporting countries. The commercial links that economic integration created help establish wide, deep wine-market channels, first within the EU, and then around the world.

Global wine also benefited from the expansion of the global free-trade system. The General Agreement on Tariffs and Trade (GATT) and then the World Trade Organization (WTO) succeeded in reducing trade barriers. Wine benefited both directly as more markets opened and indirectly as trade terms improved for machinery, technology, corks, capsules, and so forth. The global economic environment became more favorable for trade in the 1980s and 1990s, and wine's boat rose with the incoming tide.

This more-favorable environment made increased global wine trade possible, and the advent of more efficient ocean shipping using standardized containers instead of costly, inconvenient break-bulk shipments added momentum. Containerized shipping is especially significant for bulk-wine trade, where wine moves in the big steel boxes, which hold bladders containing 24,000 liters of wine each. The time was right, and wine trade spurted all around the globe in the thirty years starting in the mid-1970s but for different reasons in different regions.

New Zealand and Chile, for example, embraced globalization as part of a system of liberal market reforms. Both countries have succeeded but in different ways. New Zealand, as I've already shown, entered the global markets with premium products and has been able to maintain and even enhance their quality status. Chile, which has a long history of wine production, established a reputation for value wines and has struggled to alter this perception, even as quality has risen higher and higher.

Australia relies on wine exports to compensate for a small domestic demand base. It experienced a number of boom-bust cycles driven in part by export-market conditions. The export surge that brought Yellow Tail and Jacob's Creek to global markets was quite intentional but, as noted earlier, ran into headwinds, leading to a shift in focus to the rising Chinese market.

Georgia, Romania, and other wine-producing former Soviet countries shifted toward global markets when the collapse of their communist governments changed the structure of their markets and wine industries. Independent producers rose up alongside state wine businesses and cooperatives. Export markets in Europe and elsewhere were developed to supplement or substitute for Russia and other former-Soviet states.

Argentina embraced exports, especially to the United States and Great Britain, as domestic demand suffered both the secular decline noted earlier and periodic severe financial and monetary crises. Argentina's wine producers have managed for the most part to upgrade quality to succeed in more demanding export markets, but they still suffer from the problems of the domestic economy. High inflation rates, currency instability, and import restrictions that can affect wine production make business life uncertain in Argentina's wine sector.

The Republic of South Africa has a very old industry that was founded to make wine to provision ships sailing around the Cape of Good Hope from Europe to Asia and back. At one point, a delicious, sweet wine from South Africa called Constantia was among the most treasured wines in all the world. Napoleon had it shipped to his exile home in St. Helena. South African wine has been though many boom-and-bust cycles and virtually disappeared from global markets during much of the period of apartheid. When apartheid ended in 1994, the doors to South African wine slowly opened around the world, and now examples can be found nearly everywhere, although nothing beats traveling to the Western Cape to sample the wines on their home soil.

Globalization creates export opportunities but also lets foreign competition in the door. It increases choice, which is good, but also magnifies confusion. From the standpoint of economic crises, it has dual impacts, as well. The existence of global markets should in theory at least reduce the boom-bust cycles because imports can reduce shortage stress and exports can siphon off excess wine when production is unexpectedly high. In practice, it isn't always that simple because bulk imports and exports are not always perfect or useful substitutes for domestic products. But the global market does add some stability. Except when it does not, as when booms and busts in several important global markets align, as happened in 2017, when unfavorable weather events in several major regions at once resulted in the lowest global wine production in a generation.

WILD CARDS: PANDEMICS AND POLITICS

It is easy to see why it is so difficult to predict what will happen next in the wine industry and why, therefore, it is not very hard to turn a large fortune into a small one. There are huge secular trends that, like the tide, sweep in and out, while shorter-term "wheel of fortune" cycles churn above them, stirring things up some more. Now we add the third element, the wild cards, which are like earthquakes in their ability to alter the wine business landscape and set new trends and cycles in motion.

The COVID-19 pandemic is a good recent example of a wild card at work. It was not the first coronavirus pandemic or even the first one of the twenty-first century, but its global spread and severity and the lack of a more organized response caught the world off guard. The pandemic and the responses to it affected every aspect of the global wine market, from vineyards to cellar to transportation to consumer. One of the biggest wild cards was the closure of bars and restaurants, which are a very important sales vector for many wineries. In some parts of Europe, especially areas with large travel and tourism sectors, half of all wine is sold through the "on-premise" channels. The economic impact was severe and resulted in emergency distillation to dispose of surplus stocks in some cases.

Many wineries shifted focus from on-premise sales to off-premise retailers, such as supermarkets, and online sales. These market environments are distinctly different from bars and restaurants, however, and some wineries made the shift more quickly and successfully than others. As pandemic lockdowns eased in 2021 and bars and restaurants reopened, questions remained: To what extent would the impacts of the pandemic, such as online sales, fade? Would consumer behavior change in the long term, creating durable structural shifts?

The politics of international trade is another wild card that has stirred up global wine markets in recent years. As noted previously, wine mainly gained from the expansion of open international trade regimes in the postwar era. Even when global free-trade deals ran out of steam after the disastrous Seattle WTO meetings in 1999, bilateral free-trade agreements, such as those between Chile and China and between the United States and South Korea, frequently included terms that favored wine interests.

So it came as something of a shock when wine found itself caught in the middle of trade disputes that centered on other industries or issues. Thus, for example, the tit-for-tat trade war between China and the Trump administration resulted in China imposing high tariffs on US wine, effectively closing down this export market. Wines from several European countries were targeted when US trade barriers were raised in response to airplane subsidies and other issues. China imposed tariffs of more than 200 percent on Australian wine in 2021, which effectively closed Australia's top export market. Officially, the tariffs were an "antidumping" measure meant to offset unfairly low export prices, but the average price of Australian wines sold to China was actually surprisingly high. Dumping is a notoriously overused rationale for tariffs, and it was widely believed that this action, which devastated the Aussie wine industry, was in fact retaliation for remarks made by Australian officials about China's policies toward the Hong Kong democracy movement.

Wine was caught in the crossfire in Brexit, when Great Britain resigned its place in the European Union on January 1, 2021. The Brexit agreement was perhaps the first international trade negotiation intended to reduce trade flows between nations rather than increase or redirect them. Brexit reversed the event that I've chosen to signal as the start of wine's global era, and it is too soon to know what the final impact will be.

From an international economic standpoint, the European Union is defined by its four freedoms: free movement of goods, free movement of services, free movement of people, and free movement of capital. Britain's status as the center of the global wine universe depended on all four freedoms. Brexit at minimum throws sand in the wheels of what was a very efficient wine industry machine.

WILD CARDS: FOREIGN EXCHANGE RATES

Foreign exchange rates are the prices of one country's currency in terms of other currencies. On the day I'm writing this in 2021, for example, €1.00 can be exchanged for about $1.18 in US currency. One British pound exchanges for about $1.38. Both the euro and pound are much more valuable (they buy more dollars in this case) than they were a year before. The exchange rate is important because it affects the price of all of a country's goods and services relative to the rest of the world. If the US dollar rises in price on foreign-exchange markets, for example, all US products, including wine, will cost more to foreign buyers in terms of their own currency. A strong dollar thus discourages US exports. Because a strong dollar means foreign currencies are relatively weak, the same logic suggests that imported goods and services are cheaper and US imports of everything, including wine, will rise.

When the dollar's value falls, however, imports are more expensive and exports are cheaper to foreign buyers. A weaker dollar therefore encourages exports and reduces imports, all else being equal. That's the basic relationship. It is more complicated in the real world, with multiple currencies that rise and fall relative to each other by different amounts and rates of speed, but the basics will do for now. Many people mistakenly believe that a strong currency is always a good thing for a country, but you can see that the effects depend a lot on where you look. If your winery wants to export wine, then a strong dollar is a headwind. If your business imports bulk wine from abroad for your brand, then a strong dollar helps keep costs down and margins up. Even if your winery neither exports nor imports wine, you are still affected by exchange rates through their impact on imported elements of your product chain, such as corks, capsules, and maybe the glass bottles, and of course because your wine may compete in the domestic market with now-cheaper imports. Exchange rates affect businesses, whether they know it or not.

The fact that most exchange rates are variable—set by market forces rather than governments—introduces an additional element of risk into international transactions. Most daily exchange-rate changes are small, and there are financial techniques to hedge the risks, but sometimes, exchange-rate movements are very large and can have substantial impacts on wine markets.

As the COVID-19 pandemic set in during 2020–2021, for example, the US dollar fell substantially relative to the euro. This was an unexpected event (and therefore a wild card) because the conventional wisdom held that international investors would flock to the dollar during uncertain times because of the secure liquidity its deep markets promise. But there were other factors at work, including commitments by the Federal Reserve to keep interest rates very low to fight a pandemic-induced recession. And so the dollar fell instead.

Normally you would expect US wine exports to increase due to the falling dollar, but in this case, they had nowhere to go—wine sales in Europe generally fell during the pandemic because supermarket and online buying did not make up for lost on-premise sales. Because the falling dollar made imports of European wine more expensive to US buyers, many EU wine businesses found themselves in a real economic crisis. Their domestic market was cut in half by lost bar and restaurant sales; exports to the US were diminished by the foreign-exchange effect; and for some, Trump-era tit-for-tat tariffs further deepened the crisis.

DUTCH DISEASE AND PARALLEL IMPORTS

Because we are talking about exchange rates and wild-card effects, I can't resist telling you about a situation that occurred in 2010 that resulted in Australia importing its own exported wine in a process called "parallel imports." Does that sound crazy? Here is what happened.

Australia's natural-resources exports were booming at the time, so demand for the Australian dollar caused the currency to increase in value. This was bad for the Aussie wine industry because the strong currency increased the cost to foreign buyers. It was a case of what economists call the Dutch disease, where success in one sector of the economy boosts the currency value and creates headwinds for other sectors.

Some Australian wine producers sought to maintain export sales by keeping their prices low in foreign markets—absorbing some of the exchange costs to be competitive in key markets. So, in effect, they sold their wine in some foreign markets for less than they charged at home. In a few cases, the difference was so large that, when combined with the very strong Aussie currency, an Australian retailer could actually buy Australian wine in Brazil and ship it back to Australia for less than if they bought the wine directly from the local producers. Thus, ships carrying Australian wine to Brazil passed other ships taking similar Australian wine back home. The *Sydney Morning Herald* reported,

> Parallel importing is . . . hurting business as supermarket chains and some of the bigger independent bottleshop chains bypass Australian brand licensees and import from third parties in countries including Brazil, Malaysia and the US. Parallel importing hit record levels in the past year as the dollar continued to strengthen and retailers, looking for ways to drive prices down and exert control over their suppliers, became more aggressive in importing.[3]

Parallel imports are not the norm for international trade, but this case demonstrates just how much exchange rates can affect trade and wine in extreme cases. As wine has become more global, the financial elements of globalization necessarily affect it more than in the past.

WHAT'S DIFFERENT THIS TIME?

So what's different about the wine economy now? Why call out an economic crisis when it is very clear that the global wine industry, or at least important segments of it, are nearly always in crisis? Isn't economic crisis the normal condition for wine?

Yes, of course you are right, depending on how we think about what *crisis* and *normal* mean in the wine context. But does the fact that wine lurches from crisis to crisis make the problem any less important? Crisis? No crisis? You can argue both sides, but it should be clear that the wine industry faces a future full of economic risk and uncertainty because wine doesn't face *just* an economic crisis. The simultaneous existence of environmental crisis and identity crisis (aka the triple crisis) makes this a point of reckoning.

And then there is the Rumsfeld dilemma, which I've named after former US secretary of defense Donald Rumsfeld. Rumsfeld once famously divided strategic knowledge into four parts. There are known knowns, he said, which are things you know you know. Then there are known unknowns, the questions you ask but don't have answers for yet. There are also unknown knowns, which is knowledge that you don't yet realize is important. And finally, you have unknown unknowns, things you don't know you don't know but should! I hope that's clear.

From an economic standpoint, the known knowns for wine indicate high risk. There is the wheel-of-fortune cycle, of course, and also significant structural shifts between consumer generations (the boomer-millennial transition) and between Old World and New World markets. Globalization is a known unknown. We just don't know if the global markets' receding tide as trade barriers appear will be an enduring trend or not. The wild cards are the unknown unknowns, and we have experienced so many of these in the last few years that we have to wonder if more dark clouds are on the horizon. Or have they passed?

Just one thing is certain: If you want to make a small fortune in the wine business, it helps to start with a large one.

THE ELEPHANT IN THE ROOM

Wine's Identity Crisis

Wine is suffering from a serious identity crisis, and how could it not? We are living in the age of identity. Identity politics. Identity marketing. Selfies, selfies, selfies. As the princess sings in Elton John's musical *Aida*, "I am what I wear and how I dress," and what I post and who I "like." How could wine not be a part of and influenced by the identity phenomenon?

WHAT A WINE LABEL REVEALS

Come with me one last time to study the wine wall. This time, let's focus on the labels, which are the most obvious statement of a wine's identity. I know that they say that you cannot judge a book by its cover, but that's not really true. People do it all the time. Isn't the cover of *this* book terrific? Didn't it make you want to see what is inside the covers? You shouldn't judge a wine by its label, either, but everyone does it.

Some labels show bucolic vineyards or ornate, historic winery buildings. "Critter" wines show cute animals of one sort or another—frogs, penguins, eagles, squirrels. Wine names may be hard to remember, but animal images stick in the memory like those insanely addictive internet cat videos. Keep looking, and you will see that wine takes on all sorts of identities based on label design.

One of the noteworthy trends of the last dozen years has been an explosion in the number of wine brands and therefore wine labels, and this phenomenon is partly explained by the age of identity. Smart wine marketers target their products to particular consumer identities. Barefoot Wine was a leader in this trend, as I explain in an earlier chapter, and 19 Crimes succeeds despite breaking all the conventional rules because its target audience of male millennials understands how drinking wine with sad men on the label reinforces their outlaw identities. Some consumers identify in complex ways, so the number of possible identity brands is nearly endless.

Imagine if you were a Martian who fell to earth in front of the wine wall. Clearly, you'd understand that all these products were related; the basic bottle shape would give it away. But what would you make of all the different label identities? How could these products be connected? And why are some so much more expensive than others? If the "man from Mars" thought experiment strikes you as foolish, then please remember this: Every newcomer to wine is that Martian fallen to earth, and each of them either finds a way to figure out the wine wall's identity code or simply walks away.

This is an example of a sort of paradox that economists find interesting. Have you heard of the paradox of thrift? If you decide to get a better handle on your finances by saving more and spending less, then it is good for your personal economy. But when *everyone* does it, total spending, which creates total income, can fall, and everyone is *worse off*, unless there is some offsetting fiscal stimulus. In the case of wine brands, an individual wine company benefits from creating a distinctive, memorable brand, but the industry may suffer an identity crisis when so many wineries follow suit that the wine wall becomes a blur. Wine brands benefit, but brand wine (the identity of wine itself) can suffer. That's the paradox of wine brands.

THE PARADOX OF WINE BRANDS

The paradox of wine brands is perhaps especially important for the original Old World wine brands, the appellation system. Appellations are losing clout in two ways. They are under assault from above by climate change, which makes their strict regulations of grape varieties, viticultural practices, and blending formulae increasingly irrelevant. Bordeaux's acceptance of grape varieties from hotter regions is one example of how serious the issue can be and what actions are necessary to cope. Appellations are also under attack from below by regionally designated wines that are free of many of the appellation rules and so can compete in the market on the basis of proprietary brands. Many Super-Tuscan wines, which bear only a relatively low-status regional appellation, fetch higher prices than wines (often by the same producers) that display an official Chianti logo, for example.

This problem is especially noticeable here in the United States, where the list of American viticultural areas (AVAs) grows longer each year, as winemaking regions are divided into smaller and smaller plots. I'm a true dismal science Scrooge, so my first reaction is always to think about the economic value of the new designations and subdesignations whenever new AVAs are announced.

Only a few American appellations have substantial economic value in the sense that a bottle of wine is worth more if the magic name appears on it than if it doesn't. Napa is a good example of an AVA that pays. Many if not most AVA designations add little monetary value, and sometimes they might actually subtract value, generally by confusing consumers who wonder what it all means and how one is different from another.

It took me a long time to get over my focus on money and to think about other factors. In many cases, the goal of an AVA is simply identity—the desire to be something particular in a generic world. There might be a bit of FOMO (fear of missing out) in that, too. I get that. We live in the age of identity. Identity is its own reward. Why should wine be different? Another result, if not a goal, can be solidarity because having an AVA application approved is not an easy thing and requires winegrowers to work together. Once they've worked together to create an appellation, perhaps other opportunities to cooperate can be found, too. That's not a trivial thing.

A MODEST PROPOSAL

The role of AVAs in creating or strengthening identity and solidarity made me think of a little-known political-economy theory called the North Dakota plan. Its creator was the famous economist John Kenneth Galbraith, and the idea was this: The nation-state is a good thing in part because it gives its citizens sovereignty, which is valuable, especially if you haven't got it. More states would mean more sovereignty and more benefits. Okay so far?

But sovereignty is troublesome because one state's sovereign actions can sometimes threaten another state's sovereignty, and in worst-case scenarios, conflict and even war break out. How can the world maximize the good of sovereignty while minimizing the bad of war? The solution, Galbraith proposed in 1978, tongue firmly in cheek, was the North Dakota plan. Divide the world into dozens of nation-states, each about the size and shape of North Dakota. North Dakota is more or less a rectangle, if you haven't looked at a map recently, so the new borders wouldn't necessarily take into account geography or history. They'd be completely arbitrary.

There would be lots of small states—so lots of presidents, prime ministers, foreign ministers, and sovereigns. But each country would be too small to have much of an army or navy, so conflict would be limited. Their focus would have to be more on how to live together because their ability to meddle in other countries' business would be limited. I think I recall a variation on the theory where each country would be given one small nuclear device to deter enemies. The idea was that no one would ever use their nuke because, with it gone, they would be defenseless. Peace would reign supreme.

To the best of my knowledge, no one ever took Galbraith's modest proposal for a world of North Dakotas seriously, which is probably just as well. But it inspires me to propose my own satiric plan for American AVAs, which you can probably already guess. Why not maximize the number of AVAs by covering the wine country map with hundreds and hundreds of them in arbitrary shapes and sizes? I'd shape them like pieces in a jigsaw puzzle, but you can have squares or triangles if you prefer. Each one would have a name, of course, and an identity. More AVAs, more identity, and everyone is better off. What could go wrong?

Each would face a challenge, too, which would require solidarity to solve. With completely arbitrary borders—unlike the borders today that are sometimes determined by a mixture of terroir and politics—geography could not be relied on to make an AVA distinctive. The growers and winemakers within each block would have to work together to create a real identity—a common blend, style, or signature wine grape variety, for example. They'd have to work to make the AVA mean something because otherwise it would be just another meaningless, soon-forgotten shape on the map and name on the label.

The thing about modest proposals is that they are not always what they seem. The most famous modest proposal—Jonathan Swift's suggestion that impoverished Irish parents should eat their starving children—wasn't intended to encourage murder or cannibalism. It was meant to shock readers into recognizing the harsh and heartless treatment of Ireland's poor and the dire conditions they experienced. It worked, too, waking up English citizens to the reality of their government's Ireland policies.

John Kenneth Galbraith's North Dakota plan probably reflected his experiences as a diplomat in the Kennedy administration (he was US ambassador to India). He knew that big, powerful states were no guarantee of peace and prosperity—in fact, they were often just the opposite (think Cold War mutually assured destruction). His North Dakota thought experiment flipped reality in search of a better solution to world problems. No one would seriously consider my North Dakota plan for AVAs. It is ridiculous. But this is what American wine (and maybe not just American wine) could more or less look like in thirty years if current appellation trends persist. It won't happen all at once, just a couple more AVAs here and there. But it will add right up all the same, and then, well, there you are.

Maybe AVAs were the best way to establish identity back when there were only a few of them—remember that the very first AVA granted back in 1980 was not Napa (it came a few months later) but Augusta in Missouri. Maybe today, when the AVA count is in the hundreds, there are better paths to follow. If not, then the future could be a jigsaw puzzle world of wine.

Limiting their number wouldn't be enough to protect appellation brands, however. Proprietary brands with lots of marketing muscle behind them are a bigger threat, as *New York Times* wine critic Eric Asimov notes in a column about a new line of Penfolds wine, which includes two blends of Cabernet Sauvignon wines from California and South Australia.[1] They call them Penfolds Bin 149 Wine of the World Cabernet Sauvignon and Penfolds Quantum Bin 98 Wine of the World Cabernet Sauvignon. They retail for $149 and $700, respectively. Penfolds is an iconic Australian wine brand owned by Treasury Wine Estates. Its flagship Penfolds Grange Shiraz is a delicious blend of wines from different areas in Australia. Hoping to leverage the brand's success, Treasury has started including wines from other places in the lineup, so there is a Penfolds Champagne from France. Treasury has significant investments in the United States (it owns the historic Beringer Vineyards in Napa Valley, for example), so there is now a Penfolds Bin 704 Napa Valley Cabernet and a Penfolds Bin 600 California Cabernet Shiraz.

If Penfolds' Australian wines are delicious and its Napa Valley wines are delicious, too, then why not blend the two together? They might be even more delicious. But, as Asimov notes, they undermine the idea that wine should have a sense of place, an identity rooted in terroir. Somewhere-ness, one of wine's special properties (and a terroirist shibboleth), is replaced by nowhere-ness. Suppose that nowhere wine is delicious. Are you terroirist enough to pass it by? If so, then what happens to the regional identity that wine producers have invested so much to develop? Wine's identity crisis continues to unfold.

THE ALCOHOL WARS

One important part of *Wine Wars II* is that the battles aren't just about wine anymore. The bigger struggle is for alcoholic beverage market share, which includes traditional wine, beer, spirits, cider, ready-to-drink cocktails, and hard-seltzer-type products. That's always been true, but it is a more important factor now. There doesn't seem to be as large a group of millennials as there were boomers who identify as primarily wine drinkers. If millennials drink alcohol at all (and many younger people do not or are "sober curious"), then they prefer variety and switch back and forth among the different beverage categories. Wine has some noteworthy advantages in this conflict but some disadvantages, too. In the United States, for example, it is generally more expensive on a per serving basis than most spirits and beer. And while wine labels can be effective in establishing identity, they create problems in other ways.

Are you the sort of person who looks at every new garment to see where it's made (and of what material) and studies the nutritional information on the back labels of the groceries that you buy? Me, too, although I don't claim to be consistent in these investigations, and I am sure that I miss a lot. Many people take an intense interest in the products they buy, especially food and drink because they go into our bodies. Calories per serving, along with sodium, carbohydrates, and protein, are important to many people. It is interesting—and maybe a problem—that wine and other alcoholic beverages are for the most part exempt from nutritional reporting. Wine labels must tell consumers the alcohol by volume and warn them of health dangers but do not have to display ingredients, calories, or other factors that are required for juices, sodas, milk, and other beverages.

Interestingly, the popular Italian brand Stella Rosa wine is an exception to the current requirements—calories, carbs, and so forth are clearly listed. Why? As I understand it, the reason is that because Stella Rosa contains just 5 percent alcohol by volume (below a 7 percent regulatory threshold), it is regulated by the FDA as food (nutritional facts) as well as by the Alcohol and Tobacco Tax and Trade Bureau (TTB) as alcohol. Because the alcohol is so low, it is labeled as "partially fermented grape must" as opposed to wine. I am not sure that anyone buys Stella Rosa because of the nutrition information (it is one of the hottest wine brands today), but maybe the lack of such information is already affecting sales of wines in some market spaces. Consumers purchase a lot of different products, and they don't really need to buy anything that doesn't take responsibility and own its list of ingredients and nutritional profile.

I believe that wine, beer, and spirits will eventually be required to list their ingredients and nutritional data. I wonder what would happen if wine were to take a voluntary step and be more transparent now as a way to shape the narrative. I know there are some who think transparency would backfire—consumers would turn away if they knew what a bottle of wine really contains or how many calories are in a serving of Chardonnay. But look at Stella's sales.

White Claw, the ridiculously popular alcoholic seltzer product, has a nutrition label, too, and it is clear that it uses this to its advantage by exactly hitting the critical "100 calories per serving" number. When is wine going to wise up? I know that there is fear that if you tell consumers what is in the bottle in terms of ingredients, calories, carbohydrates, and so on, they will turn away. Really? Does anyone imagine that consumers think that glass of Chardonnay is as calorie-free as Coke Zero? The fact that Stella Rosa sells so much sweetish wine with the numbers plainly visible suggests that lots of wine drinkers understand the situation.

THE ELEPHANT IN THE ROOM

As things stand now here in the United States, wineries do not have to list ingredients and nutritional facts for most wines. They do have to include three things on the label, however: alcoholic strength; the presence of added sulfites, if any; and a warning about the dangers of alcohol. In other words, current US regulations tell wine buyers that the bottle includes dangerous alcohol and a dangerous chemical, sulfites, and they should beware.

The sulfite requirement has always been a puzzle because only a very small fraction of consumers react badly to sulfites. Sulfites are naturally occurring in wine and have been used to prevent spoilage since the time of the Romans. A glass of wine generally has fewer sulfites than a serving of fast-food French fries, which needless to say carry no warning label. Most people who get a "sulfite headache" are reacting to something else. But the sulfite warning endures and is part of wine's identity in the United States. More than one person has asked me why American wine has sulfites and European wine does not. The difference is not the wine so much as labeling requirements.

I would happily accept nutritional labeling, which would give wine a food identity, in exchange for the end of the sulfite warning. But the real identity problem is alcohol. Wine is an art, a craft, a science, a nutritional beverage, and a part of our cultural heritage, but to many, it is one thing only: a dangerous drug—alcohol. This is true around the world and of course in America, too, where it is part of our Prohibition hangover.

All the attention paid to wine-identity marketing risks ignoring this most important element of the identity crisis. People must imagine that the positive story of wine will tell itself. Well, let me clue you in. It won't. Someone has to tell it, or it won't be told. So I think there are lessons to be learned by studying the Wine in Moderation movement that began in Europe and has now spread to many corners of the wine world. Wine in Moderation was founded in 2008 at a time when the European wine industry faced a growing threat. It wasn't just that wine demand was falling—that had been going on for a couple of decades. And it wasn't just the global financial crisis, either, although that didn't help. It was rising antialcohol sentiments and policies that threatened wine, both as an economic activity and as an integral part of European culture.

The wine industry was slow to organize to defend itself. So much attention was given to wine-brand marketing that the antialcohol threat was mainly ignored. The fact that the positive case for wine includes a caution that sometimes it is best to choose not to drink wine might have played a part, too. Why spend money telling customers not to buy your product? But such messages are part of social responsibility. Beer can be a good role model here. If you watch European sports broadcasts, you will be sure to see the "drink responsibly" message along with huge posters promoting "0.0" alcohol-free beer alternatives.

Wine in Moderation today aims to promote a "sustainable wine culture" through its work with such regional wine industry organizations as Vinos de Chile, Unioni Italiani Vini, ACIBEV, and FEV in Chile, Italy, Portugal, and Spain, respectively. Several global wine companies (Pernod Ricard, Möet Hennessy, Sogrape) and a host of other groups, including WSET and the Institute of the Masters of Wine, now support and implement Wine in Moderation programs around the world. Wine in Moderation has moved the needle in its target regions, according to its most recent report, which is important. Once wine is reduced to an alcoholic least-common-denominator identity, then Einstein's law kicks in, and the wine wars are lost.

DEMOLITION MAN WINE FUTURE

We are getting close to the end of this chapter and book, so please humor me with a little thought experiment. What might the future of wine look like under the admittedly unlikely "straight-line trend projection" circumstances, where we take today's trends and fly them straight out to wherever they take us? Pondering this thought, I unexpectedly found myself channeling a 1993 Sylvester Stallone, Wesley Snipes, and Sandra Bullock film called *Demolition Man*. Stallone plays a police officer named John Spartan, who is put into suspended animation in 1996, only to be awakened thirty-six years into the future in 2032 in order to catch Wesley Snipe's bad-guy character.

Stallone's updated Rip Van Winkle encounters a lot that surprises or shocks him, including, in one scene, the inconvenient truth about retail consolidation run amok. Invited to dinner and dancing at a Taco Bell, he can't help but think, "Taco Bell? Really?" But it really is, as Bullock's character explains. Taco Bell was the only chain to survive the franchise wars, and now all restaurants are Taco Bells. "No way!" Way!

I don't think wine plays a part in the film, but let's keep going in this spirit and see where it takes us. The fictional John Spartan goes shopping for wine in 2032 San Angeles, and the first place he sees is a big-box MoVino store, bigger than the biggest wine-beer-spirits stores of the past but recognizably the same concept. He continues on in search for a small, specialist shop but soon runs across another MoVino. And then another and another, and slowly it comes to him that just as all restaurants are Taco Bells, all wine is now retailed by MoVino.

How did MoVino win this fictional competition over other chains? Because, in this made-up universe, they drew on the growing consolidation in distribution channels. Yes, all wine is sold by MoVino in 2032 because they are a wholly owned subsidiary of NSEW (North-South-East-West), the only company to survive the vicious distributor wars of 2025. There are lots of different superpremium brands on offer at the big-box wine store of the future, but the vast array of colorful labels and fictional names actually disguises a certain sameness. Much of the wine comes from the same few large producers, the ones who were able to secure reliable, quality grape supplies in the grape wars before 2026, when the last independent high-quality vineyards left after the big climate change spike were swallowed up. When John Spartan looks closely at the superpremium white wines he favors (because they pair so well with his favorite Taco Bell fish tacos), he slowly realizes that they are all made by a few large multinational firms in New Zealand. Just as Taco Bell conquered food, the Kiwis were the victors of the white wine wars.

The one constant of US wine-import statistics in recent years has been that New Zealand Sauvignon Blanc imports will grow, often faster than any other import category. I keep waiting for the run to end (and I know Kiwi producers who hold their breath and cross their fingers because they are worried, too). But nothing has stopped or even seriously slowed down New Zealand wine imports so far. And you know where that can lead!

What about inexpensive wine? Glad you asked, because that's where John Spartan had his harshest shock—it made him want to give up wine altogether. It seems that as grape supply became less and less secure and falling prices pushed basic grape producers to other crops, like almonds and pistachios, wineries were forced to weaken links to particular regions and then to grapes themselves. Appellations and geographic designations generally are an expensive luxury if you're not sure if you can buy the grapes you need to maintain a region-specific

brand, so they had to go. And then wine companies gave up specific grape variety designations for the wines for essentially the same reason. All inexpensive
wines in 2032 are now proprietary blends. No one knows what might be in the
bottle, box, or can or where it might have come from. Not many seem to care.

Absent place of origin and clearly identified grape-variety components, inexpensive wines evolved into branded alcoholic beverages, and once consumers
accepted that, there wasn't any reason they had to be made out of grapes anymore. The laws were rewritten to allow inexpensive wine-like products to be
made and marketed, and people lapped them up. Wine for the masses endured
but in an ersatz Taco Bell kind of way. Or at least that's where bad economic
analysis (and not enough sleep) takes you if you follow recent trends to ridiculous extremes. The future? Taco Bell? No Way! That'll never happen. Don't
worry. Go back to sleep. G'night!

WINE WARS II

It is almost time for our final wine tasting, but before I go, I think we need to
pause to consider where *Wine Wars II* has taken us and where we go from here.
The first edition of *Wine Wars* is organized around three powerful forces: globalization, commodification, and the terroirist resistance. *Wine Wars II* finds all
three forces still at work but in different ways. In particular, the power of wine
brands and the pressure of commodification seem stronger than before, making
the terroirist resistance even more important.

Wine Wars II introduces the idea of wine's triple crisis: environmental crisis,
economic crisis, and identity crisis. Although wine always seems to be suffering
one sort of crisis or another, this chaotic combination presents a challenge that
is greater than in the past. So what does the future hold for wine and for those
of us who love it? I don't know the answer, but I've found it useful to think
about different scenarios. Here are three for you to ponder as you pour yourself
another glass of wine.

I call the first scenario the golden age, and given what I have just said about
the *Demolition Man* wine, you probably think this the most unlikely possible
future for wine. And it is true that a golden age is an ambitious projection
because it can only happen if somehow the wine industry and the world in
which it is embedded can get climate change under control. Without strong
action on climate change, it is hard to see how wine's story can have a happy
ending. But the wine industry has taken the lead in climate change, so there's
hope, and I am optimistic that the economic and identity crisis storms can be

navigated, too. Why such optimism? Because I have seen how America recovered from Prohibition and its hangover. If wine can come back from that, then anything is possible.

But history doesn't always repeat itself the way we might like. Don't forget that in order for wine to recover from its low point, it first had to get there. So perhaps we are headed for my second scenario, the dark age, where environment, economy, and identity all conspire to rob wine of its vital place in society and culture. It won't necessarily be *Demolition Man* again. It could be much worse. Think about those Prohibition years and the decades that followed. Globalization collapsed. Wine's identity was reduced to its alcoholic strength. Now add the climate change crisis, and you have a dark age indeed.

Golden age? Dark age? What other futures could be waiting? Let me suggest a new-age scenario. Not new age in its "crystal-gazing" popular culture form but a really new system. New wine people (generational changes), new grapes and wines (environmental changes), new ways of thinking about what wine is and ought to be. Wine will change, but the idea of wine may change even more.

What would the new age look like? I haven't a clue. But I know that wine has survived dark ages before and somehow found a way to remake itself so that it is both relevant and loved. The path may not be direct or easy, but a way can be found. You see, even after *Wine Wars* and *Wine Wars II*, I still have grape expectations.

Now turn the page for your final wine-tasting assignment.

WINE WARS II TASTING

O ur final tasting takes us to Portugal, where we can find all the themes developed in this book and where, by our choice of wine, we can decide what we think about the likely outcome of *Wine Wars II*.

Portugal practically invented globalization, as Martin Page's fascinating book *The First Global Village* argues persuasively.[1] You can find Portuguese influences all around the world—from New England to Brazil to Angola to South Africa to India to Japan to Hawaii and more. How do you say "thank you" in Japanese? *Arigato*, which derives from the Portuguese *obrigado*, will do the trick.

Madeira, the fortified wine from the Portuguese island of the same name, was certainly one of the world's first global wines. Madeira wine is practically indestructible and so perfectly suited to global commerce in the days of sailing ships. Fortified and then treated with heat, initially in the holds of the ships themselves and then eventually in the lofts of wine lodges on the island, Madeira could safely travel the world and retain its freshness and quality. Yes, it is true that the signers of the Declaration of Independence toasted their work with glasses of Madeira wine.

Portugal is also important when we think about the power of wine brands. The popular wine Mateus Rosé, named for the famous Palácio de Mateus in Vila Real, was once one of the best-selling wines in the world and is still very popular today. And the Sandeman brand is also world famous. The distinctive figure of the Don with his cape and hat is instantly recognizable. If you visit the Sandeman Port lodges when you are in Porto, you can tour a colorful museum tracing the brand's evolution over the decades as seen through its distinctive advertising images.

Portugal is home to both famous terroir and committed terroirists. The Douro Valley has the distinction of being the world's first formally defined wine appellation, its lines drawn way back in 1756. And although Portuguese wine-makers are great innovators, they are also intensely protective of their traditions, as anyone who has visited a Port house or, even better, the exciting new World of Wine center in Vila Nova de Gaia across the river from Porto, will attest.

Portugal makes another contribution to the world of wine: natural cork bottle closures. Corticeira Amorim is the world's largest producer of cork stop-pers, and Sue and I have had the pleasure of seeing the cork forests and visit-ing Amorim cork factories both in Alentejo and near the Porto headquarters. Although it will delay our tasting by a few minutes, I'd like to tell you about our cork journey. I promise you, it will be worth the wait.

AN OPTIMISTIC IMPULSE

It is impossible to drive through the Alentejo region of Portugal without seeing the dark trees that dot the landscape. Pretty soon you notice the lines on the trunks where the bark has been harvested, and then you know for sure that you are in a cork oak (*Quercus suber*) forest, the densest concentration of these trees in the world.

Planting a cork oak tree is a statement of faith in the future. The first harvest must wait fifteen years, and then the cork will be of low quality, unsuitable for natural cork closures. The second and better harvest that yields more usable cork comes nine years later. Only nine years after that (and every nine years into the future) can the highest-quality cork be taken. Few other things in the world of wine (producing forty-year-old Tawny Port, for example) can compare to cork in terms of optimistic forward thinking.

Cork is an ancient product—the Greeks, Egyptians, and Romans all sealed their wine jars with cork. The harvesting of it is laborious handwork because each tree has its own configuration. Photos of modern cork harvests could easily be mistaken for medieval paintings.

Stepping into the Amorim factory in Coruche, you get an initial sense of moving forward in time from the Middle Ages to the Industrial Revolution. There is still a lot of handwork here. Sorting the processed cork bark pieces, for example, still requires human judgment as they are inspected and graded for quality one at a time. The key to making a profit in cork is to waste nothing, so each cork piece must go to its best use, and the waste at each step is recycled into a lower-priced product.

Almost nothing is thrown away. One item that was headed for the power-supplying waste burner was a piece of cork that was badly infected with TCA, the source of cork taint. What a horrible smell! Until a machine can consistently detect all the potential problems with cork, including TCA, cracking, insect damage, and so on, these workers' jobs are very secure. The factory was loud with the clamor of industrial machinery, as every task that could be mechanized had been. It gave me a sense of what nineteenth-century British textile mills must have been like.

Interestingly, the finest cork closures made from the best-quality raw material are hand-punched by skilled craftsmen. These corks need to be as close to perfect as possible, and so far nothing can replace the human eye for seeing just where the cork's sweet spot is (and what parts should be recycled down the line for other products).

It would be easy to think of cork just this way—a medieval product made using Industrial Revolution technology—but this viewpoint misses a lot, as we learned when we visited Amorim's second factory, near Porto. Here we saw many of the same processes as in the south, but the focus was different because our hosts wanted us to see the progress that has been made at improving cork closures and addressing the issues that allowed synthetic stoppers and screw-cap technology to make dramatic inroads in this market.

Innovative production processes and seriously obsessive attention to detail have now all but eliminated the incidence of detectable TCA contamination in Amorim corks throughout the product line, which is a big deal and came only after intense and costly research and process rethinking. But that was not good enough, so Amorim unveiled NDtech corks. Amorim scientists guided us into the controlled environment, where we saw the NDtech (think nondetectable TCA levels) process at work. NDtech really does individually inspect each and every cork that goes through the process and guarantees them all to be TCA-free at human-sensory-threshold levels.

I find it interesting that cork is so many things at once. It is a natural product, of course, but one that is necessarily harvested and then processed by hand and manufactured using machines and processes from a variety of periods. It is also increasingly a technological product. Making excellent cork closures is complicated, as we saw at the Amorim factories, and doing so profitably is even more complicated. We were impressed with the way that every scrap and bit of cork is put to use in closures and other cork products, and every ounce of value is realized. Environmental and economic sustainability go hand-in-hand.

Meeting the challenge of synthetic and screw-cap closures has not been easy for cork producers, who faced an economic crisis and saw market share disappear to the competition. Hard work, expensive research, and technical innovation have turned this around, however, and now many consumers and wineries who moved away from cork in the past are taking a new look.

So cork is a way to think about wine's triple crisis, which obviously is not limited to wine. The TCA taint that once made cork so vulnerable to competition is now all but eliminated. The cork industry's role in battling climate change is also clearly established. I think it is fair to say that cork is still working through its identity crisis issues, as we all are. But, as I note earlier, you have to be an optimist to plant a cork tree, and more and more of them are planted every year.

THE TASTE OF *WINE WARS II*

So how do you feel about the future of wine after reading these pages? Here are suggestions of delicious Portuguese wines to help you make up your mind.

Are you still fresh and ready to celebrate? Then have the aperitif they drink in Porto, a White Port and Tonic. Dry White Port is an underappreciated treat; Taylor's Chip Dry White Port is a favorite. Try it on the rocks with tonic and a bit of citrus and mint. Refreshing! And you can find it ready-made in 250 milliliter cans that are as convenient as they are delicious.

Do you feel confused or uncertain? Do you need to give these important issues more consideration? Then maybe you should have a philosopher's wine to help you think things through. I'd recommend a nice Tawny Port by Graham's or Sandeman. The ten-year-old bottling is great, but if you can afford it, the twenty will be even better.

Or are you ready for a terroirist challenge? Portugal has many interesting regions and wines beyond Port and the always-popular Vinho Verde. I challenge you to look deeper into Portuguese wines and see what new discoveries await you. I spoke at a wine and sustainability conference in historic Évora a couple of years ago and got to know Alentejo and its wines a bit. The reds were deep and intriguing, especially those made with Alicante Bouschet. Try Herdade do Mouchão if you can find it. But we were really grabbed by the white wines, blends of native varieties. The region is so hot, so how can they make such vibrant white wines? A paradox! Tasting the Alentejo white wines triggers a memory, as wine often does.

One of the highlights of the conference was a dinner that featured a group of burly men with hands that showed years of hard work who sang the famous polyphonic Cante Alentejano that is unique to this region. It was a moving experience to hear the soft singing coming from such an unlikely source. Another paradox! And it was pure joy when we learned that the singers were winegrowers—members of the Vidigueira cooperative. And to top it off, we were drinking their excellent wines. What an experience!

So which wine do you choose? Celebrate? Contemplate? Explore? Speaking only for myself, I suggest you try them all! Cheers, and thank you for reading *Wine Wars II.*

NOTES

CHAPTER 2: GOT WINE?

1. See Thomas Pinney, *A History of Wine in America: From Prohibition to the Present* (Berkeley: University of California Press, 2005) for the most comprehensive analysis of America's Prohibition problem and the continuing hangover.

2. Assuming that wine bottles held four-fifths of a quart.

3. Hugh Johnson, "The Wines of California," in *History in a Glass: Sixty Years of Wine Writing from* Gourmet, ed. Ruth Reichl, 155–61 (New York: Modern Library, 2005).

4. I use Robert Mondavi as a symbol of the rising fine wine movement in America starting in the 1970s in the same way that I used Gallo as a symbol of the post-Prohibition rebirth. Obviously, there were many more winemakers involved. See Pinney's *History of Wine* for a more complete account.

5. See George M. Taber, *Judgment of Paris: California vs. France and the Historic 1976 Paris Tasting That Revolutionized Wine* (New York: Scribner, 2005).

6. Karl Storchmann, "Wine Economics," *Journal of Wine Economics*, Volume 7, Number 1, 2012, Pages 1–33. Storchmann made his "Milk is all over" comment during a presentation at a meeting of the American Association of Wine Economists in June 2014.

A TOAST TO *WINE WARS II*

1. Under the terms of the merger between Möet Hennessy and Louis Vuitton, the combined company name is spelled out as Möet Hennessy Louis Vuitton but abbreviated as LVMH. Yes, I know that's confusing, but there you have it.

CHAPTER 5: THE CENTER OF THE UNIVERSE

1. Wine market data in this chapter is taken from International Organisation of Vine and Wine, *State of the World Vitivinicultural Sector in 2020* (Paris: International Organisation of Vine and Wine, April 2021).

CHAPTER 6: MARTIANS VERSUS WAGNERIANS

1. Thomas Pinney, *A History of Wine in America: From Prohibition to the Present* (Berkeley: University of California Press, 2005), 367.
2. Pinney, *History*, 367.
3. Pinney, *History*, 367–68.

CHAPTER 7: THEY ALWAYS BUY THE TEN-CENT WINE

1. The wine is officially called Charles Shaw Wine. Charles Shaw was a Napa Valley fine wine producer who experienced business reversals some years ago. Franzia bought the well-regarded brand, which he repurposed as an extreme-value product.
2. The data cited here comes from NielsenIQ's regular reports in *Wine Business Monthly*, a wine-industry publication. NielsenIQ doesn't measure all wine sales in the United States—restaurant (aka on-premise) sales aren't counted, for example, and neither are many big-box-store sales. But what they do keep tabs on, which includes supermarkets and convenience stores, provides a revealing picture of what consumers are doing. The numbers here are from 2021 and look at sales of wine in glass bottles only, excluding bag-in-a-box, cans, and other alternative packaging formats.
3. Catharine Paddock, "Pleasure Experience of Wine Goes Up with Price," *Medical News Today,* January 15, 2008, www.medicalnewstoday.com/articles/93947.php.
4. Johan Almenberg and Anna Dreber, "When Does the Price Affect the Taste? Results from a Wine Experiment" (working paper 35, American Association of Wine Economists, April 2009), www.wine-economics.org/workingpapers/AAWE_WP35.pdf.
5. Rob McMillan of Silicon Valley Bank is frequently credited with coining the term *premiumization* to describe this phenomenon.
6. George A. Akerlof, "The Market for Lemons: Quality Uncertainty and the Market Mechanism," *Quarterly Journal of Economics* 84, no. 3 (1970): 488–500.

CHAPTER 8: OUTLAWS, PRISONERS, AND THE GREAT ESCAPE

1. I wrote about Hemming's study in "Vinonomics: The Mouton Cadet Index," *Wine Economist*, August 10, 2010, https://wineeconomist.com/2010/08/10/vinonomics -the-mouton-cadet-index/.

2. Richard Hemming, "Vinonomics v3: the wine price index, " *JancisRobinson .com* (23 July 2013) (URL: https://jancisrobinson.com/articles/vinonomics-v3-the-wine -price-index).

3. Yellow Tail data is taken from Felicity Carter, "Casellas at the Crossroads," *Meininger's Wine Business International*, October 10, 2007, www.wine-business-international.com/Company_Profiles_Casella_at_the_crossroads.html.

4. See W. Chan Kim and Renée Mauborgne, *Blue Ocean Strategy: How to Create Uncontested Market Space and Make the Competition Irrelevant*. Boston: Harvard Business School, 2005.

CHAPTER 9: *MONDOVINO* AND THE REVENGE OF THE TERROIRISTS

1. Matt Kramer of *Wine Spectator* is frequently credited with the "somewhere-ness" definition of *terroir*.

2. Jonathan Nossiter, however, is an American who comes across as French in the film: soft-spoken, multilingual, wearing distinctively continental clothing. He is the son of author and journalist Bernard Nossiter and grew up in France, Italy, and other countries. Ironically, Nossiter is in some ways to film what Rolland is to wine—a flying entrepreneur.

3. This is the original French title of Olivier Torrès's excellent book, with the collaboration of Dorothée Yaouanc, *The Wine Wars: The Mondavi Affair, Globalization and "Terroir,"* trans. Kirsty Snaith (New York: Palgrave Macmillan, 2006).

4. Dogs are featured prominently throughout the film. *Mondovino* did not win the prestigious Palme d'Or at the Cannes Film Festival, but it did win the Palme Dog, for best dog film. Seriously.

5. This is taken from a comment Nossiter makes in the director's narration to *Mondovino*.

6. Even Nossiter says this in his director's commentary on the DVD of the film.

7. The province of Roussillon, with which Languedoc if frequently linked, completes the arc.

8. It is interesting to note that Jean-Charles Boisset is married to Gina Gallo of the Gallo wine family. They live with their twin daughters in the old Mondavi house in Napa. The wine world is a small world after all!

9. Jonathan Nossiter, *Liquid Memory: Why Wine Matters* (New York: Farrar, Straus and Giroux, 2009). Original French edition published as *Le Goût et le Pouvoir* [*Taste and Power*] (Paris: Bernard Grasset, 2007).

10. These quotes are taken from Nossiter, *Liquid Memory*, 103.

CHAPTER 10: WE ARE ALL TERROIRISTS NOW

1. The quotes in this section are from Mitch Frank, "When Winemakers Attack," *Wine Spectator Online*, May 26, 2009, www.winespectator.com/webfeature/show/id/When-Winemakers-Attack_3080.

2. "Unleash the War on Terroir," *Economist*, December 19, 2007.

3. See Carolyn Wyatt, "French Wine-Growers Go Guerrilla," *BBC News*, June 17, 2007, news.bbc.co.uk/2/hi/6759953.stm. You can view a video of CRAV activists making the threat here.

4. Joseph Schumpeter (1883–1950). His best-known book on creative destruction is *The Theory of Economic Development*, first published in German in 1911. The English translation appeared in 1934.

5. Karl Polanyi (1886–1960). His best-known work is *The Great Transformation* (1944).

6. Michael Veseth, ed., *The New York Times Twentieth Century in Review: The Rise of the Global Economy* (New York: Routledge, 2002).

7. Jean-Robert Pitte, *Bordeaux/Burgundy: A Vintage Rivalry*, trans. M. B. DeBevoise (Berkeley: University of California Press, 2008).

8. This section is drawn from chapter 10 of Mike Veseth, *Around the World in Eighty Wines: Exploring Wine One Country at a Time* (Lanham, MD: Rowman & Littlefield, 2017).

9. "Impact Seminar Snapshot: Treasury Wine's Clarke on the Globalization of Winemaking," *Shanken News Daily*, March 25, 2015, http://www.shankennewsdaily.com/index.php/2015/03/25/12004/impact-seminar-snapshot-treasury-wines-clarke-on-the-globalization-of-wine-marketing/.

10. Deborah Parker Wong and Giancarlo Gariglio, eds., *Slow Wine Guide USA 2021* (Parker, CO: Outskirts Press, 2021).

CHAPTER 11: SILK ROAD TERROIRISTS

1. Thanks to Bob Calvert for this insight.

2. Jeannie Cho Lee, "Language of Taste," *Decanter* (July 2009): 78–79.

3. Cynthia Howson and Pierre Ly, *Adventures on the China Wine Trail: How Farmers, Local Governments, Teachers, and Entrepreneurs Are Rocking the Wine World* (Lanham, MD: Rowman & Littlefield, 2020).

4. Jane Anson, "Anson on Thursday: Vineyards on the roof of the world," *Decanter .com* 30 April, 2013. (URL: http://decanter.com/wine-news/opinion/news-blogs-anson/ anson-on-thursday-vineyards-on-the-roof-of-the-world-759/).

5. Li Dimei, "Marselan: The Future 'Signature' Grape of China," *Decanter China*, March 31, 2017.

A TERROIRIST TASTING

1. Jancis Robinson, Julia Harding, and José Vouillamoz, *Wine Grapes: A Complete Guide to 1,368 Varieties, Including Their Origins and Flavours* (New York: Ecco, 2012).

CHAPTER 12: THIS CHANGES EVERYTHING

1. Giuseppe di Lampedusa, *The Leopard*, trans. Archibald Colquhoun (New York: Pantheon Books, 1988), 40.

2. The Wine Intelligence study was prepared for a 2019 sustainable winegrowing summit. For a summary of the report, see Wine Institute, "New Consumer Research Presented at First US Sustainable Winegrowing Summit Shows Strong Interest in Sustainable Wine," accessed October 10, 2021, https://wineinstitute.org/press-releases/ new-consumer-research-presented-at-first-u-s-sustainable-winegrowing-summit-shows-strong-interest-in-sustainable-wine.

CHAPTER 13: HOW TO MAKE A SMALL FORTUNE

1. See Turrentine Brokerage, "Turrentine Wine Business Wheel of Fortune," 2020, https://turrentinebrokerage.com/wine-wheel/.

2. Kym Anderson, Signe Nelgen, and Vicente Pinella, *Global Wine Markets 1860 to 2016: A Statistical Compendium* (Adelaide: University of Adelaide Press, 2017).

3. Adele Ferguson, "New Year to Bring Cheaper Cheer," *Sydney Morning Herald*, December 23, 2010.

CHAPTER 14: THE ELEPHANT IN THE ROOM

1. Eric Asimov, "A Wine from Nowhere," *New York Times*, June 23, 2021.

WINE WARS II TASTING

1. Martin Page, *The First Global Village: How Portugal Changed the World* (Alfragide, Portugal: Casa Das Letras, 2002).

ACKNOWLEDGMENTS

It's been a long journey from that first conversation on the Silverado Trail to the book you have in your hands today. I am indebted to dozens of wine-industry people who have taken time to help me understand their business; to all the readers who have encouraged my work and offered constructive criticism; to the many wine-industry groups who invited me to speak and to learn about their regions; and to the University of Puget Sound, which supported my early research efforts. I could try to list all the individuals who have guided me on this path, but it would be too long, and inevitably I would forget someone. So let me thank just two special people who have been at the heart of this work from beginning to end.

My wife, Sue Veseth, has been an integral part of this enterprise right from the start. One of the great pleasures of these wine economics projects has been the opportunity for Sue and me to work together after careers spent working in different fields. Sue is a fountain of fresh ideas and a valuable source of constructive criticism. Sue is much better than I am at asking the key question and drawing out revealing answers. I literally could not have done all this without her.

I first met Susan McEachern when I was writing my book *Globaloney* and contacted Roman & Littlefield to see if they would like to publish it. Since then, we have worked together on *Globaloney* and *Globaloney 2.0* and then the wine economics books *Wine Wars*; *Extreme Wine*; *Money, Taste, and Wine*; and *Around the World in Eighty Wines*. Susan got the ball rolling for this book and then announced her retirement. I know she has left me in good hands at Rowman & Littlefield, but I will miss working with her. I wish her all the best in her active retirement life.

One final note of thanks: This book did not make itself. I appreciate the expertise and support of the professionals at Rowman & Littlefield: senior executive editor Charles Harmon, production editor Naomi Minkoff, and copyeditor Nicole Guinan.

SELECTED REFERENCES

Akerlof, George A. "The Market for Lemons: Quality Uncertainty and the Market Mechanism." *Quarterly Journal of Economics* 84, no. 3 (1970): 488–500.

Anderson, Kym. *Which Winegrape Varieties Are Grown Where?* Adelaide: University of Adelaide Press, 2020.

Anderson, Kym, Signe Nelgen, and Vicente Pinella. *Global Wine Markets 1860 to 2016: A Statistical Compendium.* Adelaide: University of Adelaide Press, 2017.

Cooper, Michael. *Wine Atlas of New Zealand.* 2nd ed. Auckland: Hodder Moa Beckett, 2008.

Howson, Cynthia, and Pierre Ly. *Adventures on the China Wine Trail: How Farmers, Local Governments, Teachers, and Entrepreneurs Are Rocking the Wine World.* Lanham, MD: Rowman & Littlefield, 2020.

International Organisation of Vine and Wine. *State of the World Vitivinicultural Sector in 2020.* Paris: International Organisation of Vine and Wine, April 2021.

Lee, Jeannie Cho. "Language of Taste." *Decanter,* July 2009, 78–79.

Levinson, Marc. *The Box: How the Shipping Container Made the World Smaller and the World Economy Bigger.* Princeton, NJ: Princeton University Press, 2008.

Nossiter, Jonathan. *Liquid Memory: Why Wine Matters.* New York: Farrar, Straus and Giroux, 2009.

———, dir. *Mondovino.* New York: THINKfilm, 2004. DVD.

Page, Martin. *The First Global Village: How Portugal Changed the World.* Alfragide, Portugal: Casa Das Letras, 2002.

Pinney, Thomas. *A History of Wine in America: From Prohibition to the Present.* Berkeley: University of California Press, 2005.

Pitte, Jean-Robert. *Bordeaux/Burgundy: A Vintage Rivalry.* Translated by M. B. DeBevoise. Berkeley: University of California Press, 2008.

Robinson, Jancis, Julia Harding, and José Vouillamoz. *Wine Grapes: A Complete Guide to 1,368 Varieties, Including Their Origins and Flavours.* New York: Ecco, 2012.

Taber, George M. *Judgment of Paris: California vs. France and the Historic 1976 Paris Tasting That Revolutionized Wine.* New York: Scribner, 2005.

Torrès, Olivier, with the collaboration of Dorothée Yaouanc. *The Wine Wars: The Mondavi Affair, Globalization and "Terroir."* Translated by Kirsty Snaith. New York: Palgrave Macmillan, 2006.

Veseth, Mike. *Around the World in Eighty Wines: Exploring Wine One Country at a Time.* Lanham, MD: Rowman & Littlefield, 2017.

———. *Extreme Wine: Searching the World for the Best, the Worst, the Outrageously Cheap, the Insanely Overpriced, and the Undiscovered.* Lanham, MD: Rowman & Littlefield, 2013.

———. *Globaloney: Unraveling the Myths of Globalization.* Lanham, MD: Rowman & Littlefield, 2005.

———. *Globaloney 2.0: The Crash of 2008 and the Future of Globalization.* Lanham, MD: Rowman & Littlefield, 2010.

———. *Money, Taste, and Wine: It's Complicated!* Lanham, MD: Rowman & Littlefield, 2015.

———, ed. *The New York Times Twentieth Century in Review: The Rise of the Global Economy.* New York: Routledge, 2002.

———. *Wine Economist* (blog). https://WineEconomist.com.

———. *Wine Wars: The Curse of the Blue Nun, the Miracle of Two Buck Chuck, and the Revenge of the Terroirists.* Lanham, MD: Rowman & Littlefield, 2011.

INDEX